EVERYMAN, I will go with thee,
and be thy guide,
In thy most need to go by thy side

Everyman's
Good English Guide

Harry Fieldhouse

J M Dent & Sons Ltd
London, Melbourne and Toronto

First published 1982
© Harry Fieldhouse, 1982

This book is set in 10½ on 12pt Linotron Sabon by
Western Printing Services Ltd, Bristol

Printed in Great Britain by
Biddles Ltd, Guildford, Surrey, for
J M Dent & Sons Ltd
Aldine House, 33 Welbeck Street, London W1M 8LX

British Library Cataloguing in Publication Data

Fieldhouse, Harry
    Everyman's good English guide.
    1. English language – Usage – Dictionaries
    I. Title
    423   PE1625

ISBN 0-460-04518-0

Contents

Introduction

Though English expression works along settled lines it is an un-usual writer who can get through half a page of composition without hesitating over one of its numerous points of choice, dispute or confusion. Should this spelling be used rather than that one? What is the standard phrasing? Does this word really mean what it looks as though it means? Then in speech there are queries about the language's erratic pronunciation, which are so inadequately answered by even the best dictionaries. Doubts of this kind may affect no more than a small part of an extensive language, but they are nonetheless distracting to those aiming at good English rather than just the passable. This book offers guidance on what seem the commonest uncertainties and misunderstandings, old and new. It also outlines in a separate section some formal notions, mainly grammatical but also stylistic, of a kind long neglected in the schoolroom and virtually inaccessible to the nonspecialist anywhere else.

Does it all matter? Is correctness necessary? It is true that what the speaker or writer is getting at is usually apparent even when inaccurately expressed. But then bad cooking will sustain life. Ill-fitting clothes will provide cover. Slow trains will get there in the end. Hit-or-miss communication may come off more often than might be expected, but for those content with it this Guide can hold no interest.

It is fashionable to question whether there is even such a thing as correctness. Ordinary people undoubtedly believe there is. They regard dictionaries as authorities on what should be said and look them up in search of rulings. Modern dictionaries however have largely abdicated this role. Their compilers follow a "descriptive" policy. Holding that language is a consensus, they are reluctant to prescribe one form rather than another. Their function, as they see it, is to record indiscriminately whatever is widely said, right or wrong. Scholarly as this may sound, it is rather like deducing the Highway Code from the way drivers and pedestrians actually behave. It turns dictionaries into guides to prevailing malpractices among the ill-informed.

The novelist and critic Kingsley Amis makes a practical suggestion about this. He writes: "In the introduction to the *Concise Oxford Dictionary* the editor explains what he calls his usage labels, which appear in the main body of the dictionary between a word and its definition: for instance '*(joc.)*: jocular, used only in humorous or playful style; *(vulg.)*: vulgar, used only by those who have no wish to be thought either polite or educated' .... What about '*(illit.)*: illiterate, used only by those who have no wish to write accurately or vigorously'?"*

However intended, this is an idea that deserves to be taken seriously. Some palliative is needed for the consensus mania, with its spurious air of underpinning by majority rule. Quite apart from being impractical as a test, because there is no way of keeping up with its changes, consensus has a destabilizing effect on the language. It encourages errors to multiply till acceptance becomes irresistible. For example the unqualified recording of the colloquial *dicey*, found in newer dictionaries (instead of *dicy*, as spelling convention requires), acts to unsettle the spelling of comparable words like *icy/chancy*.

The destabilizing effect is striking in pronunciation. Longer schooling and expanded college intakes have introduced thousands to words that are not part of the currency of their home surroundings. All of us are more inclined to guess how to say a new word than to look it up. Hence many bad guesses have come into circulation. These go into dictionaries dignified as "educated usage", part of the so-called "educated consensus".

Haphazard changes like these are welcomed by some commentators as a sign of vitality. Others contend that changes, if not desirable, are anyway inevitable. What is inevitable about them? New words are obviously needed for new things or new ways of looking at old things, but why new ways of saying old things? The more widely English is spoken in the world the more necessary it becomes that it should be spoken in the same way. Differences should be discouraged, because intelligibility depends on sameness (not "richness" or "variety", the alleged benefits of local turns of phrase). Standard English, already noted for its flexibility, stands in need of nothing so much as conservation. What it is getting from many who should be its keepers is a licence for redevelopment.

Where choices are made in this Guide conservation is among the tests. So the established sense is preferred to the upstart, the

*The State of the Language, edited by Leonard Michaels & Christopher Ricks, published by University of California Press.

native term to the trendy import, the informed pronunciation to the latest guess. Then, in general, the spoken idiom is taken as a better guide than the written way of putting it. Consistency is an important test, but the most important is brevity. Other things being equal the shorter word or phrasing is always better than the longer, and the only justification for extra letters, syllables or words is extra meaning. Besides, the writer or speaker who takes care to be economical with words is driven to be equally concerned with the accuracy of their meaning. So there is much to be achieved by what might seem mere tidying-up measures. After all, accuracy and economy in writing, along with clarity in speech, are all that can reasonably be asked of linguistic expression.

As for more ambitious reforms of English, they are hardly worth contemplating. If generations of dispute have been unable to produce agreement on "split" infinitives what chance is there of, say, regularized spelling? There is similarly no future in challenging individual usages that are already part of the language. The most that can be realistically attempted is acceptance of convenient variants and resistance to change for the sake of change. What has to be taken into account is that language is an extension of personality as well as a tool of communication. Fashion, whim and temperament will leave their mark on it just as they do on food, clothing, shelter and other ostensibly practical matters. We are not dealing with an exact science, despite the scientific trappings of linguistic study.

People interested enough to dip into a book like this will be familiar already with many of the points it makes and may well wonder at others it omits. It is impossible to keep track today of every current confusion or aberration. Broadcast muddles alone could fill their own book. One could go on about *literature* rhymed repeatedly with *mature* (instead of with the last syllable of *nature*), and this from a leading literary don in a BBC cultural broadcast. Even the Prince of Wales' wedding has left its linguistic memory, what with the ITV commentator's pronunciation of *balcony* as in *Balkan*. Murphy's Law, "If anything can go wrong it will", gets all the confirmation it needs from the English of today. When people say, as some do, that mistakes are no commoner than they used to be, every serious editor and every attentive listener knows this to be nonsense.

It only remains to account for the author's presumption. My readiness to pass judgement at a time of "anything goes" comes of long practice. For more than two decades manuscripts of all kinds received by national publications have passed through my hands daily. They have ranged from readers' letters and beginners' stories to professionals' articles and eminent authors' books. Editing these has given me as good an opportunity as comes to any man of literary inclination to notice recurring slips and perplexities. It has also suggested the paradox that so little trouble is taken to refine the practical use of words at a time when so much is taken to get mere word puzzles right. But I believe there are those who would take the trouble if they knew where to turn for help. This Guide is meant to provide it.

1982   Harry Fieldhouse

Grammatical terms

Technical words are kept to a minimum in this Guide, but it has not been practical to restrict them to those in common enough use not to be thought of as technical, like *sentence/plural/noun*. Language contains so many repetitive features that labels are needed to avoid continual explanations. Reminders of what the terms used in the Guide mean will be found in various entries in Part II, as summarized here:

Basic word functions are listed in PARTS OF SPEECH.

For sentence structures like *subject/object/complement* see ANALYSIS, and also SENTENCE PATTERNS.

For the many terms to do with *verbs* see TENSES and the full list of other entries under VERBS.

Punctuation devices have individual entries, all listed under PUNCTUATION.

For *gerunds* see INFINITIVE CONSTRUCTIONS. Separate entries cover such processes as COMPARATIVES/ELLIPSIS/ PROFORMS.

Anyone looking up words and phrases in Part I will hardly ever need to turn to the more analytical Part II, unless the interest has been stimulated to probe deeper.

Pronunciation key

Wherever possible pronunciation is shown in this Guide by rhymes with familiar words or phrases. Where there is no convenient rhyme, words are respelt according to the simple system below, in which the capitals A/E/I/O/U stand for the sounds of the vowels' names, and other sounds are represented by the letters listed (right). The only non-alphabet symbol used is the well-known upside-down *e*(ə). Stressed syllables are printed in italic.

This arrangement is not enough to cover every sound, but rather than invent symbols that would not be self-explanatory the Guide fills any gaps by reference to specimen words like those below. See Part II for fuller treatments.

Usual alphabet letter	Vowel sound as found in words like	Good English Guide
a/A	*a* (stressed) / *able* / *day* / *maid* / *they*	A
a/A	*am* / *as* / *add* / *can* / *have* / *pal*	a
a/A	*ah* / *are* / *art* / *heart* / *aunt* (Brit.)	ah
—	*air* / *fare* / *there* / *pear* / *scarce* / *wary*	Aə
e/E	*be* / *bee* / *sea* / *seize* / *ski* / *quay* / *he*	E
e/E	*egg* / *get* / *head* / *berry* / *bury* / *them* / *said*	e
—	*a* (unstressed) / *about* / *china* / *better*	ə
—	*herd* / *heard* / *sir* / *hurt* / *word* / *her*	ə̄
i/I	*I* / *eye* / *tie* / *sigh* / *buy* / *by* / *why* / *ice*	I
i/I	*in* / *it* / *fiddle* / *busy* / *women* / *silly*	i
—	*ear* / *here* / *near* / *real* / *pier* / *aeon*	iə
o/O	*oh* / *go* / *so* / *sew* / *slow* / *oboe* / *though* / *mauve*	O
o/O	*on* / *off* / *cough* / *what* / *yacht* / *laurel* / *ox*	o
—	*all* / *awl* / *taut* / *thought* / *lord* / *four* / *door*	aw
—	*how* / *now* / *brown* / *cow* / *out* / *doubt* / *hour*	ow
—	*boy* / *oil* / *quoit* / *noise* / *soya* / *foyer*	oi
u/U	*you* / *yew* / *use* / *nude* / *view* / *few* / *neuter*	U
—	*too* / *to* / *do* / *true* / *zoo* / *sue* / *soup* / *blew*	oo
u/U	*up* / *cut* / *but* / *mother* / *son* / *touch* / *blood*	u
—	*put* / *push* / *wool* / *would* / *sugar* / *full*	—
—	*poor* / *sure* / *tour* / *dour*	—
—	*fool* / *pool* / *rule* / *ghoul* / *school*	—

Consonant sounds as in words like

b/B	*but/back/rub/probe*	b
c/C	(see *k* or *s*)	—
d/D	*did/add/ado/aid*	d
f/F	*fix/offer/if/philosophy/frail*	f
g/G	*gun/ago/big/vague/exact*	g
g/G	(see *j* where applicable)	—
h/H	*her/horrid/ahoy/who/whole*	h
j/J	*jay/jam/age/dodge/hinge/gin*	j
—	*beige/vision/rouge/equation*	—
k/K	*king/erection/quay/cat/act/elk/flex*	k
l/L	*love/elder/old/bell/ale*	l
m/M	*man/mother/arm/am/omen*	m
n/N	*nun/nomad/own/on/into/annul*	n
ng	*singing/long/longer/tongue*	ng
p/P	*pea/peep/ape/stop/pick*	p
q/Q	(see *k*)	—
r/R	*red/arrow/river/reverie*	r
s/S	*sun/boss/race/base/cigar/science*	s
s/S	(see *z* where applicable)	—
—	*show/shop/sugar/nation/ocean/chute*	sh
—	*church/catch/ancient/nature*	tsh
t/T	*tea/yet/duty/star/pistol/kettle*	t
th	*the/then/than/bathe/other/father*	th
th	*thing/bath/earth/throttle/author*	—
v/V	*vain/victory/vote/of/over/wave/have*	v
w/W	*we/wait/when/sweet/quite/witch*	w
x/X	(see *ks, ksh* or *gz*)	—
y/Y	*yes/you/view/few/yacht/nude/onion*	y
z/Z	*zoo/crazy/easy/dogs/ruse/accuse*	z

Part I
Words in Particular

a/an *An* hotel/*an* historic occasion etc are rarely heard but still frequently written. The persistence of **an** instead of **a** in such settings seems to be owed either to a belief that it is "more correct" or to imitation of *an* hour/*an* honest man etc, both mistaken motives. Only words beginning with a vowel sound require **an**. In *hour/ honest* (and *heir/honours/honourable* etc) the *h* is silent and the initial sound is a vowel – hence **an**. In *hotel/historic* (and most other words spelt with an initial *h*) the *h* is sounded – hence **a**.

The rule of **a** before a consonant sound applies equally of course to words beginning with a vowel letter but pronounced as though they began with a *w* or *y*, e.g. *a onetime star/a used-car salesman/a ewe*.

Note: except when it is spoken on its own, **a** is always pronounced ə, as in the first and last syllables of "aroma". (See VARIABLE VOWELS in Part II.)

able/ability See CAPABLE (which has the same general sense but differences of usage).

acronym Term for a word, usually a title, contrived from initials (or bits) of several words making up the full version, e.g. *NATO* (North Atlantic Treaty Organization). Among many cumbersome names deliberately simplified into acronyms are:

> *GATT* (General Agreement on Tariffs & Trade)
> *VAT* (Value Added Tax)
> *WHO* (World Health Organization).

The same process yields words for new technology:

> *radar* (radio detection and ranging)
> *laser* (light amplification by stimulated emission of radiation).

Acronyms do away with full stops between initials (putting them in is not only unnecessary but wrong), a convenience that is spreading to sets of initials like:

> *PTO* (please turn over)
> *RSVP* (répondez s'il vous plaît)
> *EEC* (European Economic Community)
> *TV* (television).

None of these can be pronounced as a word but they are just as familiar as abbreviations as they are when spelt out. It seems sensible to leave out stops in all sets of well-known initials.

actual/actually These are overworked words, though not so over-worked as *real/really*, which mean the same. Desire for emphasis may excuse the phrase *in actual fact*, but **actual** is defined as "existing in act or fact" (*Oxford English Dictionary*). A fact cannot become more of a fact by being described as either actual or factual. This is one of those phrases that pass in speech but not in writing.

administer See MINISTER.

adoption/adaptation The noun derived from the verb *to adopt* is **adoption**. This has led to an expectation that "adaption" can be derived from the verb *to adapt*. The word, though often seen, does not exist. What is meant of course is **adaptation**. It only goes to show the pitfalls of prediction, since the verbs are alike in all other respects (*adopted/adapted* etc). The confusion is abetted by the similarity of sense where something is adopted for use (i.e. taken up) and something else is adapted for use (i.e. modified, then taken up). So what is adapted is often adopted too.

adverse/averse Despite similarities of sense and appearance these adjectives are unconnected. **Adverse** = unfavourable/detrimental (*Winter brought adverse conditions*). The sense of **averse** is "disin-clined"/"unwilling", hence "against" (*He is not averse to bending the rules*). Both words take the preposition *to* in adjective phrases (*conditions adverse to progress*), though **averse from** is sometimes still advocated on the ground that the original meaning was "turned away". After two centuries **averse to** is established. Unlike **adverse**, **averse** cannot modify a noun, e.g. *an adverse verdict*, but not "an averse mood".

aerial/antenna In radio etc the usual English word is **aerial**. Though less widely used in North America the term is also known there, rivalled by **antenna**, a salesman's or technician's word for the same thing.

affect Often confused with EFFECT (q.v.).

afterward/afterwards Though *afterward* is the older term, **after-wards** is the usual.

aggravate It means "to make worse" (i.e. graver), as in *aggravate the situation*, but it has a long popular history in the sense of "irritate"/

"annoy". The era of youth culture (1960s and 1970s) contributed *aggro* (=annoyance), a slang contraction of *aggravation*. By now the primary sense of **aggravate** and its derivatives is unlikely to be understood except by the literary.

aim at/aim to   In the sense of addressing a target the verb **aim** is always followed by **at** (*Aim at the bullseye*), but this does not make **to** wrong in other senses (*We aim to make this railway pay/. . . at making this railway pay*). **Aim to** is on a par with the use of **aim** as a noun: *Our aim is to make the railway pay.* Objectors are misled by supposing that the word's meaning derives from weaponry, which it does not. Anyway, **aim to** is already unbudgeable in both British and American usage.

all/all of   Shakespeare wrote: *All the world's a stage and all the men and women merely players.* Lincoln said: *You can't fool all of the people all of the time.* Is there some subtlety governing the choice of **all** or **all of**? In instances like these, where **all** precedes *the* (or *this/that/those*), the inclusion of **of** is a matter of taste – it is not necessary but it is not wrong. It is only before pronouns that **all of** is required (*all of me/all of you*). Elsewhere, till recently **all of** was uncommon in British use. Now, influenced by American example, it is more frequent. As the additional word is superfluous to the sense this is a bad habit.

The American preference for **of** is presumably owed to Lincoln's Gettysburg speech. But **of** was essential to his rhetoric to match the key phrase "some of the time", in which **of** is not optional. (See also PRONOUNS [6] in Part II.)

all right/alright   No rational objection is possible to **alright**, which merely follows the precedent of *already/altogether/although* etc. The word is widely used in the British Isles and even more so in North America, though **all right** is better esteemed in both. The choice would hardly be worth comment if **alright** were not so liable to give offence – presumably because, like a split infinitive, it is an irregularity the layman can recognize.

altar/alter/alto etc   A consistent pronunciation of *al* in such words would be a boon to many. As it is, some words beginning with *al* followed by another consonant require a pronunciation as in "olive", others as in "alphabet", and others as in "awl". It is thought ignorant to confuse them.

Like "olive": *altar/alter/alternate* and derivatives.

Like "alphabet": *altitude/altimeter/alto/altruist* and *album/ alcohol/alkali/allegory/allergy/alley.*

Like "awl": *altogether/almighty/always* and all compounds of *all.*

alternate/alternative etc   The essential meaning of **alternate** and its derivatives is one or the other but not both together. *Alternating* electric current (AC) flows first one way, then the other. A consultant attending a clinic every other day is there on *alternate* days. If a second consultant is there the other days, they attend *alternately,* perhaps offering patients an *alternative,* i.e. a choice between the two. These are exact uses, respected by careful writers.

The loose use of **alternative** in the sense of "possibility" is regrettable but old-established. It rests on the idea of a choice that excludes several other possibilities, a sense not conveyed by "choices"/"options" etc. It is also encouraged by the lack of a suitable adjective, besides "other". Hence such liberties as *the search for alternative sources of energy* (i.e. excluding present types)/*There are several alternatives to choose from* (i.e. but only one choice possible)/*The alternatives are too fearful to contemplate* (i.e. whatever they are alternative to is the only acceptable choice). These may be debasements of the coinage but they are not wanton. As for phrases like *We have no other alternative/There is only one alternative,* their illogic is on a par with . . . *no other choice/. . . only one choice* – i.e. no choice exists.

although/though   Though can always be substituted for *although,* but **although** cannot always be substituted for *though.* (*His wife was kind to me. I didn't like him, though* – here *although* is not possible). As **though** is also commoner in speech, and shorter too, **although** may reasonably be regarded as redundant.

alto   See ALTAR for pronunciation.

amateur   When the sense is of amateur as opposed to professional the word is stressed on the first syllable. In the earlier and now uncommon sense of a private connoisseur or enthusiastic student of any speciality the stress is applied to the last syllable.

among/amongst   Prefer **among**. Amongst is an anachronism, not only longer to write but harder to say, whether followed by consonant or vowel. Similarly, prefer *amid* to *amidst,* and *while* to *whilst.*

analogous A tripwire for those who model their pronunciation on the associated noun *analogy*, which rhymes with "allergy". **Analogous** has a different *g*, i.e. hard *g* as in "asparagus". Several reputable dictionaries omit to mention this distinction. It is an adjective probably best avoided in speech, since the right *g* will puzzle the ignorant, and the wrong *j* will offend the knowing. In a more familiar word like *obligation*, of course, nobody hesitates over the change of *g* from *oblige*.

antagonist Means "adversary" / "opponent", and is derived from an obsolete sense of *antagonize* (which now means "to provoke / incur hostility"). **Antagonist** is not a variant of *protagonist* (q.v), though the belief that it is may account for the widespread misunderstanding of that word.

antenna See AERIAL.

anyone / everyone / anybody / everybody / nobody etc These words all refer to people. They are compounds of two words, which should be kept separate whenever the reference is to anything else. Thus: *Any one of those bombs might go off / I want you to check the invoices and clear every one of them / Every body is delivered to the assembly line after painting.* (See also NONE / NO-ONE. For use of plural pronouns / possessives in referring back to *anyone* etc see PLURAL / SINGULAR CONFLICTS in Part II.)

apartheid Afrikaans word meaning "separateness", applied to the policy of racial segregation in South Africa. It is commonly mispronounced as though it were German, particularly by outsiders professing familiarity with conditions there. Afrikaners say it *əpah-tAt* (rhymes with "part eight").

apparatus Pronounced *apərAtəs* (like "rate us"), not *apərahtəs*. The pronunciation with the third syllable like "rat" is only American.

apparent / transparent Though both used to rhyme with "parent", **apparent** now always rhymes with "arrant", and so should **transparent**. The same stress (second syllable) and the same vowel apply to *apparently / transparently / transparency*.

applicable etc One of a number of words under pressure to change from the established pronunciation of informed speakers because so many uninformed speakers assume the stress to be on the second syllable. Like *applicant*, **applicable** is normally stressed on the first syllable, along with *explicable/despicable*.

apposite   Sometimes mispronounced apəzIt (with long *i*), presumably to help differentiate it from *opposite* (opəzit). As there is an alternative in *apt* for the terse, and *appropriate* for the multi-syllabic, any difficulty is self-inflicted.

apricot   The first syllable rhymes with "ape", but a rhyme with "cap"/"map"/"sap" is the preferred American rendering.

arch/archi etc   The sense of "chief"/"principal" is shared by an old adjective and a prefix, both spelt "arch". Where **arch** occurs in this sense, as in *archbishop/archduke/arch rival*, it is nearly always rhymed with "march". But in many words that start with **arch** the spelling is coincidental and the origins and pronunciation are different. Examples: *archaeology/archaic/archive*. A safe generalization is that wherever **arch**, as in these, is followed by a vowel the pronunciation should be as in "arc"/"ark". This happens in *archangel/architecture/architrave/archipelago*. Everybody recognizes the obvious exceptions: *archer/archery/arched* etc.

aren't   Contraction for *are not*, and also – but only in questions – for *am not* (*Aren't I right about that?*). These uses are normal in speech and acceptable in writing. Apart from the exception mentioned there is no contraction for *am not*. "I aren't", like "ain't" (which was once respectable for both *am not* and *are not*), is either dialect or ignorant.

aristocrat   The stress is on the first syllable, not the second, though this variant is common in U.S. speech. The associated words both have different stresses: *aristocracy/aristocratic*.

around/round   **Round** can be adjective (*the Round Table*), noun (*life in the round*), preposition(*they ran rings round us*), or adverb(*pass the hat round*). **Around** can be preposition or adverb, and could be substituted in only the last two examples. In speech **round** probably remains the usual choice for preposition or adverb, but it is losing ground under American influence to **around** (*Why don't you come around tonight?*). This trend may be too far gone to be reversed, which is a pity, as **around** disturbs speech rhythms with its extra syllable.

arouse   See ROUSE.

arse/ass etc   The time-honoured word for what the *Oxford English Dictionary* defines as "the fundament, buttocks, posteriors or rump of an animal" is **arse** (rhymes with "farce"). From it is derived *arsy-tarsy* (upside down/arse upwards), a modern variant of *arsy-versy*. Still used with hesitation other than informally, **arse** tends to be sidestepped by resort to supposedly politer words like *backside/ bottom*. The euphemisms current in the U.S. are *ass/fanny*, each a cause of international misunderstanding because in Great Britain *ass* means either a donkey or a fool and *fanny* = vagina.

artist/artiste   The word **artist** suffers from art's difficulty of never having been satisfactorily defined (the poet-sculptor Eric Gill considered art indistinguishable from craft). In general **artist** is taken to mean a painter or, less readily, a sculptor. In a secondary sense it means anyone the speaker or writer wants to commend for displaying artistry, i.e. skill in a matter of taste. Into this category may come anyone from novelists and choreographers to tailors and cooks (*He cuts his suits like an artist/An artist of the kitchen*).

The word **artiste**, pronounced ah*tEst* and applicable to either sex, helps to relieve the pressure on **artist** by separating entertainers who perform in public. This makes a convenient distinction for onlookers but tends to be resented by performers. They rightly sense its effect in distancing them from the flattering aura of **artist**, especially what is phrased in showbiz publicity as "creative artist". The award-winning actor Anthony Quinn once asserted on British television that playing a part written for an actor is the same "creative" process as carving an original sculpture.

So **artiste** has yet to achieve general acceptance, and **artist** continues to be appropriated by comedians/jugglers/musicians/dancers/actors, as seen in showbiz terms such as *artists and repertory* (A & R)/*Artists' entrance*.

as   This word functions as conjunction, adverb, preposition, or pronoun. For the controversy over whether *like* can share the conjunction role see LIKE/AS. For the misuse with *equally* see EQUALLY (AS). A similar point is the substitution of "the same that" for *the same as* in sentences such as *She caught the same bus home that she had* *taken to work in the morning.* Here *that* is unidiomatic, and *the same* should be balanced by as: . . . *the same bus as she had taken to work.* Similarly:

> *Everything looks the same as it did before* (not *that*)
> *Is that watch the same one as you had before?* (not *that*).

When **as** is a pronoun there is a similar temptation to substitute *which*, e.g. in settings like

> *Mr Smith has been with us many years, as is well known*
> *Mr Smith works long hours, as do all of us*
> *Mr Smith, as we know, works long hours.*

In all these **as** is idiomatic, and *which* would not be.

Two prepositional uses are *as to/as for*, with the sense of "as regards"/"with regard to". *As to* is redundant, particularly before *whether* (q.v.)/*why/how*, or replaceable by a more idiomatic preposition like *about*.

Another pair of prepositions with shared sense is *as from/as of*, the first British, the second American. Both are jargon and mean no more than "from" (*The new schedule is in force as of/as from today*). The phrase *as of right* is a fashionable contrivance for the established "by right", and adds nothing to the meaning.

ass See ARSE.

assist/assistance It says something about the market for the long word that **assistance** has weathered several centuries despite rivalry from *aid* and *help*. But the word has come to be associated with jargon: *National Assistance* (= Poor Law)/*power assistance* (copywriter's term for servo mechanisms, now usually just "power" or "powered")/*Can I be of assistance, Madam?* (shop talk). Similarly jargon was the origin of *shop assistant/personal assistant*, now established commercial terms.

American idiom accepts **assist** as a noun (*With an assist from the fire department she escaped*). This usage is unnecessary but comparable with that of *help* in *You are a help/The money was a help.* Usually **assistance/help/aid** are all abstract nouns, unable to follow an indefinite article (*a/an*).

As verb, **assist** is also better left to officialese and jargon. A legitimate and ancient sense is that of *assist at* (= to be present at/take part in a ceremony), as in *In his hereditary capacity the duke assisted at the Coronation.*

assure/ensure/insure etc   These variants now have distinct if related meanings. (All have the same root and in French one word serves for all three.) **Assure** = to make someone sure (*She assured him/ gave him her assurance she would send him the book*). **Ensure** = to make certain (*He ensured that he would hear the postman by turning off the radio*). **Insure** = to protect against loss etc by paying for a guarantee of compensation, i.e. by taking out an *insurance* policy (*She insured the book before she posted it*). Where *assurance* lingers on in this last sense, as in old companies' names (*Prudential Assurance Co.*), it is an archaism. **Reassure** = to restore confidence (*He was reassured by what she had done*). In many contexts *assurance* and *reassurance* are interchangeable (*He slept better for her reassurance/assurance*).

at this time   In the sense of "in those days" this is a straightforward phrase (*There were few printed books at this time*). In the sense in which it has become a modern cliché, as in *"The nation must exercise restraint at this time," said the Senator*, it is a pretentious substitute for *now* or *at present*. Worse still is "at this moment in time". These are American imports that deserve to be resisted. We have enough wordy expressions for *now*, e.g. "for the time being".

ate   Rhymes with "let"/"get"/"set", not with "fate"/"hate"/"bait".

attribute/contribute/distribute   Only **attribute** can be a noun and it is only as a noun that *at*tribute is stressed on the first syllable. All three words are verbs and as such all three are stressed on the middle syllable: *attribute/contribute/distribute*. Politicians, economists and commentators, who are particularly given to holding forth about contributing and distributing, are continually muddling these up. The only forms that escape garbling are *attribution/contribution/distribution*, which all have the same stress – on the third syllable (atri*bU*shn).

aught   See NAUGHT.

authoress   Normal feminine of *author*, resented by feminists for irrelevant sexuality. Nevertheless it remains useful for contexts where sexuality is the point, and saves resort to "female authors"/ "women authors" etc. Besides, if *actress* why not *authoress*?

averse   See ADVERSE.

await See WAIT.

awake/wake/awaken/waken etc These verbs all refer to the process of emerging from sleep and with so many to choose from it is
natural to look for shades of meaning. In fact they are all interchangeable, though some writers try to restrict **awake**(*awoke/
awoken*) to intransitive uses. The safest form is **wake**, with or
without *up*, which has the past tense *woke* and past participle
woken. This cannot be faulted in any of the possible senses, i.e.
intransitive* as in *I woke/I woke up*, transitive* as in *You'll wake
the children/... wake up the children*, and passive as in *I was
woken (up) by the thunder* (= roused). In the sense of "rouse" the
forms **waken/awaken** are common, but unnecessary, though
awakening is the usual noun in the metaphorical sense (*He never
used to be interested in Egyptology but the Tutankhamun exhi-
bition was his awakening*). **Awake** is the adjective form, but in
preceding a noun it is usually coupled with an adverb, e.g. *a
wide-awake observer*, not "an awake observer". **Wakeful**, another
associated adjective, means unable to sleep properly.

axe/ax British obstinacy has resisted the spelling "ax", recommended by the *Oxford English Dictionary* in its earliest volume
(1882). This is now regarded as an Americanism, though it is
British spelling that has deviated.

back out/back up/back of etc *To back* is an old-established English
verb with the usual accumulation of phrases: *He glared at her and
she backed away/If you've signed the contract you can't back out
of it/Let's park here – back in where that car is moving out/The
road's blocked – we'll have to back up the hill/The nut is too tight –
back it off a bit*. Despite this variety British usage rejects the
American **back up** as a synonym for "reverse" (*You'll have to back
up and turn around/Where is the fuse for the back-up lamps?*). It
also rejects **back of/in back of** (despite *in front of*) as an adverb
or preposition instead of "behind".

backward/backwards The only spelling for the adjective is **backward** (*Bushmen are backward people*). Either form can serve as an

---

*Transitive = taking an object. Intransitive = not taking an object.

adverb (*We seem to be going backwards/backward*), with no discernible preference.

balustrade See BANISTERS.

banal Of the acceptable pronunciations a rhyme with "canal" is the most convenient, and consistent with the noun *banality*. A less puzzling word, and so to be preferred, is *commonplace*.

banisters Not "bannisters". The word usually means the side uprights of a staircase plus the handrail they support. The use of *banister* as a single upright is dying out. *Baluster*, of which **banisters** is a historic corruption, still survives but mainly in technical use. A *balustrade* is not a staircase, but a stone structure of pillars and coping, usually lining a roof or balcony.

base/basis The plurals of these nouns are spelt the same but pronounced differently: *base*, bases (*bAsiz*)/*basis*, bases (*bAsEz*). Both words mean foundation or bottom, with **basis** preferred for theoretical structures (*the basis of the argument*). Only **base** can act adjectivally (*a base number/the base fasteners*).

bas-relief = low relief, a term that would no doubt have taken over if the word (part of the vocabulary of sculpture) were in non-specialist use. It would avoid anxiety about the pronunciation, which in fact rhymes with "mass relief". This is one of several awkward terms brought into wider use by rising interest in archaeology. Its French spelling is owed to reimportation, as the word existed in English long before (usually *bass-relief*). It ought to have lost its fussy hyphen at least.

because of A concise and useful construction, often despised, perhaps in ignorance of its unassailable antiquity. *I only did it because of you/He came in because of the cold/Because of all the excitement the stew boiled over* – these are direct, immediately understood, irreproachable. The use of **because of** here is an obvious improvement on *as a result of/on account of/owing to* etc which are more likely to be found in writing, especially of a formal kind. But the notion exists that this prepositional use of **because of** (introducing an adverbial phrase) is somehow inferior to *because* on its own as a conjunction. To suit this view the examples would have to be reconstructed as: *I only did it because I wanted to please* *you/He came in because it was cold/Because it was forgotten in all the excitement, the stew boiled over.* Such elaboration, though minor, is enough to show the difference between natural idiomatic expression and literary composition.

been The stressed pronunciation rhymes with "bean", as in *Where have you been?*, but "bin" is normal where the word is unstressed or lightly stressed, as in *What have you been doing?* This is also the American sound.

befriend Does not mean "make friends with". The common definition is "to act as a friend to", but even this misses the point, as befriending is more specific. Only those in some sort of need as compared with the befriender can be befriended. The prince can befriend the pauper but it would take unusual circumstances for the pauper to befriend the prince. Typically the befriended are victims and the befriending takes the form of help. So *After the accident she was befriended by neighbours*, but *The new tenant made friends with the neighbours.*

behemoth Mainly a literary word, probably because of doubt about how to say it – bih*Em*əth (*th* as in "earth"). It is a biblical word now denoting any outsize animal, just as *leviathan* denotes any outsize sea creature.

behind See BACK OF.

beloved As a participle, as in *The good doctor was beloved by all*, the word rhymes with "loved" – which could just as well be substituted. As an adjective, confined mainly to professions of affection, as on tombstones (*. . . beloved wife of . . .*), **beloved** has three syllables (bi*luv*id). So it does as a noun, usually faintly mocking (*Is Mark bringing his beloved?*).

below See UNDER.

benign See MALIGN.

beside/besides As prepositions they have different senses. **Beside** means "by the side of", as in *I do like to be beside the sea/She was beside herself with grief* (out of her wits)/*If you can't say anything nice about a person, come and sit here beside me* (Alice Roosevelt

Longworth's joke). **Besides** = except/in addition to, as in *There's nobody here besides me/Besides us there'll be two other couples.*

But **besides** also functions as an adverb, meaning "further"/ "else", as in *Besides, it isn't true/We did all that and a lot more besides.*

better   For *We had better hurry/We better hurry* etc see IDIOM in Part II.

billion   In Great Britain a billion traditionally = a million million. This was the value given to it by the French academics who coined the term. Later the French revised the meaning to a thousand million, and this remains the value in France and in North America. In Great Britain financial journalists and international businesses are increasingly adopting the same standard, which is also the EEC norm.

binoculars   Short for "binocular glasses", which now survives only in technical use. The word **binoculars** is always plural (*These binoculars are strong*). As with *spectacles/glasses* etc the singular form is **pair of** (binoculars). The *bi* refers to the two eyes necessary for binocular vision, also called "stereoscopic". It is a fallacy that it refers to the two eyepieces, as is sometimes contended, and that "pair of binoculars" is therefore a tautology because *bi* already means two.

blessed/blest   Verse and traditional phrases are the only uses left for **blest** (*Well, I'm blest!/Blest if I will/the Isles of the Blest*). Otherwise **blessed** is the spelling for the past tense, participle and adjective. Pronunciation: **blessed** is pronounced "blest" when it is a past tense or participle (*The priest blessed them/He has blessed them*), but it has two syllables when it is an adjective, as in *a blessed nuisance* (*bles*id), occurring before its noun. Such uses are generally ironic. **Blessed** is occasionally a noun (*the blessed of this world*), with optional pronunciation as one or two syllables.

bloke   See chap.

bogy/bogey/bogie   One pronunciation (*bO*gi), three spellings, four meanings. **Bogy** (plural *bogies*) is a bugbear (*Here comes the bogyman*), or something picked from the nose. **Bogey** is a golf term for a standard score. **Bogie** is a pivoting undercarriage of a railway coach.

both/both of   See ALL.

brain/brains   Anatomically the brain is singular, and so it is in normal grammar. But established popular phrases take it to be plural, perhaps modelled on *wits*. Hence *He's got no brains/I'll beat his brains out/She's the brains of the family* etc.

breakthrough   A useful recent term – or it would be if headline writers could refrain from coupling it with *major*. No minor breakthrough is ever recorded, but "major breakthrough" is already a cliché. The word is not an absolute (see UNIQUE) but it does not need qualification. A breakthrough is enough. One has either broken through or one hasn't.

Britisher   American term for a British person, sometimes used in dialogue in British fiction to denote a foreign speaker, as the British never use the word of themselves. There is no practical equivalent of *Englishman/Welshman/Scotsman/Irishman* to cover British Isles or United Kingdom origin. *Briton* is considered at best literary, at worst self-conscious. The native idiom uses the adjective **British**. Hence some equivalents: *He's an American/He's British, They're Americans/They're British, Two Americans/Two British* etc. No word exists differentiating citizens of the United Kingdom from other citizens of the British Empire or Commonwealth.

broad/wide   These can be regarded as interchangeable except in standard phrases. **Broad**: *broad shoulders/... back/... chest/ ...-minded/... humour/... accent/... hint/... daylight/as ... as it's long.* **Wide**: *a wide berth/the ... world/... open/... interests/... of the mark.*

broadcast/forecast etc   The verbs are formed on the model of *cast*, and have no inflection (variant) for the past tense. *We broadcast* could be either present or past, and the tense must be deduced from the setting. Curiously, this rarely causes misunderstanding, which makes one wonder why we cling to the few inflections we do have. *He/she/it broadcast* (or *forecast*) is of course always past tense, as the present would be *broadcasts* (*forecasts*). The past participle is the same as the past form, and the present participle is regular (*broadcasting/forecasting*).

broil   Old English verb now surviving mainly in North American usage, and meaning "to grill". In the kitchen **broil** invites confusion with "boil", but its lineage – derived from the French *brûler*, to burn – is impeccable.

buffet There is an English verb and a borrowed French noun. The English verb with the sense of "knock about" (*The waves buffet the ship*) rhymes with "stuff it". The French noun for a refreshment bar or an informal meal served from a sideboard rhymes with "woo Fay" (*boo*fA).

burgle/burglarize The short form is British, the long American. Both are derived from the noun *burglar*, the American in a regular way, the British in a way that would be denounced as irregular if the Americans had done it.

bus/buses/buss/busses etc The idea that brotherly love can be promoted by uprooting children from their home areas and sending them by bus to attend classes in different children's home areas has produced many problems. One of them is how to spell the verb for sending them that way. Are they *bused* or *bussed*? Headlines like *Parents in Bussing Protest* threaten to make the double *s* spelling standard in America, and it has quickly gained a foothold in Great Britain, ever susceptible to transatlantic fashions.

According to the rules for spelling verb endings (see SPELLING/ ENDINGS in Part II) the verb **to bus** should double its *s* to yield *busses/bussed/bussing* – or so it might appear. But [1] this rule has rarely been followed by *chorus*, an exactly comparable noun acting as a verb (*choruses/chorused/chorusing*). It is more often than not ignored too by the more recent *focus*. Then [2] there is already a verb **to buss** (*busses/bussed/bussing*) meaning to kiss (from the French *baiser*). So there is no need to distort *bus* into *busses* etc, and there is good reason not to because of confusion with the other kind. The *Parents in Bussing Protest* might well be up in arms about an amorous teacher.

Pronunciation being unaffected by the choice, **buses/bused/ busing** can be legitimized.

cagey See DICE/DICEY for spelling irregularity.

calipers/callipers The more reasonable spelling is the original **cali-pers**, since the word is a corruption of "calibre" (i.e. calibre compasses). The extra *l* is presumably slipped in to help the pronunciation of those who do not know the origin and might suppose the first syllable to rhyme with "kale". But what with *calendar/calamity/calico* the precaution seems superfluous. **Caliper** is the standard spelling in the U.S. and a common variant in Great Britain. The word is also used as a euphemism for legirons.

cannot   For the "can't help laughing" idiom see IDIOMS in Part II.

capable/capability   Not fully interchangeable with *able/ability*. People are *capable of doing* but *able to do*. A capable person is an able person, but *able* has no equivalent to **capable of** (bravery, fraud etc). *Capability* and *ability* both mean "capacity"/"potential" but **capability** is generally applied to the non-human kind (hence Capability Brown, the landscape gardener who saw "capability" in terrain).

caring   This adjective is the opposite of *uncaring* (which means "not giving a damn"). It means "giving a damn", not "having in one's care"/"looking after". There is no adjective derived from *care* for that sense (*careful* means only "taking care"). This has been found inconvenient in the era of the Welfare State, with its proliferation of social workers, health visitors, probation officers and other employees, all purportedly taking care of aspects of their clients' lives, yet lacking a cosmetic term to describe their contribution. **Caring** is currently being misappropriated to fill the gap. It occurs in phrases like "the caring services", where the suggestion of being emotionally concerned may not be a bad confusion, from the point of view of fending off official economy drives.

carry out   An old metaphor now misused as a circumlocution, especially in official prose. **Carry out** saves the unimaginative the bother of picking the appropriate verb from *do/make/hold* etc. But why carry out a surgical operation when you can *do* one, carry out a search when you can *make* one, carry out an inquiry when you can *hold* one? Should Nelson have signalled that England expected every man would *carry out* his duty? Duty is *done*, as is research/construction/excavation/redecoration etc. Surveys are *made*, as are investigations/corrections/modifications etc. So are examinations, except the academic kind, which are *held*, as are elections. To check the spread of **carry out** a determined counterattack should be carried out, or better still *fought*.

castor/caster Castor is always right – as a kind of oil, a kind of sugar, a swivelling wheel used on furniture etc – but **caster** cannot be called wrong when applied to sugar, as it often still is. **Caster** comes from a container like a pepperpot, from which suitable sugar can be poured or *cast*.

caviar Prefer this shorter spelling to *caviare*, one of many historic versions with no particular claim.

censor/censure As these both smack of authority and disapproval careless writers find no difficulty in confusing them. To **censor** is to intercept and examine written or graphic material intended for publication, with a view to banning any part in conflict with official policy. (It is not censorship when material is rejected by whoever is ultimately responsible for publishing it, like an editor, film producer, or publisher.) To **censure** is to blame/reprove/condemn. The pronunciation as well as the sense differs: censor (*sensə*), censure (*senshə*).

ceramics The smart word for pottery, especially when this is held to be an art. Pronounced *sə*ra*m*iks. One established use is in the term "ceramic tiles", where the adjective presumably distinguishes them from slate tiles or vinyl tiles – surely unnecessarily, as tiles are taken to be ceramic unless otherwise specified. (See also PORCELAIN.)

chamois The alpine animal is pronounced *sham*wah. But the soft leather made from its skin and used among other things for washing car bodies is pronounced *sham*E (rhymes with "mammy").

chap/bloke/guy etc Of the many friendly variants of *man/boy*, a few can be accepted as having risen above slang or even informality. **Chap**, like *fellow*, is used at all levels of conversation. It generally implies a favourable or at least tolerant attitude on the part of the user, e.g. *nice chap/funny chap/odd chap/rum chap*, but rarely *nasty chap* etc. The lack of neutrality rather than the taint of slang limits its use in writing. In U.S. usage **guy** is close to achieving the same level of acceptance. In British usage it is universally understood and often used, but is regarded as an Americanism. **Bloke**, which is British, remains slang.

    Chap derives from *chapman*, originally a dealer, later a customer. The old sense survives in the slang use of *customer*, "a rum customer" etc, i.e. an odd person to deal with.

chassis   The same spelling serves for both singular and plural, but the pronunciation changes: *shas*i (singular), *shas*iz (plural). The adoption of the French word for frame in the sense of a supporting structure for vehicles is a bequest from the days of French prominence in car pioneering.

check up / on / in etc   The verb *to check* has taken on particles to mark various shades of its meanings, but has now reached the stage where its verbal phrases themselves have more than one meaning. The word's main everyday meaning is "to bring to a halt", as in *Bad habits need to be checked / The advance has been checked*. Another basic sense is "to make sure by examining", as in *Check whether there's any milk in the fridge*. **Check up** was an early variant in this sense (*Is there any milk? / I'll check up*) but now seems in retreat. To the question *Is there any milk?* the answer now is just as likely to be *I'll go and check*. So **check up on**, a form that has pained many, may yet give way to the simpler **check on** (*Is there any milk? Better check on that*) or the more recent **check out** (*Better check that out*).

   Check out however has another meaning as the converse of **check in**. Thus: **check in** = to make one's arrival known (*Check in at the airport an hour before departure*); **check out** = to take formal leave, particularly to settle the bill etc (*Mr Smith checked out of the hotel an hour ago*). But both forms have additional senses: *Please check in your valuables with Reception* (= deposit – mainly American usage, which also accepts *Check your coats here*) / *The suspect checks out* (= stands up to verification).

   Also possible is **check over** (*The engine seems erratic – would you check it over?*), presumably an imitation of "look over" / "go over". *Check* is still far short of *to get* as a spawner of phrases and at least these elaborations follow normal practice.

chic   Pronounced shEk, not shik or as in "cheek" or "chick".

chiropodist   Every possible rendering of the *ch* seems to be tried – as in "chivalry" or "china" or "chimera". The right sound is k.

choice   See ALTERNATE / ALTERNATIVE.

circumstances   "Under the circumstances" is not wrong, but is better reserved for use where the circumstances are conditional to the action: *I had no option under the circumstances / Under the circum-*

stances you didn't take long/She was lucky to get a seat under the circumstances etc. Where mere situation is expressed the natural construction is "in the circumstances": *In the circumstances of the era barons ruled like local kings/It was not the first time he had been in such circumstances/In the circumstances you describe I suggest you consult a lawyer* etc.

When in doubt prefer "in the circumstances", which is consistent with *in the situation/event/conditions* etc. *Circumstance* in the singular is sometimes used as a variant of "situation", but in the phrase *pomp and circumstance* it preserves an earlier meaning: "ado"/"fuss"/"stir".

clamour/clamor etc   This word is typical of a set of words with endings spelt *our* in the British Isles and *or* in American English. Others include *favour/glamour/humour/honour/labour/vigour*. The *or* spelling is regarded as alien in British usage but the fact is that words that have already dropped the *u*, or never had it, outnumber those with *our*. They include *actor/author/doctor/error/horror/liquor/terror/vendor*. This then is hardly suitable ground for patriotic attitude-striking.

What is more, the *u* is regularly dropped in various inflections of such words, like *clamorous/glamorous/glamorize/honorary/humorous/laborious/invigorate*. In the light of these concessions to uniformity, preservation of *clamour* etc looks more like obstinacy than concern for tradition, especially as pronunciation is unaffected either way.

clandestine   Means "secret" or "undercover", either of which expresses the sense better, besides avoiding the risk of mispronunciation (klan*des*tin).

classified   As applied to information this is a contraction of *classified as secret*. As non-secret information is considered to be *unclassified*, **classified** makes a knowing substitute for *secret* for those who want to show familiarity with institutional jargon. Anybody else should be satisfied with *secret*.

clench/clinch   No longer interchangeable, these variants have distinct senses. **Clench** (noun and verb) is a tight grip. **Clinch** (verb, *clincher* noun) is to settle a deal/argument etc. But **clinch** retains its old sense in the phrase *in a clinch* = in a close embrace/grip.

clerestory Various exotic pronunciations have been applied to this ancient word, but the right one rhymes with "clear storey". It is also what the word means (a storey of a building, usually a church or hall, with windows but no floor).

clew See CLUE.

cloth/clothe/cloths etc Though **cloth** is by definition the material from which *clothes/clothing* are made, the word is little used in that sense any more. The commoner term for the fabric of women's dresses etc is *material*, and in menswear the terms *suiting/suit-length/fabric/material* are all more readily used by laymen than *cloth*. The names of particular weaves or yarns are also used on their own (*worsted/jersey/corduroy* etc), and *textiles* is used as the technical term for woven fabric in general.

A **cloth** in its commonest sense is any piece of fabric suitable for either cleaning (*Have you got a cloth I can wipe the mirror with?/ Let me go over that with a cloth*) or covering (*tablecloth/altar cloth* etc). A **cloth** can also mean "a kind of cloth" (*The mill had a display of its cloths*). **Cloth/cloths** rhyme with "moth"/"moths".

The verb **to clothe** (rhymes with "loathe") has *clothed* as its regular past tense and participle, *clad* being archaic. The noun *cladding* now generally refers to rigid outer coverings, like armourplate or stone facings. The noun **clothes**, always plural, used to rhyme with "close" (i.e. klOz), but the *th* is sounded nowadays, with difficulty. Though the word normally means "garments", it means something else in traditional compounds like *bedclothes* (i.e. sheets etc, not pyjamas).

clue/clew In the sense of information pointing towards a solution to a problem **clue** is now the invariable spelling in Great Britain, though **clew** still occurs in America. The change, as so often, has obscured the origin of the term. **Clew** is a ball of thread, especially the one Theseus unravelled in the Greek myth to retrace his way out of the labyrinth.

coach etc The usage of **coach** to mean a single-decker private or long-distance bus (what would once have been called a *charabanc*) is peculiar to Great Britain. *Bus* covers these senses elsewhere, including double-deckers of course. British use of **coach** is derived from *motor-coach*, a term taken from *railway coach* – a superior passenger carriage. This sense has transferred to airliners in American usage, which has **coach** as a euphemism for standard-price seats (i.e. not first-class compartment).

cocoa/coconut etc   The nuts have nothing to do with **cocoa**, which is itself an ancient misnomer for powdered cacao bean. There is no chance of correcting the spelling of **cocoa** but at least the threat of "cocoanut", once real, has been beaten off. **Coconut** is now the standard spelling for the nut of the coco palm, and this success has caused a corresponding reverse for *cokernut*, a phonetic spelling that came to be preferred in the trade for reducing confusion.

coitus   Pronounced in three syllables (*kO*-it-əs), not *coy. . .*, as young encyclopaedia scavengers tend to assume.

colander/cullender   The first is the usual and historic spelling. The second is an unwanted but fairly widely used phonetic version of it.

collision (in collision with)   When vehicles etc *collide*, British newspapers report the event with the odd phraseology *A car was in collision with a taxi/motorcycle/car/lamppost* etc. The natural way of putting it would be *A car collided with a taxi* etc, but this has legal risks. It imputes responsibility to one vehicle rather than the other. Even if the facts are correctly stated it prejudges what may be the issue in legal proceedings. The awkward **in collision with** is considered neutral and therefore legally safe. This is no reason for allowing it to survive unchallenged.

   In the first place it is indefensible in cases where only one of the parties was capable of colliding, let alone of suing, as in *A car was in collision with a lamppost*. In the second place natural phrasing and neutral reporting are not incompatible. No blame is implied in any of the following constructions: *A taxi and a car collided/A taxi had a collision with a car/A taxi and a car had a collision*. If these are considered too great a departure, the established formula can be converted into English by the simple addition of *a*: *in a collision with*.

combat/combatant etc   These words, dying before World War II, have been revived with a changed pronunciation. The first syllables were once sounded as in "cumbersome" but now they are phonetic. In **combat** the noun is *kom*bat, but the verb is usually *kom*bət. **Combative/combatant** are *kom*bətiv/*kom*bətənt. Military uses responsible for reviving these words include *combat troops* (U.S.)/

unarmed combat (martial art)/*non-combatant*. In non-military use the verb **to combat** generally occurs as a change from "resist" (*We must combat these tendencies*).

comparable/incomparable   The pronunciation should not be modelled on *comparison/comparative*, but it often is. Both **comparable** and **incomparable** are stressed on the syllable *comp*: komp*ə*r*ə*bl/ inkomp*ə*r*ə*bl.

comparative   With *comparison* as a model "comparitive" is an understandable spelling mistake, but a mistake all the same – and a common one.

compare to/with   The prepositions are not interchangeable. When the sense is "liken to" (find points of likeness between the essentially unlike) the usage is **to**, as in *Shall I compare thee to a summer's day?* Where the sense is of comparing notes (assessing differences between the like), the word is **with**, as in *How do the takings compare with yesterday's?* So the form usually required is **compare with**. It is also the only possibility when the verb is intransitive, as in *Her singing compares with that of Maria Callas* (i.e. stands comparison with).

Still, it would be foolish to pretend that these distinctions are generally observed. People tend to use whichever preposition first comes into their head, and this is **to** more often than **with**. *Comparable to* is much the commoner adjective construction, though *comparable with* is usually what is meant.

complement/compliment   A **complement** is a completion. A **compliment** (once the same word and still pronounced the same) is a gesture of approval, usually flattery or congratulation but sometimes a gift. Both words are verbs as well as nouns. The nouns are both stressed on the first syllable. The verbs, according to dictionaries, are stressed on the final syllable, but this distinction is rarely observed. For an overworked metaphor of **compliment** see TRIBUTE.

composite   The final syllable does not rhyme with "sight". As in *apposite/opposite* the *s* is pronounced as z and the *i* is short: komp*ə*zit.

conduit   The long-standing pronunciation of this word, meaning a pipe or channel to direct liquid or cable, rhymed with "fund it".

Evidently not enough people knew about this, as in the course of a few years this pronunciation has been entirely replaced by a literal rendering of the spelling. So now the word is pronounced like "conned wit" (*kon*dwit).

conjurer / conjuror As this noun is formed from the verb *conjure* the spelling **conjurer** is the natural form. It is also at least as common as **conjuror**, which may owe its currency to analogy with *juror*.

connection / connexion Etymologists prefer the older spelling **connexion**, but attempts to restore it by the *Oxford English Dictionary* and *The Times* etc have made no headway. **Connection** is now the standard spelling, which was only to be expected once the verb was established as *connect* (it used to be *connex*). The same fate has befallen *inflexion / reflexion*, both of which are now spelt *ction*. The *xion* ending must be regarded as obsolete, except in *complexion* (which cannot be spelt the other way). Pronunciation is unaffected (kshən).

conscript The notion that the verb form ought to be changed to *conscribe* is a lost cause. Making the verb like *describe / inscribe* would only show up the noun. Should a **conscript** then become a "conscription", or a *description / inscription* change to "descript" / "inscript"? It is not an issue to pause over, since it is settled.

consensus As well as being commonly misspelt with a *c* in the middle ("concensus") the word is a victim of misuse in phrases like *general consensus* or, worse, *general consensus of opinion*. **Consensus** has nothing to do with *census* but shares origins with *consent*. It means a collective or general opinion, as in *The consensus of readers was that writers should use words accurately / Discussion produced a consensus that early reform was unlikely*. Specifying "general" or "opinion" is like talking of "wet water", since these characteristics are intrinsic to the meaning of the word.

consider (as) etc One of the senses of **consider** is the same as "regard as", prompting **as** to be mistakenly tacked on. The equivalents are:

> *They regard him as trustworthy*
> *They consider him trustworthy.*

Note that **consider** does not require *to be*, often slipped in in such settings (. . . *to be trustworthy*). The idea that the addition makes for better written English is false – **consider** is one of a class of self-sufficient verbs like *think/find/reckon/declare*.

In a second sense **consider** = review/give consideration to, as in *Let's consider the facts/Juries retire to consider their verdicts*. In this straightforward use **as** becomes permissible to introduce a phrase describing the area of consideration. Hence *In my next talk I intend to consider Churchill as a strategist/She sings well but, considered as an actress, she is still a beginner*.

considerable The basic sense of **considerable** (and of *considerably*) is "worth considering". Unfortunately overuse in the figurative sense of "worth considering because big" has obscured this neutrality. An item can be worth considering for its smallness as well as its bigness. A small saving might be worth considering but if described as a "considerable saving" it would be taken to be a big one. Similarly things can be worth considering for aspects unconnected with size, but this sense would no longer be conveyed by **considerable**.

The word has joined the company of vague and overblown indicators of medium-size bigness like *substantial/sizable/significant* (q.v.), the sort of word intended to disguise the user's inadequate information, as seen in *The Prime Minister can count on a considerable renewal of support/A tactician of considerable resource/Things improved considerably*. Nine times out of ten, as in these examples, the effect gains and the sense is unchanged by throwing **considerable** out.

considering Besides being the present participle of the verb *to consider*, **considering** has an independent life as a preposition. So do some other present participles like *regarding/failing/concerning/including*. In the following example **considering** functions normally as a participle: *Considering how late it was, he decided to return home*. Here *he* is the subject of the sentence and *considering* is related to this subject – that is, *he* was doing the considering. This is demonstrated by a simple reordering of the sentence: *He, considering how late it was, decided to return home*.

In the next example **considering** is not related to the subject: *Considering his previous offences he was let off lightly*. Again the subject of the sentence is *he*, but it is not *he* who was doing the considering. Nobody is specified as considering, and what is meant is *in view of his previous offences*. This construction, theoretically ungrammatical because the participle is unrelated, has been sanctified by the centuries. Idiom has granted an immunity from prosecution and grammar has made the best of it by redefining **considering** in such contexts as a preposition. The same process earlier regularized *owing/during/notwithstanding/according/pending* and some other present participles not often recognized as such.

An additional liberty is permitted to **considering**. This is an elliptical usage, as in *That was a good show, considering.* Considering what? We are not told, and the inferred meaning is *all things considered.* Again grammar is satisfied, this time by classifying **considering** as an adverb.

The following examples illustrate the prepositional use of some other present participles: ***Regarding*** *your application for an interview, would 3 p.m. on Friday be convenient?/* ***Failing*** *a reply from you by the end of the week, legal proceedings will be started/* ***Granting*** *your contention, there is still another difficulty.*

In all these instances the participles are unrelated to the subject of the sentence and must be regarded as prepositions. (For a comparable use of present participles as conjunctions, see PROVIDING.)

consist in/consist of   The British Isles *consist of* Great Britain and Ireland. Water *consists of* two parts of hydrogen and one of oxygen. **Consist of** is the commoner term and is interchangeable with *comprise.* Where **consist in** differs is in referring to an aspect rather than the whole: *The strength of the language consists in its flexibility/The appeal of a thriller consists in its suspense.* So the sense of **consist in** is "has its essence in", and the phrase usually applies to non-material things, unlike **consist of**.

constable   This is one of many older words in which the *o* is traditionally pronounced like a *u*, e.g. *son/won/done* rhyme with "fun", *money/honey* with "funny". **Constable** has long been wavering, perhaps because all other words with a stressed first syllable spelt *con* rhyme it with "on", like *constant/continent/convoy.* **Constable** is now normally pronounced like them, though the older sound is still heard in court and in U-speech (q.v. in Part II).

consummate   The adjective **consummate** (kənsumət) means "accomplished"/"skilled", as in *with consummate ease/a consummate liar/a consummate performance.* The verb **consummate** (konsəmAt) means "to fulfil", as in *His appointment consummated* *his ambitions/How many brides and grooms are too tired after a long wedding reception to consummate the marriage?* (fulfil it with sexual intercourse).

The verb's past participle *consummated* stresses the first syllable(*kons∂mAtid*). The noun is *consummation* (konsəm*Ashn*) – remember Hamlet's *consummation devoutly to be wished*, i.e. fulfilment/outcome.

content/contentment   In *Let's hope he'll content himself with half a loaf* **content** is an obsolescent verb meaning "to be satisfied" (the more natural expression is *be content with*). It is the source of *contented/contentment* etc. All these are stressed on *tent*, and so is the phrase *heart's content*, where **content** is a traditional variant of **contentment**.

In *What is the content of the document?/We emptied the contents down the drain* **content(s)** is the noun of *contain*, and is set apart in speech from the other sense by a stress on *con*. **Content/contents** are not freely interchangeable. The singular refers to the kind of contents (e.g. coal), while the plural refers to the specific contents (e.g. two tons of coal, or the whole of whatever is in the container).

contribute etc   For stress see ATTRIBUTE.

controversy   The word itself has become a matter of controversy. It is a victim of people given to guessing how to pronounce a word new to their vocabulary. Guesses overlook that **controversy** is part of the set of words *controvert/controversial/controversially/controversialist*. These are consistent not only in sense but in not stressing the second syllable (i.e. trə not *trov*). People unaware of the relationship blunder in with kən*trovə*si, encouraged in Britain by broadcasters whose policy is to flatter ignorance. The way the words should be said is: *controversy* (*kon*trəvēsi)/ *controvert* (*kon*trəvət)/*controversial* (kontrəvēshl)/*controversially* (kontrəvēshəli)/*controversialist* (kontrəvēshəlist).

convince/persuade   We can be **persuaded** to do something or **persuaded** to believe something. This ought to be enough, without demanding the same versatility of **convince**. "She convinced me to go shopping" is ridiculous, not only because *convince to* is un-idiomatic but because **convince** is a verb concerned with the convic-tions, which hardly arise in decisions about whether to go shopping. Nevertheless *convince to* is an American tradition to which British usage show signs of succumbing.

The attraction is that **convince** is a stronger word – there are always clients for any intensification of meaning – and in some contexts the words are interchangeable. In the following pairs the only difference is the additional emphasis of **convinced**:

> *convinced of the truth/persuaded of the truth*
> *convinced that this was true/persuaded that this was true*
> *she convinced me/she persuaded me.*

There is a clear distinction however between **persuade to** and **convince that,** as in

> *They persuaded me to stay for dinner*
> *He convinced me that eating sugar is unhealthy.*

The difference of application is obvious and the difference of construction is a convenient reminder.

Copenhagen "Copen*hah*gen" is a mock-Teutonic mispronunciation, heard only from those who suppose the word to be shared by the natives. In fact **Copenhagen** is an anglicism, and does not exist in either Danish or German (*Köbenhavn*). (For a similar pitfall see MUNICH.)

cos Not recognized or even mentioned by most dictionaries except as a variety of lettuce. But though left out it is a word spoken more widely than thousands of words that get in. It is the spoken contraction of *because*, pronounced kəs, and often written in colloquial imitations as in *I can't go 'cos I'm busy.* The optional inverted comma denotes the missing syllable *be*.

As modern dictionaries have long held that their function is not to judge but to record what is said, their neglect of such an everyday term is remarkable. The *Oxford English Dictionary* only lists the word as a contraction of *cosine*, besides a lettuce. *Webster's New Collegiate* adds another contraction, for *consul*. Only the *Longman Dictionary of Contemporary English*, among leading popular dictionaries, lists **cos** as a contraction of *because*, calling it "informal". If it is informal it is no more so than *aren't/don't/I'm* and similar contractions used as first choices in most kinds of English speech. Like them it tends to fit spoken rhythms better than the full version.

It is true that **cos** is not accepted in written English, except as already noted, but writing is always slower than speech in recognizing realities.

cosy/cozy   Cosy is the British spelling, cozy the American.

council/counsel   Both sound the same but they are not interchangeable in writing. A **council** is a committee or conference, and a member of a council is a *councillor*. **Counsel** is advice, as in *take counsel/keep one's counsel*. Its use in the plural is limited to rhetoric or poetry(*From whom all holy desires, all good counsels . . . do proceed*). Someone who counsels is a *counsellor*. A *counsellor-at-law*, i.e. a barrister, is referred to as **counsel** (*I want counsel's opinion*), both collectively and in the singular (*Defence counsel was Mr Carson/His side had three counsel*). Hence QC = *Queen's Counsel*, a senior barrister, not to be confused with *Privy Councillor*, a member of the largely formal British governmental body, the Privy Council.

courtesy/curtsy   All the *court*-type words except these have their first syllable pronounced kawt, e.g. *court/courtly/courting/courtesan*. In **courtesy** and its derivatives *courteous/courteously* it is kə̄t, and so it is in **curtsy** (a corruption of *courtesy* in which the middle syllable has been lost).

covert/overt   A deceitful pair. **Covert** (= secret/concealed) is all that it seems, pronounced like "cover" with an added *t*. **Overt**, its converse (= open/unconcealed), lays a trap with a different vowel and stress: Ovə̄t.

cozy   See COSY.

crayfish/crawfish   Imprecise terms for small shellfish of the lobster type, dating from the centuries before the species had been accurately identified. In Great Britain **crayfish** is the usual form, and "crawfish" is considered to apply to some obscure foreign creature. In North America **crawfish** is the equivalent of *crayfish*, applying in particular to freshwater local species.

crescendo   Though widely misused to mean a peak of sound, a **crescendo** is in fact a musical passage of gradually increasing loudness. Sound etc cannot logically be said, as it often is, *to rise to a crescendo* or even *to reach a crescendo*, since the rise and the reaching are part of the crescendo.

crisis   The plural is *crises* (rhymes with "cry seas").

criteria/criterion Only the plural is **criteria,** and "this criteria"/ "what is your criteria?" etc are howlers. Muddling *this criterion/ these criteria* is what comes of overambitious reaching for a long word when the same sense could be expressed safely with a familiar short one: *test/standard.* (See also MEDIA/MEDIUM.)

crochet An uncomfortable import with regular spelling of its derivatives but irregular pronunciation. *Crochet* (*krO*shi)/*crocheted* (*krO*shid)/*crocheting* (*krO*shiing). The *t* is silent throughout, as it is also in *ricochet* (q.v.).

crotch/crutch **Crotch** now generally refers to the fork of the body, **crutch** to the prop (originally forked) used by the lame. In British usage, though not in American, **crutch** is sometimes used for both senses.

crummy Colloquial adjective denoting disapproval: *It was a crummy party/This crummy watch is slow/They made an offer but the terms were crummy.* The word once meant "crooked" or "crumpled", as applied to a cow's horn or a stick. It now has the general sense of "defective"/"unsatisfactory"/"inferior".

crutch See CROTCH.

cry/crier For spelling see DRY.

culinary A term more often written than spoken (*the culinary arts*) and probably more often pronounced wrong than right. It is *kU*linri.

cullender For spelling see COLANDER.

curb/kerb The spelling **kerb** (i.e. kerbstone) is a British peculiarity limited to the sense of a stone edging to a road. In all other senses of restraint or check, whether as noun or verb, **curb** is the only form. In the U.S. it covers **kerb** too.

curvaceous A facetious coupling of *curve* with the solemn ending *aceous,* which suggests zoological terminology (*crustacean/crustaceous*). The word is already indispensable as a more explicit alternative to *shapely,* applied to girls' figures.

czar/tsar   Both spellings derive from the Latin *Caesar*, but only **czar** provides a reminder of this historical link. As it is also nearer to the English pronunciation (zah) it has a better claim than **tsar**, which seems to have been copied from the French.

It is curious that either word should still be in frequent use so long after monarchy was abolished in Russia, especially as the title was not officially borne by the autocrat after Peter the Great substituted *imperator* (emperor). But **czar** remained the popular term and was also preserved in the secondary title of *Czar of Poland*.

dais   Still shown in dictionaries as rhyming with "ace", but now normally pronounced as two syllables: *dA*is.

dare/daresay etc   As a verb **dare** can be treated in two ways. [1] Straightforward verb with regular inflections (*dares/dared* etc). In this form *to* is necessary with any infinitive following it, as in *He dares to put it to the test/He dares to take the chance*. [2] Auxiliary verb for questions and negatives with only two forms, *dare/dared*. These require no *to* in a following infinitive (*Dare he risk it?/He dare not take the chance*). There is no need for confusion, as questions and negatives can always be put in the regular way, e.g. *Did he dare risk it?/He did not dare take the chance*. The verb *to need* has the same pattern.

Daresay, spelt in one word, is an accepted form with no past tense, but it virtually only works with *I/we* as in *I daresay you're hungry/We daresay he did his best*. In such phrases no daring is implied and the sense is equivalent to *I expect/imagine*.

data/datum   Because **datum** is rarely used the mistake can easily be made of assuming that **data** is the singular form (*Is the data complete?*). In fact **data** is always a plural (*Are the data complete?*) and an individual item is usually referred to as *one of the data*. For a similar confusion see MEDIUM/MEDIA. *Stratum/strata* are another comparable pair, but less common.

deal/a good deal   Ancient noun able to serve as an adverb when qualified by the adjectives **good/great** (*We go out to dinner a good deal*). This idiom is comparable with *a lot* (*He worked on the car a lot*) and with the colloquial use of *lots* (*I love you lots*). It is also the model for slang constructions like *She went a bundle on him*.

The original sense of **deal** is "portion"/"amount" – hence the use of the noun in what are now standard adjectival phrases, *It gave us a great deal of trouble* (= much)/*There was a good deal of quarrelling* (= much). In all these uses the noun is unusual without the adjectives **good/great**. *It caused me a deal of worry* etc is heard, but more typical is *There's a great deal to be said for democracy*.

In later senses of a bargain or a hand of cards **deal** can of course stand on its own (*It's a deal/Do we have a deal?/It's your deal/What a rotten deal*). The sarcastic expression *Big deal!* (i.e. "Call that important?") derives from these.

dear/dearly As in many similar older pairs, e.g. *high/highly, strong/strongly*, one form – **dearly** – is always an adverb (*She loves him dearly*)but the other – **dear** – is not always an adjective. It can be an adverb too, as in *That mistake cost him dear*. People who do not understand this are given to adding *ly* to any adverb that looks like an adjective – hence the spread of *firstly* (q.v.). This process has gone so far with **dear** that the form only survives as an adverb in a few phrases like *Buy cheap and sell dear/I'll see he pays dear for interfering*. (See also HARD/HARDLY.)

debacle This word is (a) not widely used, (b) not widely understood by those who use it, and might be (c) better not used at all. The intended sense is usually "crash"/"collapse"/"breakdown" – surely a sufficient choice already. This is the figurative French sense of the word, often taken to justify a French pronunciation as in *débâcle*. The basic sense though is a breakup of ice with attendant flooding. No English equivalent exists for this, and perhaps only geologists have felt the lack. They first imported the word and are entitled to go on pronouncing it like "oracle."

debut/debutante If debutantes are usually referred to as "debs" it is because the pronunciation has been anglicized to debU/debUtont, not dAboo/dAbootont. The colloquial effect is in fact nearer the French than the newsreader version, besides being easier on the English tongue. Both words have been borrowed long enough to need no acute accent (*débutante*).

There is no English verb form from **debut**, but *make a debut* is no hardship, except apparently for American showbiz writers (*How starlet debuted in Hollywood*). (See also DEPOT/DETOUR.)

decade   The informed pronunciation rhymes with "chequered", not "decayed". Unfortunately many people do not recognize the word in this form and find it harder to say than "decayed" or "deck aid". One or other of these versions seems likely to take over.

decimate   Does not mean to reduce *to* a tenth, but to reduce *by* a tenth. It derives from an ancient Roman practice of executing every tenth soldier for mutiny etc. No matter how often this is explained it seems unlikely that **decimate** will stop being used to mean mass indiscriminate destruction.

decorous   This is the adjective form of *decorum*, meaning " seemly in behaviour". It does not belong with *decorate/decorative* etc and has a different stress. **Decorum/decorous** are both stressed on *cor*, and so is **indecorous**.

definite/definitive etc   Definite is a useful adjective meaning "defined", hence "certain"/"fixed"/"exact" – or it would be if it were not debased as a mere conversational emphasizer (along with **definitely**), e.g. *Since his fall he has a definite limp*/*She's definitely the best swimmer*. Writing with any claim to quality prunes **definite/ definitely** as superfluous or even distracting in such examples.

   Definitive, not to be confused with *definite*, means "conclusive"/ "final"/"complete", as in *This book is the definitive account* (= one that cannot be improved on)/*The Pope's rulings are definitive on doctrine* (= final definitions)/*The definitive painting of the movement* (= the key expression).

deliberate   An example of stress varying with sense. **Deliberate** the adjective, meaning "on purpose", has stress on the second syllable (di*lib*rət). The verb, meaning "to ponder"/"think over before deciding", has secondary stress on the last ((di*lib*ərAt).

delimit   Means the opposite of what it appears to mean, i.e. to put a limit on, not to take one off. The verb *delimit* is a piece of traditional officialese. In expressions like *The extent of the territory is delimited by treaty* it means that the boundary/frontier is settled, i.e. the limits have been defined. So a *delimited boundary* is an accepted or official boundary – which is what it would be called in normal speech.

delusion/illusion etc   Both words refer to mistaken beliefs and are largely interchangeable. **Illusion** has the special sense of a visual deception (hence *illusionist,* a conjurer). The verb *to illude* is now in disuse, and **delude** serves for both senses.

demise   The vowels of **demise,** long anglicized, are the same as those of "devise".

demon/demoniacal etc   In popular phrases like *demon driver/demon bowler* **demon** is a noun used as an adjective. The choice is presumably made because nobody is sure what the adjective is. Is it *demonic/demoniac/demoniacal?* The answer is **demonic** (di*mon*ik).

A **demoniac** (di*mOn*iak) is someone possessed by an evil spirit, and the same word functions as an adjective. **Demoniacal** (d*Emon*/əkl), a favourite of hyperbolists, is a more impressive version of the adjective. As these subtleties are not widely understood there is little profit in straying from **demon/demonic/possessed.**

denigrate   Rhymes with "any grate" (not d*En*/gr*At,* a contemporary blunder).

deny   See REFUTE for distinction of sense.

dependant/dependent etc   A common spelling trap. A **dependant** is someone **dependent** on someone else (*The deceased had no dependants*). The noun **dependant** is the only word in the set spelt with an *a.* The others are *dependence* (the condition of being dependent), *independence* (= freedom), and *dependency* (a country not yet independent).

depot/detour   Two anglicized specimens with unpredictable pronunciation. **Depot** rhymes with "Aleppo", except in American English (d*Ep*O). **Detour** rhymes with "sea tour". (See also DEBUT/ DEMISE/DEBACLE.)

deprecate/depreciate   These are easily confused in writing. **Depreciate** (rhymes with "appreciate" – *c* sounded as sh) = diminish. **Deprecate** (stressed like "extricate", i.e. *dep*rik*At*) = disapprove. Strictly it means to express disapproval, so that its sense amounts to "protest mildly" (*The delegation deprecated lawlessness/The police chief deprecated the growing use of firearms*).

In general **deprecate** and its offshoots are literary words that would be better replaced by simpler ones, e.g. *Most of the reviews were deprecatory* (= disapproving)/*He is too self-deprecatory*(= self-critical or modest).

Depreciate is usually intransitive, as in *During inflation money depreciates* (diminishes in value)/*Has Churchill's standing depreciated?* (diminished in esteem). In transitive use it moves closer to the sense of **deprecate**, as in *I do not intend to depreciate Churchill's reputation* (= belittle/disparage). Here again the alternatives are improvements on the original.

deprive/deprived/privation etc   A man who has never owned a yacht may be said to lack a yacht, but he cannot be said to be **deprived** of one. To deprive is to take something away from somebody. Loss is the essence of the word's meaning. Similarly **deprivation** is a lack of something you formerly had, or would have had but for some outside cause (e.g. *deprived of a normal childhood by sickness*). It is not the same as **privation**, which means lack of life's necessities or comforts (e.g. shortage of food/clothing/heating). Nor is it the same as just being poor, or not as well off as others. The difference, however, is all too easily bridged by the idea of "deprived of opportunity", which has unlimited scope for those so minded. Privation can then be attributed to and equated with deprivation. Anyone lacking what he believes he should have, or what social reformers believe he should have, becomes one of "the deprived", and a sufferer of "social deprivation". Thus two useful words with clear meanings become loaded words, only to be used with caution. (See also PRIVILEGE/UNDERPRIVILEGED.)

derisive/derisory   A derisive remark is one that derides. A **derisory** remark is one that deserves derision. It is the difference between *laughing* and *laughable*. But this is a distinction no older than the 20th century. **Derisory** used to be a synonym of **derisive**.

despicable   First syllable stressed. (See APPLICABLE.)

despite/in spite of   These are interchangeable prepositions, as in *England is attractive in spite of the weather/. . . despite the weather.* As the shortened form, **despite** ought to be the first choice. Unaccountably it is less widely used than the phrase **in spite of**, especially in common expressions like *in spite of everything*.

desert/dessert   Considered in the plural there are three different nouns here:

[1] **deserts**, the Sahara kind (*dezəts*).
[2] **deserts**, what is deserved (*dizə̄ts*), used only in plural
[3] **desserts**, puddings/afters etc (*dizə̄ts*).

As [2] and [3] sound the same their confusion in writing is hardly to be wondered at. *He got his desserts* is a classic howler.

destined   Not a substitute for "intended". *A cache of petrol bombs has been found in Brixton. Police believe the bombs were destined for new street battles* (*Daily Express*). The bombs may have been so intended but they cannot have been **destined**. Their destiny was to be intercepted by the police, as events showed. The British bobby is often described as "wonderful", but not even he can redirect destiny.

detract/distract   Detract, like *subtract*, means "to take away from". Only usage separates the two. *Subtract*, used in calculation, is reserved for precise quantities, while **detract** is figurative, as in *The author's plagiarism must detract from his reputation*. It means in effect "to diminish". **Distract** means "to take the mind off" – equivalent to *sidetrack*, though the words are not connected.

devolution   For pronunciation see EVOLUTION.

dice/dicey   Ironic use of the purple phrase *dicing with death* has led to a colloquial adjective derived from **dice** and meaning "risky". On the model of *ice/icy, spice/spicy*, not to mention *chance/ chancy, lace/lacy, race/racy*, it is obvious that this word should be spelt "dicy". Words ending in *e* drop the letter when accepting a *y*, as demonstrated by *bone/bony, craze/crazy, haste/hasty, smoke/ smoky, wave/wavy*. Yet dictionaries as steady as the *Oxford Paperback* have taken to giving **dicey**, and also *pricey*, without even offering a regular alternative. Presumably these are intended as neutral reproductions of popular muddles (another is *cagey*, instead of *cagy* like *mangy*). But before long the surplus *e* will be complicating the spelling of established words, yielding other unaccountable variants like *price/pricey/pricier* etc. Such is the effect of neutrality. What is scholarship for if not to draw attention to popular irregularities?

Note that **dice**, used as both singular and plural in the British

Isles, was originally the plural of *die* – a noun still current in American English.

did   For "didn't used to" see USED (TO), and for "didn't ought to" see OUGHT.

differ from/with etc   The verb *to differ* and its offshoots are constructed with various prepositions along settled lines. Things and people **differ in** appearance/merit/views etc. In these respects they **differ from** each other. One or more **differ with** others about something, a construction paralleled by *disagree with/quarrel with*. Or they may be said to **differ** – reason unspecified. The participles *differing/differed* follow the same patterns.

   Difference: people in disagreement are said to have a **difference with** each other. Things that happen to people however make a **difference to** them. After **different/differently** the prepositions **to/from** are both used:

> *She thinks differently to/from you*
> *This colour is different to/from that.*

From, with its suggestion of apartness rather than convergence, tends to be preferred.

   A further possibility after **different/differently** is **than**. This is now regarded as an Americanism, despite historical endorsement by leading English writers. But as **different than** also has a respectable model in *other than* there is not much of a case for resisting it. In fact it offers convenient short cuts like *We're going to do it differently than anyone else has ever done it* – a construction that saves the rigmarole of *(differently)* **from the way in which** *(anyone)* . . . etc.

diplomat/diplomatist   Now that **diplomat** is seen in *The Times* of London the pretensions of **diplomatist** can be reckoned a lost cause. **Diplomat** has long been the usual word anyway, and is just as old-established as its rival.

discomfit/discomfiture   Two words best avoided altogether, as even if the writer has a correct understanding of the sense the reader is unlikely to share it. Neither word has anything to do with comfort or the lack of it. **Discomfit**, the verb, means "to defeat in battle" – hence to *thwart*, a much better word to use. **Discomfiture** is the noun for such defeat or thwarting. If what is meant is "upset"/"put out"/"disturb", the required word is either a choice from among these or *discomfort/disconcert*.

discomfort   The word may be a noun or a verb. There is no such word as "discomforture". (See DISCOMFIT.)

discreet/discrete   Discrete is not an alternative spelling but a different word. It is a technical word in music, pathology, logic etc, meaning "separate", as opposed to *concrete* (= continuous).

disinterested/uninterested   Ignorant use of **disinterested** is rapidly destroying the word's useful distinction from **uninterested**. **Disinterested** means "free from self-interest"/"impartial" (*He was able to take a disinterested view of the quarrel*). **Uninterested** means "lacking in interest"/"indifferent" (*She's uninterested in mechanical things*). **Uninterested** is little used, the usual forms being *not interested* or *uninteresting* (*She's not interested in mechanical things – she finds them uninteresting*). This may account for the mistaken resort to **disinterested**.

disparate/disparity   British dictionaries agree on a first-syllable stress for **disparate** (as in "desperate"), but *Webster's* prefers the second syllable (as in "this parrot"). It is not a word much used in speech, but under the influence of *disparity* (rhymes with "this parity") the second version is more often heard nowadays than the first, perhaps because the word is more recognizable that way.

dispatch/despatch   The case for **dispatch** is stronger on both etymological and phonetic grounds. The spelling **despatch** is a misinformed imitation of the French *dépêcher*, which is not the origin of the word.

dispel/expel/repel   There are areas of the language with not enough words and others with too many. **Dispel/expel/repel** belong to one of the overendowed. **Dispel/expel** both mean "to get rid of", **dispel** being applied to the abstract (doubts/anxieties/hopes etc), **expel** to the concrete (idlers/cheats/waste materials etc). **Repel**, to force back, is simply a synonym for "repulse". Currently *repellent* is more fashionable than *repulsive* (*The play's theme was repellent*).

distinct/distinctive etc   These are not interchangeable, and their differences are perhaps seen best through counterparts derived from the verb *to distinguish* (= to differentiate). **Distinct** = distinguishable, as in *There's a distinct flaw in this mirror/Chalk is distinct from cheese.* Hence **distinctly** = distinguishably. **Distinctive** = distinguishing, as in *His car is sprayed a distinctive shade of brown.* The adjective *distinguished*, as in *Such a distinguished man*, means a man distinguishable by reason of eminence/success etc (the sense is always favourable, except when ironic).

distract See DETRACT.

distribute etc For stress see ATTRIBUTE.

disused/unused etc Anything disused has been formerly used. Anything unused has not yet been used. **Disused** occurs usually as an adjective next to its noun, as in *a disused coalmine/a disused railway track. That coalmine is not used/. . . no longer used* would be preferred to *That coalmine is disused*, but the commonest form is *That coalmine is in disuse.* There is no such noun as "unuse", and hence no parallel phrase, the gap being filled by phrases like *lack of use/want of use.* **Unused** has two forms: [1] pronounced with the *s* as a *z* and meaning "not in use", [2] pronounced with the *s* sounded as such and meaning "unaccustomed", as in *They were unused to the climate.* (See also USED TO.)

doubt whether/doubt that These are not interchangeable in question or negative sentences, where only **doubt that** will do: *I don't doubt that the doctors know what's wrong/She never doubted that he meant well/Did you doubt that he spoke the truth?* In other sentences **doubt whether** is normal: *I doubt whether the doctors know what's wrong/She doubted whether his intentions were good.* The idea that the choice depends on the intention of whoever expresses the doubt, i.e. whether he intends to confirm or disavow it, no longer stands up, though it may have been sound once. It was advocated in the first Fowler manual, *The King's English*, but abandoned in the second, *Modern English Usage*.

draught/draft The original word is **draught**, which retains the majority of senses, such as current of air/beer on draught/draught horse/draught board. The spelling **draft** is confined to a provisional version of a written document/a banker's draft/a military posting or detachment (in the U.S., conscription). The same applies to the words as verbs. Someone who *drafts* written documents is a *drafts-*

man, but a *draughtsman* is someone who draws, not writes. *Draughtsmanship*, an obscure quality often held up for admiration by picture fanciers, means no more than skill in drawing.

due to/owing to   These phrases are not interchangeable in careful writing, though the distinction between them tends to be ignored in speech. **Due** is an adjective and, unlike **owing to**, cannot serve as a preposition. So *Due to the rain we stayed at home* is wrong because *due* is an unattached adjective – it does not describe either *we* or *home*. *Owing to the rain we stayed at home* is correct because **owing to** has come to be accepted as a preposition (though *owing* originates as a participle of the verb *to owe*).

   As **due to** is liable to be wrong and **owing to** is not, the simple solution is to stop trying to use **due to** where **owing to** could fit. In general any sentence beginning *Due to . . .* will be wrong. But there are proper uses for **due to** in sentences like the following: *There's a payment due to her/The disaster was due to lack of forethought/The credit due to his achievement is rarely acknowledged.* In all these examples the adjective *due* is clearly attached to a noun.

duffel   The coat with attached hood and toggle fastenings is named after a town, noted for its cloth, near Antwerp in Belgium. The spelling is **duffel** (not "duffle").

each other   In *They dread each other's relatives* and any possessive use of this phrase **other** is singular ("others'" is wrong). The idiomatic word order is *They respect each other*, not *They each respect the other/Each respects the other.* "One another" is interchangeable with **each other**.

   It is a superstition that **each other** should be restricted to references to not more than two. (See also PRONOUNS in Part II.)

east/eastern etc   See NORTH/NORTHERN.

ebullient   The second syllable (*bull*) rhymes with "dull", not "pull" – i*bull*yənt.

economic/economical   Economic is the adjective of *economics*, the study of the production and distribution of wealth, formerly called "political economy". So an economic issue etc is an issue of economics and normally has nothing to do with economizing. **Economize/ economical/economically** are another set meaning "behave thriftily"/"thrifty" etc (*She's an economical housekeeper/They live economically*). As there is no adverb equivalent to **economic** confusing use is sometimes made of **economically** in this sense too.

Edward/Edwardian Edward rhymes with "redwood", **Edwardian** with "bawdy 'un". Neither has a second syllable rhyming with "bard", a modern fad.

effect/affect etc Commonly confused. The senses are illustrated in the following: *The building is **affected** by damp* (= damp is having an effect on the building) / *The peeling wallpaper is an **effect** of the damp* (= a result) / *Repairs must be **effected*** (= put into effect / done) / *The **effects** will be far-reaching but they won't **affect** you.*

A different sense is conveyed by the set **affect/affected/ affectedly/affectation**, i.e. to do for effect. Hence *She **affects** the brogue, though she is not Irish / Her brogue is an **affectation** / He overdoes his politeness – it's **affected**.*

In the plural only, **effects** can also mean property (*His personal effects*).

So **effect/affect** are both verbs, with **affect** capable of two different senses. Only **effect** is a noun, but it too has two different senses.

effective/effectual etc   There is a glut of words like these but the only ones needed are **effective/effectively/effectiveness** and their negatives **ineffective** etc. The rest are superfluous variants, e.g. *effectual/ ineffectual/efficacy/efficacious*.

Effective, the adjective of *effect*, means "practical"/"having an effect", as in *Is prison effective? Does it deter? / He lacks the title but he's the effective boss* (the boss in effect). *Effective today* etc is American officialese for "with effect from today etc".

Of the superfluous specimens, **ineffectual** is often used for human inadequacy (*My husband is always ineffectual in a crisis*), but has no advantage over **ineffective**. **Efficacious** is rare, perhaps mainly remembered for the jingle *She invented the vegetable compound, efficacious in every case.* It only means "effective".

Note that *efficient/efficiency* share the essential meaning of **effective/effectiveness**, but their emphasis is on desirable effects, which the others do not necessarily imply.

egoist/egotist Despite schoolroom attempts to differentiate between these, both words have the same popular meaning: someone who overdoes the use of *I* and/or is too taken up with self. If a choice has to be made **egotist** is to be preferred, leaving **egoist** to represent a believer in academic theories of *egoism*. In all similar words the first syllable rhymes with "egg" (e.g. *ego*/*egocentric*).

eight/eighth If *eighth* kept in step with its neighbours *seventh*/*ninth* it would be spelt "eightth". Instead it is spelt without a second *t* but pronounced with it. (See also TWELFTH.)

either/neither "You say eether and I say eye-ther". The song settles the pronunciation issue – it is a matter of choice. But *E*thǝ (*th* as in "other") is commoner in America, /thǝ in Britain.

The other recurrent query about these words is whether to follow them with a verb in the singular or plural. The strict sense of **either/neither**, i.e. "one or the other" and "not one nor the other", requires a singular, as in *Either of these choices **is** correct*. But the grammar is often blurred where the mental picture is of two rather than one, as in *Neither of them know(s) what they are talking about*. Here *they* is unavoidable for lack of a more suitable pronoun (except as will be noted), and there is no convenient way of matching the second half of the sentence to the first half. It becomes a matter of choice again how the conflict is disguised.

The effect of the mental picture on speech is that **either/neither** are probably more often treated as plurals, e.g. *Though they are Japanese neither of them take their shoes off inside the house*. The sense here is "both of them don't" – a wording not permitted by idiom. Where a grammatical solution is available it tends to sound academic, as in *Neither of them knows what **either** is talking about/... knows what **he or she** is talking about ... knows what **he/she** is talking about* (where the alternatives are of the same sex).

So plural verbs are inevitably resorted to to smooth over the differences. Considering the latitude allowed to collective nouns (q.v.) in the matter of plurals it is nothing to fuss over. (See PLURAL/ SINGULAR CONFLICTS in Part II).

eke out A phrase apparently fated to misuse. It does *not* mean to have a thin time (*He eked out his last years in seclusion*) or make something last longer than usual (*He eked out his wardrobe by going without new clothes*). **Eke out** = to supplement/to render adequate by addition. The notion of addition is essential. Hence: *He eked out his wardrobe with patches of waste material/Her pension was eked out with the income from occasional baby-sitting.* The thing eked out is always the thing added to.

elder/older etc   As a noun meaning a senior or a senior official, **elder** is still useful (*Your elders and betters/the elders of the church*). As a member of the set **elder/eldest**, particularly in adjectival use, it perpetuates the sort of distinction that is not worth making. **Older/oldest** convey the same sense as **elder/eldest** but usage reserves the last for seniority within a family. Unfortunately even this distinction is inconsistent. So while *the elder daughter/an elder son/the son's the eldest* are the preferred forms, **elder/eldest** cannot be substituted in *She's older than her brother/Her sister-in-law is older though/She's the oldest then.*

Such subleties deserve to fade into disuse and there are signs that this is happening. **Older/oldest** are gaining ground and **elder/eldest** are perhaps mainly used by parents about their own children (*Jane's my eldest*).

elevator/lift   Exhibit A for Anglo-American differences. In the sense of a hoist for grain however, **elevator** is the earlier term and is still used in common. **Lift**, regarded in Great Britain as though it were the original (with **elevator** an aberration), dates from the introduction of serving hoists in hotels and mansions in the mid-19th century. Though the term was used much earlier in coalmines, it denoted an entirely different technical device there – which may be why the word was avoided when **elevator** was coined. **Elevator** is generally understood in the U.K., though **lift** puzzles North Americans.

emulate   Not a synonym for "imitate", as is widely assumed. **To emulate** means "to vie with"/"to imitate competitively"/"to try to outdo at the same thing". Whether the correct sense is understood widely enough to make the word worth using is doubtful.

enable   This verb, meaning "to empower/authorize" (hence *an enabling Act*), must be constructed with a full infinitive (i.e. including *to*): *Your kind offer of accommodation enabled me to enjoy a longer holiday/Their official papers enabled them to pass the police roadblock/The wait between trains will enable us to get a snack.* It cannot be used as a simple alternative to "made possible" or

"facilitate", e.g. *I wanted to stay longer and your offer enabled it.*
This should be rephrased to . . . *enabled me to do so.* No passive
form (*I was enabled to* . . . etc) is in use.

encyclopaedia/-edia The spelling **encyclopedia** is general in
America (an exception is the American-produced *Encyclopaedia
Britannica*) and common in Great Britain. The older spelling with
ae (already a simplifaction of *æ*) will presumably be superseded, as
has happened in *medieval.*

endemic/ephemera/polemic etc In all these, and their derivatives,
the stressed *em* is pronounced as in "epidemic", i.e. rhymes with
"them", not "theme".

The difference in sense between *epidemic* and **endemic** is that
the first is a temporary outbreak of disease etc, while an endemic
disease is native or locally prevalent.

enough/sufficient/sufficiently There is no difference in meaning
but **enough** has peculiarities of positioning. As an adjective **enough**
can go before or after its noun (*There'll be enough time to relax
later/. . . time enough to relax later*) – it now goes more often
before. Also as an adjective **enough** cannot be preceded by an article
(*a/the* etc), unlike **sufficient.** So *Have we enough stock/store
enough/supply enough/reserve enough?* but *Have we a sufficient
stock/store/supply/reserve?*

As an adverb **enough**, unlike **sufficiently**, always follows the
verb or (where there is one) the object of the sentence: *Every
virtuoso practises enough/No virtuoso can practise his playing
enough.* In these examples **sufficiently** could go at the end or, in the
second one, in front of *practise.* When qualifying an adjective or
another adverb **enough** goes after the word, while **sufficiently** goes
before it (*hard enough/fast enough/big enough/appalling enough,*
but *sufficiently hard/sufficiently fast/sufficiently big/sufficiently
appalling*).

Enough is much the oldest of these English words, the commonest in familiar phrases, the crispest, and the natural conversational choice. The preference for **sufficient(ly)** noticeable in some
writers and public speakers must be due to either a taste for formality or a lack of confidence in handling **enough.** For the artifici-
ality of **sufficient(ly)** compare *That will be enough/That will be
sufficient* or *Are you sure you've tried hard enough/Are you sure
you've tried sufficiently hard?*

enquire   For preferred spelling see INQUIRE.

ensure   See ASSURE.

envelope   The verb *to envelop* (rhymes with "develop") has been part of the language since Chaucer. So attempts to hold out for a Frenchified pronunciation of the noun **envelope** (*ong*vəlOp instead of *en*vəlOp) seem excessive – the more so since the noun itself has been used in English for more than two centuries.

environment   The primary meaning of this word is "environs"/"surrounding region". The recent modern sense, which has all but obliterated it, is owed to the ecological lobby's success in popularizing a term confined previously to biologists. It now means the surrounding physical conditions in general.

ephemera   For pronunciation see ENDEMIC.

epitome/forte etc   The English pronunciation of adopted foreign words ending in an articulated *e* is chaotic. Some, like **epitome/hyperbole/apostrophe/anemone**, continue with the *e* sounded as a separate syllable, as in *ipit*əmi. Others are remodelled, so that **syndrome** rhymes with "aerodrome". Still others waver. **Furore** sometimes has three syllables and sometimes two – in the U.S. it is spelt *furor*. **Forte** in the musical sense takes after its Italian forebear in having two syllables (rhymes with "forty", not "Fort A"). In the sense of a strong point it should rhyme with "fort", as the *Oxford English Dictionary* gives it, since its French original has only one syllable. But since it has an *e* on the end it is swiftly recognized as a foreign specimen and given a rhyme with "forty" for safety's sake.

equally (as)   These two do not go together. If the need is felt to strengthen *as* in constructions like *He's as good as you are* the required word is *just*, not *equally* (*just as good as*). Equality is built into the construction *as . . . as*, and does not need to be specified again. If **equally** is to be the writer's choice he does not need *as*. Thus *You and I are equally guilty*, or *You are as guilty as I am*, or *We are just as guilty as each other* etc (but not *We are equally as guilty*). The misuse comes from clutching at **equally** and trying to force it into another word's pattern of phrasing instead of sticking to its own.

equip See FURNISH.

erstwhile Still resurrected for solemn effects or heavy humour, but for which the word might be decently buried. It only means "former".

erupt/irrupt Only **erupt/eruption** are now in everyday use. **Irrupt** is in fact a different word, meaning to break into, whereas **erupt** means to break forth. As both have the same pronunciation the spellings are occasionally confused.

especial/special etc The adverbs **specially/especially** have a clear difference of meaning. **Specially** = on purpose. **Especially** = in particular. The two adjectives **special/especial** carry either sense, with **special** the more usual form. The distinctions are largely confined to writing as the words are hard to tell apart in speech. The unstressed first syllable in **especial(ly)** usually gets submerged.

These examples illustrate the difference between **specially/ especially**, but reveal some overlaps:

> *He came home early specially* (to see the children before bedtime)
> *He came home especially early* (= particularly early/earlier than usual)
> *The part was made specially to fit*
> *You cooked this specially for me?*
> *The French especially take cooking seriously*
> *You all looked especially smart.*

In phrases like *made specially for Fortnum & Mason*, **especially** could be substituted, because any such product could also be described as made for the firm in particular. (But *made especially for* would not exclude making for others too.) Doubtful areas like this simply reflect the inherent closeness of *on purpose/in particular* etc.

essential See UNIQUE.

euphemism/euphuism A euphemism is a politer or more palatable substitute for an obvious term, as in *Final Solution* (= extermination)/*physically handicapped* (= cripple)/*Supplementary Benefit* (= dole)/*capital punishment* (= death penalty)/*corporal punishment* (= flogging)/*recidivist* (= habitual criminal)/*obesity* (= fatness). Ours is an age of euphemisms.

Euphuism, a word sometimes confused with **euphemism**, would be better locked up in dictionaries. It means a particular kind of elaborate high-flown language known only to literary critics – and not to many of those.

ever Because **ever** forms part of words like *whatever/whenever/ however/whoever* etc some people mistakenly write it as a compound word every time it occurs next to a word like *what/when/ how/who*. This policy overlooks the sort of sentence where **ever** can be separated and repositioned, e.g. *however* is not what is meant in *However can I thank you?*, which could be rearranged as *How can I ever thank you?* If repositioning is possible **ever** should not be part of the compound. In such sentences the function of **ever** is simply to add emphasis, like *possibly/at all*.

When **ever** is properly part of a compound it occurs mainly in subsentences. The possible compounds are with *who/whom/ what/when/where/which/how*. Grammatically these words can usually be replaced by the **ever** version in subsentences, but its selection varies the sense: **ever** shows that the word to which it is attached is intended in an indefinite or generalized sense, as in *Give them whatever they want/He writes to us wherever he is/Let's finish it however long it takes*. (These examples can be compared with . . . *what they want/ . . . where he is* for a more restricted sense.)

Some of the **ever** words have other functions. *Whatever* acts adjectivally in *You have no patience whatever. However* (q.v.) acts as a conjunct in *The rain stopped. However it soon started again.*

everybody/everyone etc For when to separate into two words, see ANYONE. For use of plural pronouns/possessives in referring back to **everybody** etc see PLURAL PROBLEMS in Part II.

evolution/devolution/revolution As *evolve/devolve* follow the model of *revolve* it might be expected that **evolution/devolution** would be rhymed with **revolution**. By purists, so they are. But much the most usual pronunciation of **evolution** sounds the first syllable as "Eve". Being a more recent word in popular use **devolution** wavers between the two, with the "Eve" version probably the commoner.

except/except for Should **except** be followed by **for**? When **except** is a simple preposition **for** is usually unnecessary, as in *Every room has been cleaned except (for) the kitchen/We're all ready except* *(for) Grandma.* **For** is preferred when **except** starts a sentence: *Except for Grandma we're all ready/Except for the kitchen every room has been cleaned.* It is also required [1] where the sense is "without", as in *I don't know what I'd have done except for you,* and [2] where the item excepted differs in kind from the one cited, as in *The bar was deserted except for a few regulars* (the regulars are of a different order from the bar). In all these examples *but* could be substituted for **except**.

When paired with *that,* **except** functions as a conjunction, as in

I would have phoned except that I couldn't get change.

Here *that* is often ellipted.

exceptionable   See UNEXCEPTIONAL.

executor/executive/executioner   In their different ways they all *execute.* An **executor** sees to the execution of a (last) will. An **executive** executes the policies of an employer/business/institution – he is an executive officer as opposed to an administrative officer or clerical officer. An **executioner** executes the sentence of the court, i.e. the death sentence.

expel   See DISPEL.

explicable   Stress first syllable. (See APPLICABLE.)

exquisite   Stressed like "requisite"/"perquisite", on the first syllable (*ex*, not *quis*). Guessers seem to find the second syllable more comfortable, though there are plenty of other models for stressing the first, like *exercise/exorcist/extricate/extirpate.*

face up to   When an expression survives general denunciation by the literary it may be because it fills a genuine gap. **Face up to** is said to use three words to do the work of one (*face*). But are *facing the facts/facing the future* etc the same thing as *facing up to the facts/facing up to the future?* The verb on its own conveys nothing of the frame of mind in which the facing is done. One can face the future with hope, confidence, despair or fear. To **face up to** it implies effort and resolve.

fair/fairly The phrases *fight fair/play fair/won fair and square* show that **fair** can function as an adverb and need not necessarily be replaced by **fairly**, the regular adverb. But this latitude is limited to traditional phrases like these. Only **fairly** would do in a sentence like *Let's divide up all the leftovers fairly*. The sense in all instances is "honestly"/"according to the rules".

But colloquially **fair** is common in another sense, equivalent to "really", as in *She fair told him off/The car fair tore past*. This use is on a par with "didn't half" (*She didn't half tell him off*), i.e. it is a colloquial application of the word and cannot be made formal by substituting **fairly**, as is often tried. In fact when this is done the effect is liable to be unintended, as in *The two boxers fairly knocked each other about* (which suggests a concern for the rules rather than a mutual pasting).

fall/autumn As a synonym for **autumn** the word **fall** is no longer used in Great Britain but is the everyday word in the U.S. Contrary to popular British belief, **autumn** is not unknown there, just less widely used.

fantasy/phantasy etc These are no longer alternative spellings. **Fantasy** and its offshoots are normally spelt with an *f*. Two survivors of the earlier style are *phantasm* (= an imagined vision, not a phantom) and *phantasmagoria* (once a trade name, now applied to a succession of phantasms).

farther/further Any distinctions between these two words are arbitrary. Neither of them is the original comparative of *far*, and though **far/farther/farthest** are sometimes taken for a set in senses of distance, **far/further/furthest** are more widely used in all senses. This may be because **further** etc is safer, having senses not shared by **farther**. Thus **further** (as adjective) = additional, (as adverb) = moreover/furthermore, (as verb) = to promote/help along. It also yields the noun *furtherance* (= advancement).

Some people make the distinction *I go farther* (in distance)/*I go further* (in argument etc), but this is whimsical. The practical approach is to treat **further** as the norm.

fatal/fatalist/fateful Earlier senses of **fatal** (= destined/inevitable etc) have been swamped by use of the word to mean "deadly"/"ruinous". But **fateful** = destiny-laden, and **fatalist** or -**istic** = conforming with the doctrine of fatalism or inevitability.

fed up With its image of overfullness this may not be the most elegant of adjectival phrases, but it is respectably formed and indispensable in such uses as *What's the matter – you look fed up?*. It covers *bored/tired/miserable* at one go. The only cause for grammatical offence is when the phrase is followed with an ignorant *of* instead of its proper preposition *with*. So *I'm fed up with the weather/I'm fed up with staying in* are irreproachable, while *I'm fed up of . . .* is intolerable.

fertile/missile etc It is a source of much harmless merriment to the British that Americans pronounce **fertile** to rhyme with "turtle", and **missile** with "missal". This divergence unfortunately extends to many more words, including *facile/fragile/docile/ductile/ prehensile/projectile/tactile/volatile*. Americans pronounce all these words on the pattern of "turtle", while British speech follows the pattern of "I'll"/"smile"/"file".

British consistency has been achieved by harmonizing *ductile/ tactile*, which were once exceptions. So it is a pity that American consistency has been achieved by moving in the opposite direction.

few/a few etc The grammatical peculiarities of *few* pass largely unnoticed by the native English speaker, but to begin with **few** and **a few** have different senses. **Few** = not many but some/**a few** = some but not many, e.g. *There are a few, kind sir* (= some)/*Many are called but few are chosen* (= not many).

Then **few** accepts only adverbs as qualifying words: *too few/ very few/scandalously few*. But **a few** accepts adjectives too: *a good few/a tiny few/quite a few/a very few/not a few*. All such phrases can also act as adjectives as in *a good few people/a precious few examples/not a few chances*.

fewer/less The theory is that **fewer** refers to number while **less** refers to quantity or amount. A strict interpretation thus gives

> *less chance/fewer chances*
> *less trouble/fewer troubles*
> *less noise/fewer noises*
> *less trade/fewer sales*
> *less population/fewer people.*

It will be seen that **fewer** requires a plural noun in each example, unlike **less**. But it is not as simple as that. **Less** is the normal choice with *supplies/troops*, which are regular plurals, and with *goods*, which (in the material sense) is always plural. The explanation is that such terms are felt to imply totality rather than the units comprising this. But this is a subtlety not to be expected of spoken sentences, and **less** is inevitably the usual first choice in speech regardless of reference.

Careful wordsmiths prefer to write **fewer** where appropriate, even though they may not say it. They take care over *many fewer/ several fewer* etc, but find themselves in a dilemma with "a few fewer" – to which the only solution is *a few less*.

figure etc   Since **figure** admittedly rhymes with "jigger", and its derivatives **figured/figuring** keep the same sound, there is not much to be said for making an exception of **figurative(ly)**, as in *fig*Urətiv. If there has to be any exception it is best limited to **figurine** (fig*UrEn*), a word of obvious alien origin. The unexpected staying power of the *fig*Uə version may be due to transatlantic example as, despite all the "figgerin'" that goes on in westerns, it remains first choice in leading dictionaries like *Webster's New Collegiate*. There the rhyme with "jigger" is regarded as "especially British".

finalize   Objections to **finalize** as American jargon for "finish"/ "complete" (e.g. "An ugly word, un-English, and quite unnecessary") are both wrong and futile. Wrong, because the word has a distinctive and useful sense – not just to finish/complete something but to settle the last details. Futile, because the word is obviously here to stay, its usefulness having become apparent.

first/firstly etc   **First** has been an adverb just as long as it has been an adjective, but 10 centuries are not enough to satisfy the tidy-minded. Hence the notion that **firstly** (itself of venerable antiquity) should be substituted, especially in enumeration (*firstly, secondly, thirdly* etc). But umpteen phrases establish that **first** is the normal form: *You go first/First I must have a drink/First come, first served/First catch your hare/Which came first, the chicken or the egg?*. Even in enumeration there is no cause to resort to **firstly** for consistency. *Second/third/fourth* etc can just as well be used adverbially, an idiom demonstrated by *John came first, Paul came second, Philip came third, and Roger came last*. **Firstly** is not wrong, but it is a matter of choice whether the *ly* forms are preferred to the simpler adjectival forms used adverbially.

flammable   See INFLAMMABLE.

floe A floating piece of ice, which is not the same as an *ice flow*.

folk/folks etc Through the centuries **folk** has suffered an undeniable downgrading, displaced by *people* and patronized as quaint. If not yet relegated to colloquial use, **folk** is increasingly associated with bucolic senses, as in **folklore**. Hence **folk music**, a music supposedly traditional to rural folk, though nowadays commercially produced and performed. **Folksy** is a colloquial adjective covering *unpretentious/comfortable/welcoming/honest* and all the reassuring attributes ordinary people like to apply to themselves.

    Folk and its plural form **folks** are used interchangeably – *The Folks Who Live on the Hill/The folk next door*. In American usage the plural can mean one's relatives – hence *You must meet my folks* (= *my parents* etc – not one's spouse or children).

forbear/forebear A **forebear** is an ancestor or forefather (*fore* has the same sense as in *before*). To **forbear** = to refrain from (usually some expected or deserved rebuke or enforcement). Hence *forbearing/forbore/forborne/forbearance*. A similar difference separates *forgo/foregoing*. To **forgo** = go without/renounce, whence *forwent/forgone*. **Foregoing** = preceding (*Nothing in the foregoing terms affects your financial interest*), adjective and noun.

forbid/forbade **Forbid** tends not to be used in the past tense, **forbade**, because of doubt about its pronunciation (rhymes with "bad", not "bayed"). The usual evasion is *wouldn't allow*.

forecast For the past tense form see BROADCAST.

forever It seems hard to believe that only a few years ago objections were made to spelling this as one word, e.g. a '70s manual states "The one-word spelling is to be discouraged . . .". But since the novel *Forever Amber* the resistance has been justly doomed (if *all*+*ways* why not *for*+*ever*?). **Forever** is now just as acceptable in British usage as in American.

forgo/foregoing For the distinction of meaning see FORBEAR.

former/latter As an adjective meaning "previous", **former** has a useful function (*the former chairman of the board/Lady Whimple, the former Miss Smith/He has regained much of his former energy*). As a pronoun, especially when paired with **the latter**, **the former** is a literary device intended to spare the reader repetition. But it generally achieves this by inflicting on the reader work that ought to have been done by the writer. A previous passage usually has to be reread to identify what the writer is referring to. Who needs a favour like that?

Repetition is surely a relief compared with this sort of thing: *Whether the Government should have gone ahead along the agreed course, anticipating the new risks, or whether this was the time for a full reconsideration is something that will be endlessly debated. Indecision lost the opportunity for the latter, and events took too unexpected a turn for the former.*

Reconstruction by the writer is the only proper solution to such riddles, e.g. *What the Government should have done will be endlessly debated. Should it have gone ahead along the agreed course, anticipating the new risks? Events took too unexpected a turn. Should there have been a full reconsideration? Indecision lost the opportunity.*

Most popular newspaper offices impose a ban on the use of *the former/the latter*, and understandably so.

Formica See HOOVER.

forte For pronunciation see EPITOME.

forward/forwards etc Until recently **forwards** was used in some adverbial senses, but on a basis so obscure that **forward**, already the commoner adverb (*looking forward to seeing you*), is now commoner in all senses, apart from the phrase *backwards and forwards*. **Forward** is also an adjective and a verb. As no distinction is needed in the use of the adverb the dropping of the *s* is a plus.

No consistent trend yet extends to similar words like *backwards/onwards/towards/afterwards* (q.v.). **Forward(s)** rhymes with "four wood(s)", but in nautical use **forward** is pronounced forəd.

fraction/fractional In *You could have bought that for a fraction of the price* **fraction** is taken to mean a small part. This is an instance of jumping to conclusions. A fraction is any part less than the whole but it might be nine-tenths or more. Large or small should be specified in careful writing. But then in careful writing **fraction** would probably not be used at all, since it conveys no more than "part".

Phrases like *a fractional increase* are best kept for mathematical contexts. Elsewhere they are just elaborate substitutes for *small, little* etc.

A comparable example is the use of *quality* in phrases like *quality clothes/shop here for quality*, which assume that the quality is good, though *quality* covers both good and bad.

fragile   For pronunciation see FERTILE.

frontier   Pronounced *frunt*Eə. Stress on the second syllable (frunt*Eə*), much heard in movie westerns, is an American option.

fulsome   Means just what it seems to mean, i.e. "plentiful"/"ample". The idea that it derives from "foulsome" and really means "loathsome" is a fallacy. Its derivation is what one would imagine, *full+some*, and its only derogatory sense is that of "overfull", as applied chiefly to excessive flattery etc.

It is true that at one stage of its long career **fulsome** led a double life and was also used to mean "loathsome", though whether this was due to confusion with an earlier word "foulsome" or to an extension of the sense "excessive" is uncertain. What is certain is that **fulsome** no longer has any senses but those offered above.

funereal/funerary   Funereal (fUn*Eə*riəl) means "like a funeral" (*We were moving at a funereal pace*). **Funerary** is the adjective for "to do with a funeral" (*a funerary rite*), though the noun *funeral* is more often used in this role, as in *a funeral procession/the funeral ceremony*.

furnish/equip/provision etc   These are among a group of verbs all meaning "supply" but having vague specialized applications. It is curious that items as important and various as furniture, major hardware, and food and drink, should all be described by their least typical characteristic, that of being supplied. The verb **furnish** still means to supply in general as much as to supply furniture (*Please furnish references*). **Furniture** retains the sense of that which is supplied, being applied to window and door fittings as well as household movables. So does *furnishings*, the word for household textiles.

Equip, originally meaning to fit out a ship, now means to supply any machinery or fittings, and **equipment** = anything from filing trays to a dam turbine.

Provisions (something *provided*) are bulk supplies of victuals and/or other non-durable items. **To provision** is to supply these. Some other words with the same general sense of "supply" are *fit out/outfit/purvey*. With so many to choose from it seems a pity that more exact applications could not be allotted. Better still would be a coining of more descriptive words like the un-fashionable *ironmongery/hardware/victuals*.

furore   For pronunciation see EPITOME.

further   For relation to *farther* and other senses see FARTHER.

garbardine/gaberdine   These tend to be treated as interchangeable, but the small difference of spelling marks a difference of definition. **Gabardine** is a modern worsted-type cloth. **Gaberdine** was histori-cally the word for a loose garment worn by Jews and by people supported by alms. By extension it also applied to the coarse cloth of the garment.

gala   The Durham Miners' Gala, an annual event dating back 100 years, is known to those involved in it as a *gAlə*, i.e. the word rhymes with "sailor"/"paler". This anglicized pronunciation, en-dorsed by the *Oxford English Dictionary*, is perfectly justifiable for a word that had been part of the language nearly three centuries before the miners took to it. But the spread of Continental travel has brought home the French origin of the word to many who know of Durham only for its cathedral. To mark this discovery the sophisticated have adopted *gahlə*, which has already become the standard pronunciation – another instance of outside events over-taking the coal industry.

gallant   Rhymes with "talent". Stress on the second syllable, when not ignorant, is facetious.

gaol   See JAIL.

garage   Though this quickly achieved anglicization, rhyming with "carriage"/"marriage" (*garij*), second thoughts have prevailed. The current pronunciation imitates the original French, with the second syllable's vowel pronounced "ah" and the *ge* pronounced as in "beige"/"rouge"/"vision" (a consonant sound for which no letter exists in English). This is also the usual pronunciation in the U.S., except that Americans stress the second syllable instead of the first as in Britain.

gasoline American term for *petrol*, also used in Great Britain till the French term *essence de pétrole* (petroleum spirit) was adapted instead. Petroleum itself is the crude oil, known for centuries, from which the various fuel oils such as gasoline/kerosene/diesel are extracted.

gasometer The stress is on the second syllable, gasomitə, as it is also in *speedometer*. These words should not be taken as models for pronouncing *kilometre*. They are differently derived – from *meter* (a measuring device) not from *metre* (a measure). *Kilometre*, a compound of *kilo+metre*, is stressed on its first syllable, kiləmEtə. Only American usage gives it the *gasometer* stress.

geography/geometry etc Commonly mispronounced with first syllables as jog/jom, instead of jiogrəfi/jiomətri (as in *geographical/geometrical*). (See also GRAPH/GRAPHIC.)

geriatrics/gerontocracy/gerontology etc Too recent to appear in the first Supplement to the *Oxford English Dictionary*, **geriatrics** is the branch of medicine concerned with old age, and **gerontology** is the study of old age. The adjective **geriatric**, which properly means "to do with geriatrics" (*geriatric ward/a geriatric study*), has come to mean "senile" in popular use. **Gerontocracy** = government by old men. All these words are pronounced with a soft *g* (jer-).

gipsy For spelling see GYPSY.

glacier/glacial Glacier rhymes with "gassier" (not with "racier"), **glacial** with "racial" (glAshl). The inconsistency need only trouble geologists. The layman has no occasion to say **glacial** when all he means is "icy".

glad/happy Both = joyous. **Happy** is supposed to have the primary meaning of "lucky"/"fortunate", but it is almost invariably used as the adjective of *happiness* in the modern sense of that word, defined as "pleasurable content of mind", i.e. joy.

glamour/glamorous etc   See CLAMOUR for spelling variants.

graph/graphic etc   Graph can rhyme with "laugh" (i.e. grahf) or with "gaffe", but there is no choice with **graphic**, which always has a short *a* as in "traffic". The same applies to "graph" words like *photograph/holograph* and to "graphic" ones in which the *graph* syllable is stressed as in *photographic/geographical/biographical*.

grey/gray   The standard spelling in the British Isles is **grey**, and in the U.S. **gray**. But both spellings are known in both countries and they pass without distress. The historical case for each is about equal, with **gray** preferable on phonetic ground.

guarantee/guaranty/warranty   These are the same word in origin. All have the same essential sense of a surety or promise to indemnify. **Guaranty** is obsolete in the British Isles, where **guarantee** is the normal form for both verb and noun. Both **guaranty** (usually financial) and **warranty** are current in the U.S., but **warranty** is never a verb. British usage treats **warranty** as an alternative to **guarantee** in the sense of a commercial commitment to refund payment or repair defective merchandise, but only **guarantee** would be used in such senses as *Free choice of marriage partner is no guarantee of happiness/Hard work is the best guarantee of results.*

guerrilla   The word means an armed fighting irregular, and serves as adjective as well as noun (*guerrilla war/guerrilla unit*). In pronunciation it is now indistinguishable from *gorilla* (gəri*l*ə). Equally indistinguishable today are the roles of guerrilla and terrorist, though in theory a guerrilla does not necessarily commit acts of terror.

guillotine   In a widely believed piece of popular etymology **guillotines** are so named because Dr Guillotin originated the machines to speed up the rate of executions during the French Revolution. Only the name is correct in this. Under other names similar machines had been in use in several parts of Europe long before Dr Guillotin's time. He merely advocated mechanical execution as a humane method. The French guillotine was designed not by him but by Dr Antoine Louis, secretary of the Surgical Academy. It was built by a German harpsichord maker, Tobias Schmidt, with prompting by Charles-Henri Sanson, the hereditary executioner.

gynaecology   See OBSTETRICS.

gypsy/gipsy etc   **Gypsy** is the earlier and the better spelling, with its reminder of the belief that gypsies came from Egypt. Similarly *Zigeuner* in German preserves the notion that they derived from an Asia Minor sect. *Romany*, the name of their language, suggests a Latin origin, but is in fact derived from *rom* (rhymes with "from"), the term gypsies use for themselves where they do come from: India. (See also ROMANIA/ROMANY).

haemorrhage/haemoglobin etc   The set of words once all spelt with an initial *hæmo* (= blood) is gradually shedding the *a*, so that *hemo* is already an optional simpler spelling. Unfortunately there is no comparable movement towards consistent pronunciation. The spellings **hemorrhage/hemorrhoids** indicate that the first syllable is pronounced the same as "hem". But there is not much point in making the same change to **haemoglobin/haemophilia** etc, in which the first syllable remains hEm (vowel as in "heed").

hallo/hello etc   As this is just a greeting noise, allowing individual twists, the spelling may be thought unimportant. But the standard forms are **hallo** in the British Isles, **hello** in North America. **Hullo** is now rare. Earlier forms have included *halloa* and *holla* (from which comes the American verb *holler – if he hollers let him go*). Another is *halloo*, now literary or hunting, associated with *Peel's view halloo would waken the dead,* though the original phrase was in fact *view-hollo.*

hamstring   For its forms as a verb see STRINGED/STRUNG.

handful etc   There is a superstition that the plural of this is "handsful". But as with *mouthful/eyeful/basinful* etc **handful** is a normal noun and forms a normal plural: **handfuls.**

handicapped   As a euphemism for *disabled* this seems exceptionally inappropriate, since cripples and mental defectives are not engaged in a horserace. But as the term has acquired international endorsement the main hope for its abandonment lies in the generally short life of such euphemisms. A **handicap** is a penalty imposed on competitors to equalize their chances. The word is centuries old, deriving from the name of a game and soon applied to differential weights carried by racehorses. Outside sport it has no use other than figurative. As applied to the disabled, **handicapped** is a contradiction, since their afflictions make for unfairness rather than fairness.

hang/hung/hanged   The past tense of the verb **to hang** is **hung** and so is the past participle (*I've hung the key on the hook*). The form **hanged** replaces **hung** in the sense of execution by hanging, as in *He was sentenced to be hanged/Murderers risk being hanged* and also in the exclamatory phrase *I'll be hanged if I will* etc. The distinction, once considered a test of education, is no longer so important now that murderers are more often just shut away.

hangar   An aircraft shed. Rhymes with "coathanger" (i.e. not gar).

happy   See GLAD.

harass etc   A regular candidate for misspelling and mispronunciation. It has only one *r* but is not stressed on *ass*. **Harass/harassment** rhyme with "embarrass"/"embarrassment". The American version with stress on *ass* is widely copied.

hard/hardly   Hardly is an adverb but it has not been the adverb of **hard** for generations. **Hard** acts as adverb (*try hard/work hard/think hard*) and adjective too (*hard times/a hard case/a hard winter*). In this it resembles *first/high* (q.v.). But whereas those words have *ly* versions available, **hardly** in general use differs in sense from **hard**, and is limited to "barely" etc, as in *She hardly looked at my orchids/Hardly had we arrived than it started raining.*

harem   The anglicized pronunciation rhyming with "harum-scarum" is now being abandoned, a reflection of new Western awareness of Arab realities. The usual form of restitution is *hahrəm*. Also possible is *hahrEm*, derived from a different word for the same thing.

he/her   See I/ME and also PRONOUNS in Part II.

headquarters   This is a plural noun, as in *The division's headquarters are at York/The headquarters were bombed*. But it is occasionally spelt without an *s* in adjectival senses, as in *These are the headquarter accounts/He is joining the headquarter staff*. The noun is also liable to treatment as a singular (*The division's headquarters was bombed*), a transgression that has developed far enough not to jar.

heaven/heavan The general spelling is now **heaven**.

help For the "can't help laughing" idiom see IDIOMS in Part II.

helpmate/helpmeet For once the obvious is right. A helpful companion etc is a **helpmate**. The other form arose from the phrase in Genesis *an help meet [i.e. suitable] for him*. There would be some point in keeping **helpmeet** if "suitable help" were the desired sense, but the distinction is too fine, and anyway the word is only used as a supposedly knowing version of **helpmate**.

Herculean Classicists seem to prefer a stress on the second syllable (Hək*U*liən) but this rendering is outnumbered by one rhyming with "Her-cue-lien".

high/highly As with *hard/hardly* (q.v.) these have separate senses. **Highly** is a mere variant for "very"/"extremely" (*The news is highly disturbing/a highly intelligent woman*), except in the phrase *think highly of* (= well). **High** is both adjective (*high time/high price*) and adverb (*riding high/The eagles fly high*).

him, her/he, she etc See I/ME and also PRONOUNS in Part II.

historic/historical Anything of note in history is **historic**. Anything to do with history is **historical** (*historical events* – as opposed to legendary/*historical studies/historical people* etc). The distinction is clear but as what qualifies as noteworthy is a matter of opinion the scope for overlap is wide. So **historic** tends to be used where **historical** is meant, but not vice versa. *Historicity* = "historicalness" (*The historicity of King Arthur is doubtful*), i.e. historical existence.

hoard/horde A generation seems to have grown up under the impression that these are alternative spellings for a word meaning "a large number". They are commonly, almost regularly, confused in print. They sound the same (hawd) but their meanings are distinct. A **hoard** is a cache/collection/store, usually valuable. A **horde** is a tribe or troop of nomads, usually Asiatic. So "hoards of spectators" typically muddles the image, the intended sense being of troops of people presumably. **Horde** is used mainly in the plural, which may alert the uncertain.

honour/honorary etc   For spelling peculiarities see CLAMOUR.

Hoover etc   Many trade names like **Hoover**, associated with a patent product, are now part of the language. They include *aspirin/escalator/gramophone/linoleum/celluloid/thermos/nylon/synchromesh/zip fastener*. All these once carried capital initials, and the question is when such proper nouns become ordinary nouns. Hoover's "beats as it sweeps as it cleans" patent has run out, but the word had passed into the language long before then, both as noun and verb (*Doesn't look as though you've hoovered this room*). It was so much more convenient than *vacuum cleaner/cleaner*.

The issue only concerns professional writers, who by leaving a capital off a registered name can provoke threatening letters from company lawyers. To avoid such hazards editors often provide lists of names to guide their staffs, but these easily get out of date. Recent lists would probably contain such names as *Polaroid/Magimix/Formica/Tannoy/Terylene (Dacron* in U.S.). A trader is entitled to protection for a catchy brand name, the spelling of which should be his as a matter of simple accuracy. But there is no way of prolonging the protection once the name becomes catchy enough to graduate as a generic term. Part of the price of success is that his brand name will be applied colloquially to rival products. But then, in speech, protection is unenforceable from the beginning.

hopefully   The objection to such usages as *Hopefully the bus will not be late* is a British prejudice, due to unfamiliarity with the word in a disjunct role, for which **hopefully** has many precedents. (See explanation under CONJUNCTS/DISJUNCTS in Part II.)

horde   See HOARD.

hospitable   It is the *hos*, not the *spit*, that should be stressed. Likewise with *hospitably* (hospitəbli).

houri   The rhyme of the first syllable is not with "hour" but with "dour"/"tour"/"poor", and the *h* is sounded. The word should not be applied to appetizing oriental females in general, as it sometimes is. It means specifically one of the charmers awaiting the righteous in the Moslem paradise.

housewife When applied to a needle-and-thread case the word retains the old pronunciation *huz*if – but this sense is hardly known today. In *housewifery*, another rare term, the *wif* rhymes with "whiff", as in *midwifery*.

hover Other words ending in *over* rhyme with either "over" or "lover", but **hover** is exceptional. It rhymes with the Cockney "bovver" (for *bother*).

however In *You'll never shift it however hard you try* the word is an adverb. In *I don't know how ever you managed* there are properly two separate words – for explanation see EVER. The other function of **however** is as a conjunct (q.v. in Part II), a form of adverb not to be confused with a conjunction. As a conjunct its sense is "even so"/"nevertheless"/"but" (*My mother didn't go. I, however, made the effort*). Note that despite the similarity of sense **however** is not interchangeable with *but* where *but* is a conjunction, e.g. it could not replace *but* in *My mother didn't go but I made the effort* (a common misuse is as in *My mother didn't go, however I* etc).

Some writers hold that **however** should not start a sentence, but nothing in its sense prevents that. *Even so/nevertheless*, which are elsewhere interchangeable with **however**, regularly start sentences (as does *but*). The flexibility of its positioning is shown by the following examples:

> *When she reached the closet, however, she found it bare*
> *When, however, she reached the closet . . .*
> *When she, however, reached the closet . . .* (note: the sense here is of *she* in contrast to someone else)
> *However when she reached the closet . . . .*

humanist/humanitarian A **humanitarian** is a do-gooder, as everyone knows. But who can be sure about **humanist**, a term with so many senses that the one intended can only be inferred from the context? In its commonest modern use **humanist** is an artful substitute for *freethinker/rationalist/agnostic*, i.e. it describes an outlook whose starting point is man, not god.

humour/humorous etc For spelling peculiarities see CLAMOUR.

hung   See HANG.

hyphen/hyphenate   **Hyphen** functions as a verb as well as a noun: *Hyphens are often put in words that should not be hyphened.* So there is no need for **hyphenate**, a high-flown verb form widely used in publishing – and still less for the noun derived from it, **hyphenation**, which just means *hyphening.*

I/me   etc   At some stage in every English-speaking childhood the information is picked up that *It's me*, which the child has been saying for years, is not correct. What should really be said, so it is contended, is *It's I*, which the child has never said or heard. The basis for the lifelong confusion so produced is the grammatical notion that *is* (and the verb *to be* in general) can have a subject but not an object (see LINKING VERBS in Part II).

In *It's me/It is me* **me** is the objective or accusative version of **I**. As such it should only occur as a grammatical object, which is ruled out after *is* etc. On this basis the correct form would be *It's I/It is I*, and similarly *It's he/she/we/they* rather than *him/her/us/them*.

The theory is fair enough but theory does not determine language – it only tries to account for it. Anyone who asks the question *Who am I?* will unhesitatingly answer *I am me*, not *I am I*. Similarly we all say *It's her/That's them/Was it him?* etc. These are not incorrect forms, whatever their grammatical status. They are normal forms, reflecting a natural way of thinking (which is paralleled in other languages besides English).

One exception where the theoretical versions are preferred, at least in writing, is in sentences like *It's we who have to do all the clearing up/It's they who've made the mess.* Here *who* is the subject of a subsentence and seems to jar unless it is matched by a pronoun of the same subjective case, i.e. *we/they* rather than *us/them*. This is only an aesthetic preference however, and in speech the "ungrammatical" forms remain usual.

I/me etc are also an issue in sentences like *She can run as fast as me* (or *You are slimmer than her/. . . richer than him*). It is sometimes contended that the required word is **I** (or *she/he*) on the theory that the sentence is incomplete or elliptical, i.e. what is meant is *She can run as fast as I (can)* (or *. . . she (is)/. . . he (is)*). That is one way of looking at it, but why pretend people mean something they never in fact say? *Is she as tall as me?* was good enough for Shakespeare (*Antony & Cleopatra*), and we cannot still be pretending after all this time. *Me* etc always follow *as/than* unless the pronoun is also the subject of a following verb, i.e. *She takes shorthand faster than me*, but *She takes shorthand faster than I can dictate.* The objective or accusative case is always required in pronouns following prepositions, e.g. *to me/about her/with them/ for us.*

These problems occur only with pronouns, as nouns in English – except for a handful – do not have case inflections. Considering the puzzlement caused by such instances in pronouns one wonders how we should cope if they did. (See also PROFORMS in Part II.)

idiosyncrasy Often misspelt "idiosyncracy".

idyll/idyllic With the examples of "idol" and "idle", it is not surpris- ing that **idyll** should be heard with its initial *i* pronounced as "I" – as it used to be. But today **idyll** rhymes with "did ill" (stress on first syllable). In **idyllic** the stress shifts to the second syllable.

ilk Not a word the ordinary writer should ever need to use. Its only surviving use is in traditional titles such as *Sir Iain Moncreiffe of that Ilk.* Here it stands for "Moncreiffe of Moncreiffe", because **ilk** = same. It saves repeating a place name where this is the same as a family name (but it does *not* mean "family").

illuminate/illumine etc The standard forms are **illuminate/ illumination** etc. When the intended sense is of enlightenment rather than physical lighting the form **illumine** is sometimes used, but pointlessly, since it weakens the desired lighting metaphor.

illusion See DELUSION.

immune response Medical terminology is no better as an example of clear English than the trade-union kind. When doctors talk about the **immune response** the natural meaning of the term is that the response is immune, but what they mean is that the response is one of immunity – it is the body or the part of it in question that is immune. So the term ought to be "immunity response".

imply/infer etc The difference is that **imply** means "hint"/"suggest" and **infer** means "deduce/"gather". Actions, events, circumstances, speeches **imply**. Onlookers, listeners and others **infer**. (*Does the* *prospect of a poor harvest imply dearer food? "It is too soon to draw that inference," said the Minister of Agriculture/The agent's brief did not say he could take the law into his own hands but it implied as much/When she slammed the door on him, he inferred that she'd gone off him.*)

The difference is evidently too subtle for many, as **infer** is constantly misused for **imply**. A columnist of *The Times* of London, reproached by readers for making this mistake, had the nerve to reply that **infer** was in the dictionary with "imply" as a meaning. It is only in the dictionary because so many people like *The Times* columnist get it wrong that dictionaries have to record the misuse.

impotence/impotent   Both are stressed on the first syllable, like "impudence"/"impudent". **Impotence** is the converse of *potency*, tempting the use of the obsolete form "impotency".

incomparable   See COMPARABLE.

incontinent/incontinently   Not to be confused. In modern use the word **incontinent** means "lacking self-restraint", in particular of urination (though earlier of sexual indulgences). **Incontinently** = immediately, but the word is dying and its use now is only literary.

indiscriminate/undiscriminating   Someone lacking discrimination is **undiscriminating**. This term usually refers to taste and never to lack of prejudice in racial issues. Similarly **discriminating** is an adjective for having good taste (however that elusive quality may be defined) and does not imply racial discrimination. The adjective *discriminatory* may be appropriate in racial contexts, to the extent that it refers to purposeful selection. **Indiscriminate** has nothing to do with either connoisseurship or prejudice. In practice it is interchangeable with *reckless/heedless*.

individual   Abuse of the noun as a facetious substitute for *person* etc (*Rupert is a curious individual*) is less common than it was. Individual is a useful noun in the sense of "one in particular", and the adjective has always been blameless.

ineffectual/ineffective   For usage see EFFECTIVE.

infer   See IMPLY.

inflammable A deceptive word, meaning "able to catch fire" but appearing to mean the negative. To avoid dangerous confusion the variant *flammable*, already standard in the U.S., is increasingly used in industry and ought to be adopted generally. It has an unmistakable meaning and is not a contrived form – it has been known since the early 1800s.

    Inflammable is derived from *inflame*, a verb now rarely used except figuratively, as in *to inflame the passions* (= arouse) or *inflame anger* (= incense). The negative form (= not liable to catch fire) is **uninflammable**, a linguistic subtlety workers in volatile chemicals cannot reasonably be expected to be familiar with.

inflection/inflexion For spelling see CONNECTION.

inherent Rhymes with "adheren⋯", not with "errant".

innings/inning In the British Isles and in all cricket-playing countries **innings** is both singular and plural (*I've watched many innings of his/It's time I had an innings*) and **inning** is unknown. In baseball countries **inning** is singular and **innings** is the plural.

innovate/innovatory etc If the adjective **innovatory** is not much used, at least in speech, it is perhaps because it is such a mouthful to say. The main stress, as in **innovate** (*in*əvAt) but unlike **innovation** (inəvAshn), is on the first syllable: *in*əvətri. Perhaps it is not surprising that other renderings are tried (e.g. inəvAtri).

inquire/enquire The two spellings have co-existed for centuries. The more sensible form is obviously **inquire/inquiry** which accords with *inquisition/inquisitive* and is more phonetic. **Inquire** etc is standard in American usage (with **enquire** rare), but **enquire** is the more common in the British Isles, though the *Oxford English Dictionary* prefers **inquire**.

instantly/instantaneously For distinction see MOMENTARILY.

institution/institute In all senses except some official titles the normal word is **institution**. So *The institution [i.e. instituting] of trial by jury can be traced to Norman times/Trial by jury is too much of an institution to succumb to passing fashions* but *the Institute of Psychiatry/the Imperial Institute/the Royal Institute of British Architects*. To complicate the pattern there is the venerable *Royal*

Institution (and many titles modelled on it), but its history predates this distinction.

insure   See ASSURE.

intellect/intelligence   **Intelligence** is basic brainpower. **Intellect** is what the owner does with this, his mental development and knowledge. Hence *intelligent* = quick-witted/reasonable/not stupid. *Intellectual* = thoughtful/preferring interests of the mind/brainy (because intellect is the most obvious evidence of brainpower).

intense/intensive   A difference in meaning is no longer discernible but there are differences in usage. **Intensive**, as the fancier word, is used in more solemn contexts, as in *intensive training/intensive research/intensive cultivation*. Official efforts are **intensive** (even when what is meant is *extensive*), while heat and hunger and hate remain **intense**. In general it might be said that effects and endowments are never **intensive**, whereas strivings (but not objectives) often are. *Intensely/intensively* are even less differentiated than the adjectives, and *intensely* should be preferred.

interpolate   Stress *terp*. Similarly in *interpolation*. The meaning is "to interpose or insert". A common use is in the sense of inserting misleading words or passages in other people's texts.

interrogate   Not always interchangeable with *to question*. Reports and assertions can be questioned as well as people, but only people can be interrogated. Also, **to interrogate** (stress on *ter*) is to question formally, i.e. face to face, not by mail etc.
There are two adjectives, both stressed on *rog*: *interrogatory*, meaning "to do with interrogation", and *interrogative*, meaning "questioning" and applied mainly to grammar (*an interrogative construction*). In legal use *interrogatory* is also a noun for a formal question to an accused.

into/in to   In some contexts it is wrong to write the compound form. Where **in** is part of a phrasal verb or **to** is part of a following infinitive they should be written separately. So *She went in to see him*, but *She went into his room. I looked in to tell you* but *I looked into the trouble*. Here the separated **to** belongs with *to see/to tell*.
The use of **into** to denote taking an interest in or taking part in, as in *He's into heavy music/I'm not into all that stuff*, is a col-

loquialism dating from the 1960s. But it seems to be an extension of a much earlier idiom, e.g. *That child is into everything/When it rained the dog was into his kennel like a shot.* There is a similar idiom with *out of* (*We were out of there in no time*).

invalid Pronounced *inv*əlid in the sense of "disabled"/"ill", but in-*val*id in the sense of "non-valid". In the term *invalided out*, meaning discharged from the Forces etc on grounds of ill-health, *invalided* is pronounced invə*lEd*id.

inventory The word has nothing to do with inventing, as is indicated by its proper pronunciation: *inv*əntri (not in*vent*əri). In America, where the phrase *on inventory* = in stock, the word is spoken as four syllables with a secondary stress on *tor*: invəntori.

irrefutable Stressed on second syllable (*ref*), not third. (See also REFUTE/DENY.)

irreparable Stressed on second syllable (*rep*), not third.

irrevocable The stress cannot be deduced from the basic verb *revoke*, nor from the stressing of similar words, which varies. In **irrevocable** the stress falls on the second syllable (*rev*), as in *irresolute/irrelevant/irreparable/irrefutable/irregular/irreverent.*

issue/tissue etc The double *s* in these is usually sounded as *sh*, as in *mission/fission*, so that **tissue** rhymes with "atishoo". But a pronunciation rhyming with "kiss you" has gained ground among educated speakers in the British Isles, and is preferred by the Oxford Press dictionaries.

it/its/it's To avoid the common confusion of **it's** for **its** all that is needed is to grasp that **it's** is short for *it is/it has*. To judge from the prevalence of the error this is more than is taught in school English classes. Even signwriters seem unable to master it. The difference between **its** and **it's** is like the difference between his and he's. The possessive **its** functions as both pronoun (like *his/hers/ours*) and adjective (like *his/her/our*), usually as adjective. (See PRONOUNS in Part II.)

The urge to treat **it's** as possessive is in imitation of the *'s* added to nouns to make them possessive. And as a matter of fact **its** was originally formed by this process, which provides offenders with a plea in mitigation. The converse confusion, **its** for **it's** as in *It looks as though its going to rain*, is less common but perhaps more of a nuisance to the reader, who is prompted to look back to see which noun it refers to.

It is curious that such a big difference in sense never causes confusion in speech, where there are no apostrophes to guide us.

jail/gaol   The spelling **jail** is phonetic, commoner in British use, invariable in American use, and etymologically secure. The awkward **gaol**, sole instance of a *j* sound in a word beginning with *ga*, should have died out long ago, and only lingers on because British officialdom is as slow to modernize its spelling as its prisons.

jeans   See LEVI'S.

jewelry/jewellery   As the pronunciation is always *jooəlri* the preservation of the longer spelling, to which many British writers and publishers seem devoted, is either faddism or misplaced effort. **Jewelry** is not only phonetic but just as deeply rooted in the language as the pretentious **jewellery**. It is standard in American use.

joky/jocular/jocose etc   Of these three the most-used adjective today is **joky** (not "jokey" – see DICE). **Jocose** is entirely literary and **jocular** is nearly so – it survives in solemn contexts like *The offer we received was jocular/He replied in jocular terms*.

journalese   Term of abuse for writing by a journalist, or writing published in a newspaper. It dates from a period before the Northcliffe-Hearst revolution in popular journalism and is nowadays used by people totally ignorant that it ever applied to a particular artificial style. Despite the many shortcomings of modern journalistic writing, what is published by newspapers and magazines is in general far closer to plain English than literary, business, academic, or official writing.

junction/juncture   These were once largely interchangeable but **juncture** is now limited to the sense of a convergence of events, i.e. a point in time. It occurs almost exclusively in the phrase *at this juncture*, a rhetorical substitute for *now/here/then*, as in *At this juncture I shall turn from my consideration of prospects to a report* *on recent events*. The phrase amounts to an older British equivalent of the modern American cliché *at this point in time*, and is perhaps only less irritating for being more familiar.

All the usual senses of joining together are conveyed by **junction** or *joint*. Except in the grammatical sense **conjunction** is an alternative to *junction* or *juncture*, reserved for elaborate expression (*a fortunate conjunction of events*).

kerb/kerbstone See CURB.

kerosene The original and still the U.S. term for what in the British Isles is called *paraffin*. (See also GASOLINE.)

kilogram This has escaped the stress distortion suffered by *kilometre* (q.v.), only to run into the hazard of a mock-Continental pronunciation rhyming with "key low". **Kilo** (as the word is commonly abbreviated) rhymes with "pillow".

kilometre For pronunciation see GASOMETER.

kind of For "these kind" etc see SORT OF.

lade/load Of these two associated verbs, which have the same meaning, only **load** continues in general use. Apart from specialized use in shipping (*a bill of lading* etc) nothing remains of **to lade** except the participle *laden*. Even this tends to survive only in figurative uses with the sense of "encumbered", and in compounds like *heavy-laden*. Otherwise the standard word is *loaded*.

laissez-faire This form, the imperative, is the original in the sense of economic non-interference (= roughly, "let them get on with it"). The infinitive form *laisser-faire* is now used by the French, and by those better informed about French than about history.

large/largely Though the adverb is **largely** the adjective form takes its place in traditional phrases such as *to loom large/bulk large/writ large*.

largess(e)   As the word was used by Chaucer it has not lacked time to become anglicized, yet the French spelling (*largesse*) is commoner than **largess**, which the Oxford dictionaries used to put first. The word is even subject to a foreign pronunciation, with stress on the second syllable and a *g* as in the French *je* – and this is not always done facetiously. Users unaware of its long English history are presumably anxious not to be thought unaware of the word's currency in modern French. As the sense is perfectly conveyed by *bounty* there is no reason for a dilemma.

lasso   The influence of westerns has long established the pronunciation as la*soo*, supplanting the earlier British sound (*las*oh). The spelling needs an *e* in the plural: *lassoes*.

lath/lathe/lather   Three reasons for pitying foreigners learning the language. **Lath** rhymes with "path" (not "hath"), **lathe** with "bathe", **lather** with "gather" (not "rather"). So except in American usage and certain dialects each *a* represents a different vowel sound, not to mention that the *th* in **lath** differs from the other two. The words are unconnected in sense or origin.

latrine/lavatory etc   When it comes to mentioning the "natural functions" we enter a world of euphemism. *Urinal* is about the only plainspoken word but it has limited scope. The rest, alike in dodging mention of excretion, come and go in public favour, part of an unending quest for an ideal term which periodically contributes new suggestions like "comfort station". The word currently fashionable in British use is *loo*, a medieval revival (from "gardez l'eau", a warning cry of slops about to be emptied into the street). Another ancient term that might be revived is *privy*, perhaps the least coy of the many evasions.

   Lavatory, still mentionable, and *latrine*, mainly military, both come from the Latin for washplace, a line of thought also responsible for the 18th-century euphemism *water closet* (or *w.c.*). A later American euphemism is *toilet*, widely used but condemned in U-speech (q.v. in Part II). Another theme has provided *commode* (= convenient)/*convenience* (usually *public convenience*). Then there are colloquial or facetious euphemisms like *the ladies'/the gents'/thunder box/bog/john (U.S.)*.

   Selection of the right word for the right company is a matter of judgement, as what is acceptable depends on social background.

Probably the safest choices are to be found among *lavatory/toilet* (formal) or *loo/bog/john* (colloquial).

latter See FORMER.

lay/lie/lain etc The native who can give confident directions through this grammatical thicket is no ordinary mortal. To say that there are two verbs, the transitive **to lay** (*laying/laid*) and the intransitive **to lie** (*lying/lain*), is true, but it is only a statement of the problem. Both verbs have the same sense (a third verb is *to lie/lying/lied*, i.e. to tell a lie). The differences are best displayed by setting out the parallels.

Infinitive	*to lay*	*to lie*
Present tense	*lay (lays)*	*lie (lies)*
Past tense	*laid*	*lay*
Present participle	*laying*	*lying*
Past participle	*laid*	*lain*

Examples:

lay	**lie**
present	
I lay odds	*I lie awake*
You lay the table	*They lie in wait*
She lays the blame on me	*He lies asleep*
imperative	
Lay that pistol down	*Lie down*
past	
Who laid the table?	*We lay down*
She laid an egg	*He lay quiet*
perfect	
He has laid the pistol down	*I have lain awake*
Have you laid on drinks?	*Someone has lain here*
present imperfect	
She is laying the table	*The ship is lying at anchor.*

Inevitably *laid*, as the more predictable form, is often substituted in error for **lain**. To avoid the choice a different tense is preferred as in *How long has that rubbish been lying there?* (instead of *. . . rubbish lain there?*).

The nouns **lay/lie** also cause confusion but there is no good reason for this. One will serve as well as the other. It is quite false to regard one form as more correct than the other in the phrase *the lie* *of the land*. They have been used interchangeably for ages. Nowadays **lay** is the usual American form, **lie** the British.

The difference between the two verbs is memorably demonstrated in the modern slang term *to lay a woman* (transitive) as compared with the traditional term *to lie with a woman* (intransitive).

leeward   The layman, used to *leeway* and appreciative of its phonetic spelling, is not going to be talked into changing his habits for **leeward**. Nautical tradition however rhymes **leeward** with "steward" (*looəd*), and this was long the pronunciation of the Leeward Isles.

legendary   This adjective means "to do with a legend" but is widely used to mean "well known", e.g. *The star attraction of the evening gave another demonstration of her legendary singing.* Were her songs about legends, then? Fairly certainly not. What is meant here is that the singer sang in her usual style, which was already well known or at least talked about by the audience. **Legendary**, however, makes the performance sound more extraordinary, as though she were *a legend in her own time*. This phrase is itself a piece of hyperbole, since by definition a legend is a fiction founded on history. If **legendary** is to be used with any accuracy it should at least be reserved to refer to something that could reasonably be termed a legend, i.e. something old-established but still discussed. But perhaps this is a quibble. After all, who would jib at *her fabulous singing*, yet a fable is defined as a piece of fiction founded on nothing. (See also PROVERBIAL.)

leisure/leisurely   Leisure rhymes with "measure"/"treasure", not with "seizure". There are two adjectives: **leisured** = having leisure (*the leisured classes*), and **leisurely** = characterized by leisure (*We spent a leisurely afternoon*). The adverb form is also **leisurely**, but use of the word as in *We went home leisurely* is widely felt to be uncomfortable, as though missing an extra *ly*. It tends to be avoided by phrases like *at a leisurely pace. Unhurriedly*, which expresses the sense just as well, is an even simpler solution. (See also LIKELY.)

lend   See LOAN.

less   See FEWER.

lest   Survives in rhetorical and poetic use (*Lest we forget*) but is now rare in other writing, even the formal. It would be convenient to substitute **lest** for *in case*, but each takes a different construction: *We were warned **in case we lost** our way* but *We were warned **lest we should lose** our way*. So **lest**, which looks shorter, turns out to be longer-winded.

Levi's   Trade name for jeans (denim trousers) marketed by the Levi Strauss company, but popularly used as a noun denoting jeans of any brand. As jeans are always plural, confusion is inevitable about the status of **Levi's**. Is it not a plural too, and should not the apostrophe be omitted? It may come to that, but meantime **Levi's** is an ellipsis of *Levi's jeans* (the omitted word being understood). Its eventual fate may follow that of *Harrods*, originally a singular possessive. **Levi's** can also expect to lose its capital *L*, already neglected as often as not.

libel/slander etc   Until the reform of British defamation law during the 1970s the practical distinction between these two was clear: **libel** was a published defamation, and **slander** was a spoken defamation. The further distinction that a libel could be true while a slander had to be false was a legal nicety. Now **libel** covers both forms of defamation, which at least brings it into line with popular usage. For those seeking a term with no legal implications *calumny* covers defamation in general, but implies falsity.

liberal   Except in the sense of "generous" or "open-minded" there is not much use left for **liberal**. The word no longer implies liberty, nor does it gain substance by reference to liberalism, a creed few could now define. When spelt with a small *l* **liberal** is no longer part of the currency of politics. In Great Britain the modern Liberal Party advocates interventionist policies such as profit-sharing (but not loss-sharing) in the name of "social justice". For policies characterized by a reduction or abolition of intervention the adjective today is *libertarian*.

licence/license   The noun is spelt **licence**, and the verb is **to license**. So *A licensed vehicle must display its licence*. In U.S. usage **license** serves for both forms.

lichen   The botanically minded, having discovered that this form of rock or bark fungus is not really a moss, tend to take up the word

lichen before making the further discovery that it rhymes with "liken", not "kitchen".

lift See ELEVATOR.

light/lighted/lit etc There are two verbs **to light**, one meaning "to alight" (as from a vehicle) or "to land on a surface" (hence *to light on a treasure* etc). In this sense it is a phrasal verb paired with *on*: **to light on**. The other meaning is "to ignite or illuminate". Both have **lighted/lit** as past participle and/or past tense forms.

The verb for ignite/illuminate is by far the commoner, and the adjective **lighted** has only that sense (*a lighted match*). But in both verbs **lit** is probably the commoner form whether as past tense or participle: *Have you lit the lamps?/No, but the fire is lit/I'll tell you how I lit on the idea/He guessed I had lit on something.*

In reference to illumination modern idiom avoids the word and prefers such phrases as *Put the lights on/Are the lights on?/Their hall was illuminated with something new in lights* etc.

like/as In his edition of *Strunk's Elements of Style* E.B. White writes: "*Like.* Not to be used for *as* . . . . Most carefully edited publications regard its use before phrases and clauses as simple error". The error, if error it is, lies in treating **like** as a conjunction instead of a preposition. It is the difference between *What was the show like?* (preposition) and *It was just like I expected* (conjunction), or between *Don't do it like that* (preposition) and *Do it like I showed you* (conjunction).

The contention is that in the conjunction examples **like** should be replaced by **as** (see PARTS OF SPEECH in Part II). Undoubtedly many writers make this distinction. Even modern grammarians, who never recommend or oppose, allow themselves disapproving noises about use of **like** as a conjunction. Their comments range from "informal" or "nonstandard" to (an anathema, this) "felt to be somewhat substandard". Coming from those who like to see themselves as neutral sociological onlookers these are crushing observations.

The trouble is that compliance with the restriction on **like** as a conjunction requires prodigies of mental analysis before a speaker can open his mouth. Which of the following can he say?

I need a drink, like you (okay – *like* preposition)
I need a drink, like you do (taboo – *like* conjunction)

It looks like rain (okay – *like* preposition)
It looks like it will rain (taboo – *like* conjunction. Should be
    as if)
I bet they're late, like last time (doubtful – this can be
    interpreted as an ellipse of . . . *like they were last time*,
    in which *like* is a conjunction and so taboo).
She wants a typewriter like you use (taboo unless viewed as
    an ellipsis of . . . *like the one you use* – then okay).

Since **like** and **as** share the same sense and can both function as
prepositions it seems perverse to hold out against equal treatment
as conjunctions – particularly in view of the liberties already
allowed to **like**:

They complained like mad (for *as if they were*)
She spends money like water (for *as if it were*)
I feel like going to bed (for *as if I should like to go*).

Then there are the vivid colloquial phrases *like there was no
tomorrow/like the man says/like it tells you in the book*. Such a
convenient and widespread usage is not going to be abandoned to
please grammarians or traditionalists. It is more likely to spread till
there are so many exceptions that the line can no longer be drawn.
In speech that position has virtually been reached already, and there
is no good reason to resist it in writing. How can it be wrong to say
(or write) *She looks just like her mother used to look*?

likeable For spelling see UNMISTAKABLE.

likely As with *leisurely* (q.v.) this word is felt to be uncomfortable as
an adverb. Because **likely** is also an adjective (*a likely story*) there is
an urge to differentiate its adverb form on the pattern of *surly/
surlily* – the usual way of converting adjectives ending in *ly* into
adverbs, as long as the outcome is pronounceable. But **likely**, being
already an adverb, cannot be so treated. So in Standard English,
though not in dialect, **likely** is never used as an adverb on its own,
but only in combination with another adverb, as in *most likely/
more likely/very likely/quite likely* etc: *They most likely missed the
bus/You'll quite likely get a refund*.

limelight etc Has anybody now alive ever seen the limelight referred
to in such phrases as *She's very much in the limelight just now*? It
seems unlikely. Limelight has not been used in theatres since the
coming of electric spotlights and so on. The word **limelight** there-

fore fails the basic test of imagery, that of suggesting something the reader/listener can picture from memory. Why specify a kind of light outside everyday experience?

The language is already cluttered with obscure references (see IMAGERY in Part II) and the progress of technology during the 20th century has added to the debris. Obsolete specimens still cited include *blueprint/letting off steam/mangle*.

liquefy   This spelling survives perversely, despite challenges from "liquify". The problem tends to be avoided by the spread of *liquidize* where the sense allows.

liqueur/liquor   Liqueur rhymes with "secure", and describes the strong spirit-based sweet drinks sipped after meals. **Liquor** rhymes with "licker", and as a drink refers almost exclusively to the intoxicating kind in general. But its use in this sense is mainly American, the British term being *drink*, as in *Drink was his downfall*.

literal/literally   etc   Favourite resorts in the unavailing struggle to make words mean more than they can say, as in *It was so cold I was literally freezing*. The intended sense could be more accurately conveyed by *virtually/practically/nearly/as good as/to all intents/ in effect* etc, but accuracy is not the purpose. The speaker is using hyperbole, which is acceptable, because we know he was not truly freezing (i.e. flesh hardening, blood turning to ice, body temperature dropping to freezing point). He is only trying to communicate how exceptionally cold he felt.

The trouble with such hyperbole is that it tends to obscure the valuable precise sense of **literal/literally**: "word for word". It throws doubt on whether the intended sense is exact or merely hyperbolic in such uses a *a literal translation/Don't take me literally/literally broke/literally the last of the Mohicans*. So careful writers cherish *literal/literally* and avoid wasting them on hyperbole and loose phrasing. Besides, these are words that can easily make a laughing stock of those who take liberties with them. Consider: *Surprised? She literally had kittens!/He has no guts, and that's the literal truth*.

load   See LADE.

loan/lend   The standard British forms are the verb **to lend** and the noun **loan**. But **loan** is the earlier word in both functions, and it survives colloquially as a verb in the British Isles (*Can you loan me your lawnmower?*). In the U.S. it is the norm.

locum tenens A tiresome phrase with no plural and an awkward pronunciation. *Stand-in*, which is what it means, is a more practical substitute. But **locum tenens** is entrenched among doctors, who usually abbreviate it to *locum* (*locums* by way of plural). Those who want to parade the full version should say *lOkəm tEnənz* (not ten).

longevity/longitude Irrational consonant variations are usually taken in their stride by English speakers, but a few of them cause hesitation. These offshoots of *long* are two of them. In both **longevity** and **longitude** the *g* is pronounced as *j*.

lose out See WIN OUT.

lot/lots of etc What the *Oxford English Dictionary* calls the "colloquial" use of **lot**, as in **a lot of/lots of**, is now far commoner than the original senses of the word (*drawing lots/our allotted span*). The "colloquial" use has become a standard idiom in speech, and **a lot of** (though perhaps not yet **lots of**) also passes in print. Both phrases make up for the limitations of *many/much*. They rank as slightly less formal equivalents of *a good deal/a great deal* etc (see DEAL), which are also often preferred to *many/much* for being less stilted. (For treatment of **a lot of/lots of** as singular or plural see PLURAL/SINGULAR CONFLICTS in Part II.)

The trouble with *many* (q.v.)/*much* is that they are no longer the natural words in various everyday uses, especially in speech, e.g. *I bought many oranges today* is unidiomatic, and **a lot of/lots of** should be substituted. Similarly:

> *There are many jobs I must do at home* (a lot of/lots of)
> *Many workers were off sick today* (A lot of)
> *We are risking much trouble* (a lot of/a good deal of)
> *You are making much noise* (a lot of/a good deal of)
> *Much furniture is due to arrive tomorrow* (A lot of/A good deal of)
> *There's much in what you say* (a lot/a good deal).

In the examples referring to number (oranges/jobs/workers) *a good many/a great many* could be substituted, but not *many* on its own. **A lot of/lots of** refer equally to mass or number. They too have limitations however, and cannot take over in questions such as *How many oranges did you buy?*

In negatives **a lot of**/**lots of** are possible but *many*/*much* are probably more usual (*There wasn't much noise*/*There weren't many oranges*). Formal writing, such as an official record, also prefers *many*/*much*, as in *There is much to report. Many workers were off sick today, causing much dislocation.*

Elsewhere the accepted phrase is **a lot of** etc, with **lots of** confined mainly to speech. **Lot** of course retains its earlier senses, as in *one's lot in life*/*Lot 23 in the auction*/*They paved paradise, put up a parking lot.*

loved   For adjectival use see BELOVED.

machination   The illogical pronunciation with the *ch* sounded as k, which was current earlier in this century, has given way to sh – consistent with *machine.*

Magimix   See HOOVER.

Mahomet/Mohammad/Muhammad etc   Among Arabists the favoured form is **Muhammad,** but there is no convention for the spelling of Arabic names in English. All the variants are simply attempts to imitate Arabic sounds, which the Roman alphabet is unable to represent.

Even if the Arabic form could be rendered exactly in our alphabet there would be no reason for English to adopt it. In all languages it is a normal process to spell and pronounce foreign words in any way that suits the borrowers. Only two things matter: that the name should be recognizable and that the same version should be kept in any piece of writing in which it is repeated.

All versions of **Muhammad** stress the second syllable, and among adjectival forms by far the commonest is **Mohammedan** (though the spoken sound is probably more often Məhomidn). (See also MOSLEM/MUSLIM.)

major/minor   These are victims of the relentless search for ways of suggesting greater precision than the user's reasoning has achieved, or indeed attempted. They sound more thoughtful than *bigger*/*smaller* or *greater*/*lesser*, though that is usually what they mean. So:

The major part of the town is now cut off (= greater part / Most)
Several diseases are endemic but the major affliction is
malnutrition (= worst)
Chancellor of the Exchequer is one of the major offices of
state (= most important)
Someone has to look after these minor matters (= small /
unimportant).

As there is no limit to the demand for vague indicators of bigness and smallness, **major / minor** are a growth industry:

a minor poet / a minor official / a minor anxiety (= small /
unimportant)
a major prophet / a major effort / a major breakthrough
(= big / important).

So both words serve as window-dressing replacements for humbler words and rarely function as genuine comparatives. (See also CONSIDERABLE.)

majority / plurality   In electoral terms **majority** has different senses in British and U.S. usage. A majority in a British election is the number of votes polled by the winner in excess of the number polled by the closest rival, i.e. a simple majority. This kind of majority in a U.S. election is a **plurality**, and **majority** is applied only to an overall majority, i.e. the number of votes over and above the total polled by the other candidates. **Plurality** is an ancient English term which once had the sense of more than half, but is no longer used in British politics.

malign / benign / malignant etc   **Malign** (= noxious / to defame) and **benign** (= amiable / beneficent) rhyme with "line" / "nine". **Malignant** (= inimical / virulent) rhymes with "indignant".

mannequin / model   In the sense of someone who wears clothes to show them off professionally **mannequin** has been supplanted by **model**. This is nothing to regret, as the word was a French import in conflict with the established English term *manikin*, a little man or dummy figure.

manoeuvre / maneuver   Both forms rhyme with "Hoover". **Maneuver** is the U.S. development, not recognized in the British Isles, where the only development in **manoeuvre** is that the word has dropped its digraph (*œ*).

many/many a etc   Though **many** has an obvious plural sense, idiom allows various mismatchings with a singular noun or article:

> *Many a good tune is played on an old fiddle*
> *Many's the man who wishes he were younger*
> *A great many people were there.*

These are traditional phrasings, still in everyday use, but the regular modern versions would of course be: *Many good tunes are . . ./Many are the men who . . ./Very many people . . . .*

The older constructions may be modelled on *any*, which can be singular or plural both in sense and grammar. There is also a similarity with *a few* (q.v.), another plural word used with a singular article.

margarine   There are three certainties about this invented word: [1] it was meant to be pronounced with a hard *g*, as in "Margaret", [2] in the British Isles it is nearly always pronounced with a soft *g*, as in "larger", [3] for at least 100 years it has not been applied to the substance for which it was coined. In Britain and in Western Europe it is the legal name for a butter substitute, called *oleomargarine* in the U.S., but it was originally applied to an ingredient extracted from animal and vegetable fats, later shown to have been wrongly identified.

marry   The problems of marriage begin with the verb. **To marry** has the conflicting senses of [1] performing the ceremony (*The priest married them*) and [2] becoming married (*Sheila is marrying George/Veronica says she'll never marry*). Hence ambiguities like *Sheila and George* **were married** *two years ago*. Does it mean they were in the married state at that time, but perhaps are now divorced or separated? Or does it mean that two years ago they became married, i.e. were married by an appropriate official? No guidance can be offered. The sense has to be deduced from the context.

This ambiguity obviously strikes people as unsatisfactory, since so many prefer the term *get married*, as in *Sheila and George are getting married/They got married two years ago/When we get married . . . .* This is probably the normal form in speech. But the all-purpose *get* stirs prejudice, and many feel that it is somehow less than correct, at least in writing.

Others accept a superstition that the proper form is the passive *be married*, as in *They were married by the priest* (rather than *The priest married them*) – probably because this is a convention of many British newspapers. There is nothing in either belief.

The passive is no more respectable than, say, *Sheila and George married yesterday*, both versions having been used for centuries. Nor is there anything amiss with *get married*, which is the most practical solution and the likeliest survivor.

massage/masseur/masseuse Masseur rhymes with "sir", not with "sewer", and **masseuse** (the feminine) with "sirs". **Massage** rhymes with the revived Frenchified pronunciation of "garage" (q.v.), but it is hard to pronounce that way when used as a verb and followed by another consonant. So in contexts like *Let me massage you/Massage the back of the leg*, and even in *massaged*, the more familiar English j sound (with initial d sound) tends to be substituted. (See COLLIDING CONSONANTS in Part II.)

maybe/perhaps Unaccountably **maybe** is regarded by some writers and editors as an upstart term, less respectable than **perhaps**. In fact it is at least as ancient, though less widely used before the 20th century. The two words are interchangeable without reserve. *Perchance* is an obsolete variant.

meaningful Trendy substitute for *significant* (q.v.). A typical overworked use is in *a meaningful experience*, where the sense seems to be an experience that gave the subject something to think about. Another way of putting it would be *worth while*.

means This noun retains the same spelling whether singular or plural, and takes a singular or plural verb in the ordinary way. In *The means are not justified by the end* **means** is obviously plural, just as it is singular in *That was a means to an end*. One exception in this grammatical Arcady: when **means** is used in the sense of "income"/"resources" (*a man of means*) rather than method, the word is always plural (*her means are limited*).

media See MEDIUM.

mediaeval/medieval The modern spelling is **medieval**, which is a relief. The traditional spelling was *mediæval* (with a digraph).

medium/media etc It is convenient to have a word covering the various forms of publishing, electronic and printed. Each is a medium of communication, but Victorian spiritualists had long ago cornered *mediums* for their own communicators with the dead. This left the living with **media**, the regular Latin plural of the word. It has been swiftly taken up, but many grateful users who know **media** means newspapers, television etc do not know it is the plural of **medium** or even a plural at all. They not only treat it as a singular but invent a new plural for it too:

> *Radio would be a suitable media* (medium)
> *These are the medias we recommend* (mediums/media).

Purists are entitled to be outraged. They can reasonably point out that in commercial use *mediums* is hardly likely to mean the spiritualist kind, so that no new word is needed. This is true enough but a need is obviously felt. Is torturing a fragment of a dead language (which ought to have grown used to maltreatment by now) such a bad way of meeting it?

Those wishing to avoid offending classicists have only to remember to give **media** a plural verb and never precede it with *a/this/that* etc.

meet/meet with etc   On its own **to meet** is a versatile enough verb. It is capable of transitive use (*She met him*) and intransitive use (*When shall we three meet again?*). It does not need an added preposition as in **meet up**, a pointless colloquial elaboration (*They met up in London*) with no sense in which the verb on its own cannot be substituted. Even less defensible is **meet up with**, as in *We met up with them on holiday*. This has two additional words for no additional meaning.

Then there is **meet with**, which has the traditional sense of "to experience" (usually by chance): *The dog met with a sad fate/The car met with an accident/We hope to meet with more consideration next time*. The preposition *with* seems superfluous even here, but as the phrase is of ancient lineage and established current use there is no point in complaining about it.

There is not much point either in complaining about the special American sense of **meet with**: "have a meeting (= conference) with", as in: *The President met with his advisers/When I was in New York I met with him*. This sense is never used in the British Isles but it cannot logically be objected to. On the other hand it is certainly unnecessary. The verb *confer* is what is usually needed (*The President conferred with his advisers*) – or even *see* (*When I was in New York I saw him*).

mentality/mind About the only sense in which **mentality** is commonly used is "kind of mind". Hence *I can't understand the mentality of these vandals/Doing a thing like that, it shows his mentality* etc. The word is not a multi-syllable alternative to **mind**, though poetic licence excuses Cole Porter for so misusing it in his couplet *Use your mentality/Wake up to reality*.

meticulous Just a fancy word for *scrupulous/painstaking/particular* – a recent revival inspired by the French *méticuleux*.

mezzanine As this word is borrowed from Italian its pronunciation cannot be modelled on the *zz* in "dizzy"/"jazzy", though it often is. Nor can the "nine" be pronounced like the number. The word, meaning an intermediate floor between the first and second storeys (see also STOREY), is said *metsənEn*. The double *z* has the same sound in "mezzo-soprano".

midwifery For pronunciation see HOUSEWIFE.

migraine The word does not rhyme with "my grain". Pronounced *mEgrAn*.

mileage The process of derivation from *mile* should have lost the *e* and yielded *milage* (compare *smile/smiling* or *dote/dotage*). The logical spelling however has not been accepted and hardly anyone besides *The Times* of London perseveres with it. **Mileage** is now so general that *milage* is not immediately recognizable as the same word.

mind See MENTALITY.

minister/administer These verbs have different constructions that should not be interchanged. **Minister** is no longer used in transitive senses and requires to be followed by *to*. Its sense is "to serve or help", as in *ministering to the sick/He'll be wanting his dinner, so I'll go and minister to him/Appoint someone to minister to their needs*. **Administer** is a transitive verb and means "to manage or dispense" (*We have a Personnel Director to administer the staff/ The adjutant administers the regiment/The tribunal administered a rebuke to the witness*).

minor See MAJOR.

missile For pronunciation see FERTILE.

model See MANNEQUIN.

momentarily/instantly etc The shades of meaning here are as follows. **Instantly** = at once/this instant(*Let go instantly/Orders must be obeyed instantly*). **Instantaneously** = at the same instant (*The enemy came in sight and a shot rang out instantaneously*). **Momentarily** = for the duration of a moment (*The motor stopped, but only momentarily*). In American usage, however, **momentarily** shares the sense of **instantly** in addition, and is also capable of meaning "at any moment". The British pronunciation is *mOməntrəli*, but the American rhymes with the American pronunication of "primarily" (i.e. "pry merrily").

money/monetary Since the pronunciation of **money** rhymes with "funny"/"sunny", only perversity can account for the bad habit of pronouncing the word's derivatives **monetary/monetarism** as though it rhymed with "bonny"/"Johnny".

moor/more **Moor** does not rhyme with **more** (maw), though it is often made to. It rhymes with "poor"/"tour"/"dour", and **more** with "pour"/"four"/"door".

Moslem/Muslim A handier term for *Mohammedan*, though the word in fact derives from "Islam". **Moslem** is the usual spelling, though **Muslim** is fashionable. *Moslim/Mooslim* etc have been among earlier spellings, indicating that any spelling is a mere approximation to the Arabic. (See also MAHOMET.)

mother of parliaments A phrase often misapplied to the Westminster Parliament, even by members of that parliament and parliamentary journalists, whose business it is to know better. John Bright's remark, from which the phrase is misquoted, was: "England is the mother of Parliaments". (See also PARLIAMENT.)

mould/mold In both senses (growth/model) **mould** has always been by far the commoner spelling in the British Isles. The more phonetic **mold** is the American norm.

mouthful etc See HANDFUL.

much more/much less etc   In sentences like *It was all I could do to catch the plane,* **much more** *warn you I'd be on it* the problem is when to use **more** and when to use **less**. It occurs similarly with *still more/still less*. The usual mistake is to put **less** instead of **more**, which wrecks the sense for those who work these things out. Those who do not should play safe by substituting the phrase *let alone*, which achieves the same effect without risk.

The test of **more/less** is to supply the missing words eliminated by this elliptical construction. They are of course a repetition of the first part of the sentence. Examples:

> *It was all I could do to catch the plane, (it was)* **much more** *(than I could do to) warn you I'd be on it*
>
> *The job is out of the question on that pay scale, (the job is)* **much more** *(out of the question) at last year's prices*
>
> *We must be early to make sure of a seat, (we must be)* **much more** *(early) to avoid queuing.*

Much less is correct in *I never laid eyes on the woman,* **much less** *(laid) hands (on her).*

muezzin   Has three syllables, rhyming with "Dewey's in".

Munich   Rhymes with "tunic". A guttural rendering mistakenly assumes the word to be German, but the Germans call the town *München*. (For a similar snare see COPENHAGEN).

must   See OUGHT.

mutual   Whatever services Dickens may have performed for literature he ruined the chances of **mutual**. The word can never recover its proper meaning in the face of *Our Mutual Friend*. What **mutual** means, or should mean, is "two-way"/"between two", but *our mutual friend* implies three. Strict uses of **mutual** would include: *the couple's mutual affection* (the affection of each for the other)/*the mutual fears of these nations* (the fears of each for the other). In *The dean and the bishop held each other in mutual esteem* (they esteemed each other) the sense is correct but the word is redundant. If they held each other in esteem it was obviously mutual. Similarly in *They were mutual friends*.

The sense **mutual** is too often made to carry is "in common". This is the term that should usually be substituted, as in *our mutual friend* (our friend *in common*)/*They had a mutual interest in the* *girl* (an interest *in common* in the girl – or simply *They both had an interest . . .*").

Note that *reciprocal* is not a possible substitute. It implies mutuality, but to reciprocate is to act etc in return, e.g. a reciprocal detestation depends on there being a prior detestation to return.

naive/naïf etc   For a century or more **naive** has been acclimatized to the English language. So its status as a feminine adjective in the French language is irrelevant, and to parade the masculine version *naïf*, as in *He is rather naïf*, shows familiarity with French at the cost of betraying ignorance of English. The same applies to the use of **naïveté** as a noun, when English has long since settled for **naivety**.

Anglicization has not extended to the pronunciation though. **Naive** rhymes with "nigh eve". **Naivety** is pronounced nIEvti.

named after/for etc   When a child is given a name in honour of somebody who already bears or bore the same name, the child is said to be **named after** that person. U.S. usage, preserving an alternative old construction, prefers **named for**. Under the influence of this usage book dedications are often inscribed "For . . .", whereas the verb *to dedicate* requires "To . . .".

napkin   As the older word, and also the U-word (see U-SPEECH in Part II), **napkin** may be preferable to *serviette*, but there is no case for treating *serviette* as an upstart. It was an established word in Scotland from the 15th century on, and only its French spelling is newfangled.

narcotic   Another Chaucerian term now widely taken to be American. Whereas *drug* properly means any medicine (hence U.S. *drugstore*) a **narcotic** is specifically a drug that induces sleep or stupefaction. Somebody feeling the effects of a narcotic, however, is said to be *drugged*, a term not applied to somebody who has taken medicine. **Narcotic** is uncommon in Great Britain, where anything described as a *drug* is taken to be hazardous, and *medicine* generally means something liquid.

NATO   See ACRONYM.

naught/aught/nought Only **nought**, the symbol for zero (*noughts and crosses*), continues in ordinary use. The others, **aught** (anything) and **naught** (nothing), are obsolete except in poetry and a phrase or two (*set at naught/bring to naught*). But **naught** has sired *naughty* (= misbehaving) by a process similar to the derivation of *villainous* from *villein* (serf).

necessity/necessitate etc See UNIQUE.

need/needs etc The verb **to need** has peculiarities. Like *to dare* it is a regular verb with alternative constructions for negatives and questions. Besides the regular negative, as in *It does not need to be done*, there is the alternative *It need not be done*. Similarly the regular question form, *Does it need to be done?* can be replaced by *Need it be done?*.

Note that the regular forms are constructed with a full infinitive (*to be done*) while the alternatives drop the *to* (*be done*). Note too that in the alternative **need** can convey both present or past time: *He need not do that* (= does not need to . . .)/*He need not have done that* (= did not need to . . .).

This is a simplified summary, as alternative constructions of **to need** are also usual in various contexts that are neither questions nor genuine negatives, e.g. *She need only cook for one/No one need go short/All he need do is ask*. These idioms, if not negatives, are all apparent subtractions from the needing.

Needs, besides its function as a verb or a plural noun (*My needs are simple*), is also a quaint adverb occurring only in the phrase *needs must . . .* (= it is necessary to . . .). This use is now principally facetious, as in *Needs must gather up our things and head for home*.

neither See EITHER.

nephew Often pronounced *nef*U in the belief that *nev*U is a corruption. It is the other way round.

new/newly etc The vowel sound U as in "cue" is harder to say than oo as in "coop". So there is a tendency to adopt the simpler sound in words traditionally pronounced with the other. The process is completed in *blue*, once blU, now bloo. It is past the point of no return in *sue* and *suit*, now more often soo/soot than sU/sUt. **New/newly** are always nU/*n*Uli in Standard English, but *noo/nooli* are common in dialect and in American speech.

nice/nicely   It is sometimes held against **nice** that the word is a mere all-purpose adjective of approval. This is just what makes it so useful, and accounts for the virtual extinction of its other senses. What people generally mean by **nice/nicely** is "commendable"/"pleasant". Curiously, this sense fits many traditional uses of **nice** where the strict sense is "precise"/"discriminating", as in *a nice eye for a design/a nice appreciation of the pros and cons/a nice point/a nice sense of timing*. After all, a discriminating eye and a commendable eye are much the same thing. Anyway **nice** has got beyond being a word to despise and would now be seriously missed.

niche   Rhymes with "rich", having had three centuries in England to go native.

no   After *or*, as in *They'll go ahead whether we agree or no*, **no** is the traditional form, but *not* is now general. Both are adverbs here, so it hardly matters. The other adverb use of **no** is with comparatives, as in *Things are no better*. Here the sense goes beyond "not better" and is equivalent to "not any better".

In phrases like *She didn't say yes, she didn't say no* **yes/no** are sometimes mistakenly enclosed in quotation marks as though they were direct speech. But *say no/say yes* are established phrases in which **no** is a noun, just as it is in *They won't take no for an answer/We're getting too many noes*.

nobody   Sometimes two words. See ANYONE. See also NONE.

non   Two puzzles about the prefix **non** are [1] why it is sometimes followed by a hyphen and sometimes not, and [2] when to choose it in preference to *un/in*. Both processes appear to be guided by no discoverable principle.

[1] As no hyphen is needed in older compounds like *nonsense/nonentity/nonconformist* it seems absurd to preserve one in *non-payment/non-attendance/non-combatant/non-playing* etc. **Non** is an ancient prefix and should not be treated as temporary. [2] The uncertainty about which prefix to choose is illustrated by *essential*, which occurs with all of them: *non-essential/inessential/unessential*. But most pairings with **non** are settled, if unaccountable. The choice makes no difference to the sense.

Unlike *none*, which rhymes with "nun", **non** rhymes with "on"/"gone".

none/no-one Two questions are asked: [1] how do you spell **no-one**? [2] is **none** always singular?

[1] If **no-one** is recognized as part of the *anyone/everyone/someone* set its natural spelling is "noone". But this has to be ruled out for the hint of pronunciation like "noon". At the same time the spelling in two words, *no one*, fails to distinguish the term from phrases like *No one person knows enough to be able to say/No one bomb could do such damage* (i.e. but more than one might). Hence **no-one** is the best spelling compromise.

[2] **None**, a pronoun undoubtedly derived from "no one", sometimes means exactly the same: *None but the brave deserves the fair/Help came from none other than his tormentor*. This merely confirms that the word is singular in the sense of "no person", as it is also in the sense of "nothing". But **none** is also the negative of *any* (*Has he any?/He has none*), which can be singular or plural according to context (see ANY). So **none** can also mean "not any persons"/"not any things", and this is the more usual way *none* is used.

Sometimes the sense is clearly singular, as in *None of this is any good*, sometimes clearly plural, as in *None of them are going to put themselves out*. If the user is thinking of several rather than one he is likely to choose a plural verb, especially if the noun or pronoun in front of the verb is a plural, as in: *None of them have read the notice/None of the guests want to eat yet*. (See also PLURAL/SINGULAR CONFLICTS in Part II.)

Another peculiarity of **none** is its use as an adverb in the sense of "not any". The best-known example is probably *none the wiser*. Similarly *The rules are none too clear/The sea was none too smooth/He was none the better for his holiday*.

normality/normalcy The regular noun derived from the adjective *normal* is **normality**. The spread of **normalcy** is due to President Warren Harding, who on succeeding President Wilson announced that his policy would be one of "normalcy". The word was then so unfamiliar that he was thought to have coined it, though it was already known as a technical term in science. It attracted attention as an apparent malapropism because a *cy* ending is not the standard addition to convert comparable adjectives into nouns. **Normality** (and *abnormality*) is still the norm, but **normalcy** is now common, and widely preferred in North America.

north/northern etc As with all the points of the compass, there is no reason for writing **north/northern**, or other forms, with a capital initial except when the word is part of a formal or customary title, as in *the North Pole/South Dakota/East Fife/the North of England*, i.e. the counties north of the Humber. **North/northern** (and *south/southern* etc) are interchangeable as adjectives except where custom has already settled the choice. Thus *northern France* is preferred to "north France" because it is easier to say, and *southern France* avoids confusion with *the South of France*, i.e. the Riviera. Similarly *southern Africa* is Africa south of the Equator, not to be confused with the state of South Africa.

not proven   Just as *proven* is a near-enough extinct variant of *proved*, heard only in the odd phrase (*a proven remedy*), so **not proven** exists only in Scottish law. Sassenach public speakers and others striving for effect keep it alive as a show-off substitute for the ordinary *not proved*, making sure nobody misses it by rhyming it with "cloven"/"woven". If it has to be used at all there is no good reason for departing from the vowel sound of *proof/prove/proved/proving* etc.

obliged/obligation etc   The verb **to oblige** has two conflicting senses, [1] to compel, [2] to do a favour. Compulsion is usually confined to the passive forms, as in *You're obliged to reply/The cabbie didn't want to take us there but he was obliged to*. Doing a favour is seen in examples like *We don't usually deliver but we'll do it to oblige you/M'lud, I'm much obliged*. Used as an adjective **obliging** = helpful, as in *Thanks, you've been most obliging/The staff are so obliging there*. The verb in all such instances has a soft *g* (*əblIj*).

A similar verb, **to obligate** (*oblI*gAt), is now virtually obsolete, but from it are derived the terms **obligation** (=duty/compulsion) and **obligatory** (*əblig*ətri=compulsory). There is also **obligated** (=duty-bound, as in *You've no cause to feel obligated*, which is just another way of saying *Don't feel you have to*). It will be seen that *compel/have to/helpful* etc provide alternatives for all these words.

oblivious   As the adjective of *oblivion*, which means "a state of forgetfulness", **oblivious** ought to offer no problems. It means "forgetful"/"unmindful", and like those adjectives it is constructed with the preposition *of* (*forgetful of what you told me/unmindful of what she said/oblivious of these examples* etc). What **oblivious** does not mean is "unaware", and the preposition it ought not to take is *to* (*Oblivious to what was happening he went on with his work*). Wherever **oblivious** is followed by *to* it may usually be assumed that the user has picked the wrong word. He may be oblivious of the right one, or – more likely – unaware of the difference.

obscene   The use of this word as a general substitute for "disgusting" is to be discouraged. What is disgusting is not necessarily obscene, and the obscene is only disgusting because also indecent/lewd. Poverty and wealth, fatness and thinness, overeating and starvation may all be disgusting but none is obscene, unless those concerned are given to lewdness as an outcome of their condition. We have enough words to express disgust (*repulsive/repellent/abhorrent* etc) but only one to express what **obscene** expresses.

It is possible to point to historical precedents for the wider sense. But the revived use, it can safely be said, is due to inadequate grasp of the accepted sense rather than concern for the historic.

obstetrics/gynaecology   These are not the same thing. A **gynaeco-logist** specializes in the diseases and disorders of women. An **ob-stetrician** specializes in childbirth and its associated conditions. **Obstetrics** is stressed on the second syllable. **Gynae** rhymes with "shiny", and the word is stressed on the third syllable.

of   A source of two illiterate errors: [1] confusion with *have* (as in *I should of told you*), and [2] intrusion after *off* (as in *Get off of that wall*). The confusion with *have* occurs because **of** is normally pronounced әv, and *have* when unstressed (*I should've told you*) is pronounced the same. The urge to slip in a superfluous **of** in phrases like *Can't keep my eyes off (of) you/He took it off (of) me* is common in Cockney, under the impression that it is educated.

off   Rhymes with "cough"/"doff"/"toff". The long *o* (aw) still heard in U-speech was never admitted by the *Oxford English Dictionary*, though it allowed that the sound might be longer than the *o* in *got/offer/office*.

often   The obvious model for pronouncing **often** is "soften" (*sof*n), in which the *t* is never sounded and the *o* is never stretched to aw. Both these effects plague **often**, but its usual pronunciation is *of*n.

older   See ELDER.

omelet/omelette The shorter spelling was current in the language centuries before the modern French spelling was adopted. It remains the standard U.S. form, but in the British Isles it has been entirely ousted. If any tidying-up of English spelling were ever to be attempted, the restoration of **omelet/program** etc would deserve a high priority.

on/onto/upon It is a superstition that there is a right place for **on** and a right place for **upon**. There is never a sense in which **on** is wrong. **Upon** is now a mere ornamental variant of **on**, carrying no sense of *up*. Presumably people like the sound of it, as there is no other reason for bothering with its extra syllable except in a traditional phrase like *once upon a time*.

As for **onto**, this has still not been recognized as an English preposition, despite the model of **into**. It continues to be written in two words *on to*, and jars when it is not. But if **onto** is a fault, it is a mild one.

once With its capacity to mean "one time" or "at one time", and its grammatical versatility, **once** is a useful word. *Once more/once again* is simpler than the awkward *one more time* (prevalent in U.S.). **Once** is also a convenient though uncommon alternative to *former/onetime*, as in *the once and future king/Mr Richard Nixon, once head of state*. It can serve as a conjunction too, a more emphatic form of *if/when*, as in *Once you have found her never let her go/We can rest once we arrive*. **Once** is indispensable in various common phrases such as *for once/just the once/once in a while/once for all/once upon a time/at once*.

one As the nearest English can get to a genderless singular pronoun, **one** is regrettably limited in scope. It can legitimately stand for anyone like the speaker/writer regardless of sex, as in *One does one's best for one's children*. It also works as a self-effacing substitute for *I*, as in *One doesn't mind helping when it's in a good cause*. But this is a questionable device when it disguises a personal opinion (*The Commons accepted the Prime Minister's view of the situation, but one doubts whether this was wise*).

The trouble with **one** is that once you start with it you have to stay with it. You cannot alternate with *I* etc, as in *One wonders why people do it, but I can hazard a guess*. Only U.S. usage allows a lapse into *he/her/you* etc, as in *The more one studies it, the more it reminds you...* This is just as distracting as keeping on specifying

one, in which the repetition – what with *one's* and *oneself* – soon becomes artificial and even comic. What starts as impersonal ends as self-conscious. So **one** is only practical for limited appearances.

You/we are preferred devices, as in *You/we find as you/we grow older that your/our appetite gets smaller.* Anyone sometimes has the required sense, but does not work as a substitute for **one,** as may be tested in *One would like to be generous – but what can one do when there are one's own bills to pay?.* The problem can only be avoided by rewording sentences, e.g. *The appetite is found to get smaller with age.*

only   Usually the placing of **only** makes so little difference to the sense that a wide tolerance is possible. The slogan *We're only here for the beer* could be rephrased as *We're here only for the beer* or *We're here for the beer only* without altering the message. But various degrees of ambiguity can occur if the wording is unwary, e.g. *She only plays tennis to please him.* This presumably means that the only reason she plays tennis is to please him. But it is capable of meaning that she does nothing else but play tennis, or that tennis is the only game she plays. Normally people guess which words **only** is meant to limit.

In sentences like *If only the ground staff had been careless the crash might have been avoided* the sense is not so much ambiguous as baffling (though it might be clearer in its context). Taken literally it laments that the ground staff were not careless, but the intended point is that they were not alone in being careless. So the word order should be: *If the ground staff only had been careless . . .*

Only as conjunction: in the following examples **only** is a conjunction with the sense of "but then"/"except that": *You keep saying we'll go, only you never take me/The present was lovely, only it was broken.* This is mainly a colloquial construction, but it is acceptable in writing and does not need the comma it sometimes gets after **only.**

onward/onwards   Both forms are in practice superfluous, as *on* means the same, and the distinction between the two is obscure. **Onward** functions as adjective or adverb, **onwards** only as adverb. (See also BACKWARDS.)

optimist/optimistic etc   The usual sense of **optimistic** now is "sanguine"/"hopeful", and an **optimist** is somebody with such a character or conviction. That is not what either word meant originally, and purists sometimes complain that both should be restricted to Leibniz's philosophy about this world as "the best of all possible worlds". His philosophy though has not been taken seriously since Voltaire wrote *Candide* in refutation. So today only historians of philosophy ever need to use the words in that connection, while ordinary English speakers have no other noun than **optimist** for a person who is hopeful.

option   See ALTERNATE/ALTERNATIVE.

oral   For tendency to confuse sense see VERBAL.

ought/ought not   Like *must*, **ought** is an auxiliary with only one form. It is followed by a full infinitive, whereas *must* takes a bare infinitive: **ought** to go/*must* go. In negative constructions both words are followed by *not* and neither makes use of *do*: **ought** not to go/*must not* go. This is usual with auxiliary forms (*am not/shall not/cannot/would not* etc), but perhaps **ought** is not recognized as an auxiliary. Anyway it is the only one prone to coupling with *do*, as in the expression *didn't ought to*.

   This phrase is still more often than not avoided as bad English, and even among its users there seem to be misgivings about it. The objection to it (and to *did ought*) is that the verb *do* in an auxiliary role requires an infinitive, not a past tense (i.e. *do go/did go*, not "did went"!). **Ought** is not an infinitive but a past-tense form. It was originally an inflection of *owe*, though it is now a word on its own. If this objection seems abstruse the fallback is that *didn't ought to* is a clumsy and unneeded variant. (See also USED (TO) for "didn't used to . . .".)

overt   Not pronounced like its converse, COVERT (q.v.).

owing to   Usually preferable to DUE TO (q.v.).

paradigm   An obscure word once confined to specialists, who knew what it meant and how to pronounce it (rhyming with "dim", not "dime"). It is now a fashionable jargon word, borrowed from philosophy to make a change from *example*. Invaluable for obfuscation, along with *parameter* (q.v.), which tends to occur with it.

parameter   A kind of mathematical constant, but the word is popular among the non-mathematical as an impressive substitute for *limits* or even *characteristics*. All kinds of things now have parameters no-one ever suspected before.

paranoia/paranoiac   Not interchangeable with *obsession/obsessive/ obsessed*. **Paranoia** is a persistent mental delusion in which the **paranoiac** believes himself to be either persecuted or someone famous. Anyone with a bee in the bonnet may be obsessed but he is not paranoiac. Still less is it paranoiac to warn against dangers, real or imagined, such as "reds under the bed"/overpopulation/nuclear warfare etc.

Parliament   Those who cherish parliamentary procedures and traditions to the point of wishing to share their enthusiasm tend to put themselves out to say *pahl*/Emənt. This was the pronunciation given in the *Oxford English Dictionary* (1904), though not in subsequent Oxford dictionaries. It echoes *parley* but is not suggested by early spellings like "parlement"/"parlament". Today it is a piece of pedantry, and all authorities agree on *pahl*əmənt.

partial/partially/partiality   These words have the opposite sense to *impartial* etc, i.e. they imply bias as opposed to neutrality, as in *He's partial to a glass of port after dinner/Her partiality for jewelry is expensive.*

In *a partial recovery* **partial** has another sense, that of "in part". How often this difference causes confusion is hard to know, but there is no reason to use **partial** etc like this at all. *Part/partly/in part* are capable of taking over wherever the question arises: *a partial recovery (a part recovery)/They succeeded partially (They succeeded partly* or *. . . in part).*

patent etc   Broadly the pronunciation rhymes with "latent" in the British Isles, while American usage rhymes the first syllable with "pat". Exceptions include *Patent Office/letters patent/patentee* in which official British usage follows the American. Ordinary speakers however will not get involved with these refinements. If they are British they will say *pAt*ənt, and if they are American *pat*ənt.

patriot/patriotic etc   Another case of uncertain pronunciation, and a rare instance of where the speaker can please himself. Is it "pat" as in Patrick, or "pate" as in patron? "Pat" is surely more common in Great Britain, and is consistent with the derivatives *compatriot/expatriate*. Some make a distinction between **patriot** ("pate") and **patriotic** ("pat"), which is paralleled in *patron/patronize*. In North America the scene is more settled, and "pate" is general.

pejorative Essentially a literary or declamatory word, and one calculated to impress rather than enlighten, even when confidently pronounced – which, as it is so rarely heard, it often isn't. Its traditional pronunciation is *pɛ*jərətiv, its meaning "depreciatory"/"disparaging"/"degrading"/"lowering", any of which should be preferred as being more likely to be understood. Fortunately only politicians and critics seem to use it and most say pi*jor*ətiv.

peninsula etc A word not often used, but misspelt as often as not whenever it is. **Peninsula** is the noun (*the Spanish peninsula/the Malay peninsula/South Korea is a peninsula*). **Peninsular** is the adjective, on the model of *insular* (*the Peninsular War/Peninsular unrest grows/a peninsular odyssey*). As English permits nouns to be used as adjectives **peninsula** can pass for **peninsular**, but it is a clanger to use **peninsular** as a noun (i.e. not "the Spanish peninsular").

per cent Is **per cent** an abbreviation of the Latin *per centum*? Some writers assume that it is and take care to write *cent.* (with an abbreviating full point). But it is not at all sure that **per cent** does stand for *per centum*, which was never a Latin phrase, though legal documents traditionally use it. **Per cent** may well be a corruption of the French *par cent*, and the *Oxford English Dictionary* keeps its distance from the Latin theory by never using the full point itself. Even if **per cent** did originate as an abbreviation it has been an established English phrase in speech and writing long enough for the noun derived from it to be *percentage*, not "percentumage". So zeal for preserving the full point smacks more of obsession than perfectionism. In fact there is little need to spell out **per cent** at all, as the symbol % is recognized by all who grasp the concept of percentage.

How many do so is something the writer might reflect on. Why deal in 50%/25%/10% etc when the measures are far more vividly conveyed by *half/a quarter/a tenth* etc? People do not think in comparisons with 100 but in simple proportions.

perfect See UNIQUE.

perhaps/perchance See MAYBE.

periodic/periodical In physics and chemistry the adjective is **periodic** (*periodic motion/periodic table* etc), and so it is in technical use generally. In publishing the adjective is **periodical** (*a periodical publication*) and so is the noun. In general use the speaker chooses whichever form occurs to him first, and the words are interchangeable (*a periodical housecleaning/periodic resolutions to work harder/our periodic moods* etc).

perk/perquisite Perk, slang abbreviation of **perquisite,** is now established as a word on its own in such phrases as *the perks of office/the perks that go with the job*. It means any customary material benefit enjoyed by an employee in addition to wages or salary.

persuade See CONVINCE.

petrol See GASOLINE.

phantasy Obsolete spelling of FANTASY (q.v.).

pharmaceutical etc The *c* in **pharmaceutical** is pronounced as in *pharmacy* (s). In **pharmacology/pharmacopoeia** it is pronounced as a k. Pharmacology is the study of medicinal drugs, pharmacopoeia (fahməkəpEə) is a directory of recognized drugs and doses.

phony/phoney This is thought to be a modern corruption of *funny*, but only in the sense of "sham"/"pseudo" (as in *There's something funny going on here*). In America, where it originated, the word's preferred spelling is **phony**, and so it should be in Great Britain. But when it was first imported the word was popularly taken to have something to do with "telephone", and **phoney** remains the more common spelling here. (See also PSEUD.)

piano/pianoforte Because the directions on musical scores are traditionally written in Italian it should not be assumed that Italianate pronunciations like pEahnO and fawtA are required for the familiar piano, which has been around long enough for anglicization. The player of a piano is a *pianist*, pronounced pEənist (not pEanist or pEahnist), and the instrument he plays is pronounced pEanO/pEanOfawti.

picaresque/picturesque The two have nothing in common except a spelling resemblance and colourful subject-matter. But that is enough for confusion. **Picturesque** is said of a scene striking enough for a picture. **Picaresque** is the term for a story about a rogue or rogues. So **picaresque** is a technical word unsuited for a general audience, among which it has little prospect of being understood.

picket/picquet Picket is the normal spelling in all senses (*picket fence/strikers' picket/military picket*), at least among civilians. In military usage **picquet** survives for a detachment on camp guard duty etc, but it is not used as a verb. In speech, like **picket**, it still rhymes with "ticket".

pilaff/pilau/pilao/pilaw The name of this well-known oriental rice dish is only of interest as an example of the difficulties of representing Eastern words in an agreed form. All the spellings listed are current. **Pilaff** is pronounced *pElaf* and all the others are pE*low* (as in "now"). (See also MAHOMET.)

placebo In these scientific days conversation requires familiarity with many technical terms, including those, like **placebo**, associated with medical mysteries. Even if one knows what it means (a dummy pill etc given to patients to humour them, or to a proportion of patients in a trial of a new medicine), dare one say the word out loud? There is nothing like mispronunciation for betraying depth of ignorance. **Placebo** is pronounced pləs*Eb*O. Its plural is **placebos.**

plastic/plastics We all know what we mean by a **plastic** – polyester/nylon/ABS etc – and when we say **plastics** we mean several of them. This is now established usage. But when plastics came in, in the mid-20th century (though bakelite and cellophane had arrived long before), there was an attempt to capture **plastics** as a solemn scientific name on the model of *acoustics/economics/physics*. Zealots would write of *a plastics material/plastics technology*, copying such forms as *an economics treatise/a physics theory*.

In technical literature traces of this purism survive. It is well meant, intending to avoid the theoretical confusion of *plastic material* etc, which might be taken to mean a mouldable material rather than a material made of plastic (many plastics are normally rigid, and are only capable of being moulded during manufacture). But users of English are practised at making the same word mean incompatible things without misunderstanding one another.

plethora As an ornamental variant of *plenty/abundance* etc **plethora** is ill-chosen. It originates in the medical sense of an unhealthy excess. Strictly it should be limited to such uses as *a plethora of crime/a plethora of sickly food*, though these would require a purist audience to appreciate them. Better still would be to stick to words like *plenty/abundance/superfluity*, which everybody can understand. The stress is on the first syllable, not the second.

plurality See MAJORITY for definition.

poignant In origin this is a synonym of *piquant*, but no sense of "to pierce" or "to prick" is still conveyed by it. In practice **poignant** is now just a literary word for "moving"/"touching". Also it is no longer pronounced *poinƏnt*, but *poinyƏnt*.

porage Unusual spelling of PORRIDGE (q.v.).

Polaroid See HOOVER.

polemic For pronunciation see ENDEMIC.

porcelain The smart word for *china*, which is pottery made from china-clay (originally pottery imported from China). (See also CERAMICS.)

porridge/porage The accepted spelling is **porridge**, though **porage** – one of several earlier forms – is still used commercially. The word derives from *pottage*, as in the biblical *mess of pottage*. But **porridge** now refers only to a boiled cereal, usually oatmeal.

postpone etc The *t* in **postpone** is supposed to be sounded, but it hardly ever is. The same is true of *postdated/postgraduate/postscript*. In all these the *t* of *post* is usually silent because of the difficulty of articulating a cluster of three or more consonants. (See COLLIDING CONSONANTS in Part II.)

practical/practicable The word people usually want is **practical**, but the uncertain, often reassured by the longer word, tend to choose **practicable**. **Practical** means "doing"/"putting into practice" (*She's so practical/His practical turn of mind*). **Practicable** means "do-able"/"capable of being put into practice" (*The suggestion is ambitious, but the government does not regard it as practicable*).

The word is increasingly avoided by resort to *viable* (which properly means "capable of living") and even to *on* (*That scheme of yours is just not on*).

Overlaps occur in senses like *It's not practical/practicable for me to fetch the children*. Here the issue is do-ability but only in terms of convenience, not theory. The wanted word is **practical**, unless for some reason the speaker is physically incapable of doing the fetching.

practice/practise The noun is **practice**, the verb **practise** (*Practice makes perfect, so practise and keep on practising*). U.S. usage does not make this distinction, but spells both noun and verb **practise**, as with *license* (q.v.).

preceding/precedent etc Despite **preceding**, which rhymes with "receding", the first syllable of **precedent** is sounded like "press", and the word has the same stress as "president". *Precedence* follows this model.

premier/premium Though both words are stressed on the first syllable, the *prem* in **premier** rhymes with "stem", and in **premium** with "scheme". **The Premier** = the Prime Minister, but in Australia and Canada **Premier** denotes the chief minister of a constituent state, only the federal leader being called Prime Minister.

premise/premiss Premiss is an alternative spelling, now uncommon and confined to British usage, for the sense of a postulate, or part of a proposition (q.v.) in logic, or an assumption underlying an argument. In legal documents the preliminary explanations etc, later referred to as *the aforesaid*, are the **premises**. From this use, mainly in bequests and conveyances of property, and only in the plural, comes the sense of **premises** as a building and/or grounds. The word rhymes roughly with "nemesis", i.e. prem, not prEm.

premium See PREMIER.

prerequisite Often given an unneeded hyphen, **prerequisite** is also abused by pairing with *essential* (*an essential prerequisite*). A prerequisite is anything required as a condition of something else, i.e. it is essential by definition. Users who believe in making sure their readers or hearers understand the drift by putting *essential* in front of the word can achieve the same effect by using *essential* on its own – as a noun (*Official approval is an essential of the scheme*).

presage Now used almost exclusively as a verb, *portent* (verb *portend*) being preferred as a noun. Rhymes with "message".

presently Means "soon" in British usage, "at once"/"at present" in American. The word is considered archaic in *Webster's New Collegiate Dictionary*, a condition that should be encouraged generally. A word that combines three conflicting senses is a liability.

pressure/pressurize Aviation has given us several useful words like *take-off* and *nosedive* but it can keep **pressurize**. This may be appropriate for the sense of artificially maintaining the air pressure inside high-flying airliners, but it is not needed for the sense of applying psychological pressure. **Pressure** itself serves satisfactorily in this sense: *The Minister is being pressured by his backbenchers/ Don't pressure me/Effective pressuring depends on timing*. Such use of a noun as a verb in a special sense is a normal English process, especially where the existing verb (*to press*) is already overloaded with meanings. But there are those who seem to lie in wait for new words just to be able to misuse them. They have seized their chance with **pressurize**, no doubt attracted by its extra syllable, and pressed it into service for which it is clearly unfitted, as in *The Senator said he would pressurize the Administration/Dissatisfied consumers are pressurizing the fuel industry*. This misuse is doubly objectionable. It substitutes a long new word for an existing shorter one, and it muddles a metaphor. **To pressure**, the correct term, is to apply pressure from the outside. **To pressurize** is to apply internal pressure, i.e. to inflate, which cannot be the intended image.

preventive/preventative Both forms exist, but **preventive** is the one to use (*preventive medicine/preventive measures/a useful preventive* etc).

price/pricy For spelling see DICE.

primarily Like *primary*, **primarily** is stressed on the first syllable, yielding *prImərəli*. The necessary gabbled articulation troubles some, as it does in *momentarily* (q.v.) and to a lesser extent in *summarily/voluntarily*. Funks and copycats take refuge in the ubiquitous American pronunciation, which rhymes with "prime airily" or "pry merrily", and stresses the least distinctive part of the word. People attempting multi-syllable words seem to expect the stress to fall roughly in the middle, but English is a language of exceptions, many of which stress the first syllable.

princess   Stressed on first syllable when followed by a name (i.e. used adjectivally) as in *Princess Margaret*, or by an elaboration of the title as in *Princess Royal/Princess dowager*. Stressed on second syllable when used as a noun on its own, as in *She is a princess*. An unwanted *t*-sound is inclined to intrude inadvertently, producing "printsess".

principal/principle   One of the commonest causes of spelling confusion in the language. **Principal** = chief/leading/main (*the principal minister is called the Prime Minister/The principal cause of discontent was high taxation/The principal cities of Belgium are Brussels and Antwerp/The head of this college is known as the Principal/In compound interest the annual percentage is added to the principal, i.e. the sum you originally invest*. It will be seen from these simple examples that **principal** is usually an adjective but can also be a noun. This is not true of **principle**, which is only a noun. **Principle** = a basic truth of reasoning/a moral or logical formula/ an item in a code of conduct (*The Uncertainty Principle is a starting point for modern physics/Running up debts is against her principles/He works on the principle that most people are honest/An important principle of our law is that an accused person is assumed innocent till found guilty*). A person who acts on principle is *principled*.

privacy   This is a case of "you say tomahto and I say tomayto". There is no disagreement about *private/privately*, in both of which the *i* is pronounced as in "I". So it should be in **privacy** – and in U.S. usage it is. But in Great Britain, in defiance of the *Oxford English Dictionary*, a pronunciation as in "privy"/"privilege" is more common.

privation   See DEPRIVE.

privileged/underprivileged   To be **privileged** is to enjoy an advantage/benefit/immunity. By definition a *privilege* is exceptional – if everybody had the same advantage it would no longer be an advantage. The word **underprivileged** is therefore a contradiction in terms, assuming as it does that a certain level of privilege is normal. It is a politician's or sociologist's euphemism for *poor/unemployed/ disabled* and any other category the user chooses to regard as worse off than they should be. So besides being contradictory it is also too imprecise to have any value except emotional – which is admittedly the role in which it is most often resorted to.

probable/probably Anything **probable** is also *likely* but different applications prevent the two words from being interchangeable. **Probable** requires to be followed by *that* where *likely* can take an infinitive:

> *You're likely to be the first*
> *It is probable that you will be the first.*

Note that phrases like *the probable effect/outcome/impact* etc require a present tense, while a similar version using **probably** requires a future tense. So: *The probable effect of the drought is widespread starvation* (not *will be* – the sense is *The effect that is probable is…*)/ *The effect of the drought will probably be starvation*. As an adverb **probably** has none of the limitations of *likely* (q.v.).

proboscis Probably less used as jargon for the trunk of an elephant, or flexible snout of other creatures, than as a facetious term for any prominent nose. Does not rhyme with "neurosis" – the middle syllable is as in "boss". The plural is also deceptive, not "probosces" but *proboscises* (the Latin original was "proboscides").

productivity Sometimes condemned as jargon, **productivity** survives because it is useful. It is not another word for "output", as contended by the lexicographer Eric Partridge, but for output in relation to input, i.e. productiveness, or efficiency of production.

profession/trade etc **Profession** is now so widely abused as a euphemism for *trade/business/occupation* that its abusers are probably unaware of any offence. The proper sense of **profession** is as in *the learned professions* (law, medicine, and the Church), an occupation requiring qualifications in prescribed studies, with a governing body or equivalent to oversee competence and conduct. Journalists, actors, hairdressers etc may be none the worse for lacking such arrangements but they are not entitled to dignify their breadwinning with such terms as *the profession of journalism/the theatrical profession/the hairdressing profession*.

The essence of a profession is the requirement of agreed professional standards. These cannot be characteristic of an occupation to which entry is open to anyone who can find a customer. Fixed standards may even be undesirable in changeable commercial activities like hairdressing and journalism.

The original meaning of **profession** was an avowal of a particular occupation, a sense surviving in *During the '80s he professed* *philosophy at Oxbridge* (= taught philosophy with the rank of professor).

program/programme The older spelling is **program**, which is also phonetic and shorter. It is thus preferable on every ground. As it is also standard in the U.S. it is absurd that **program** should be thought odd in the British Isles in comparison with **programme**, which is a recent imitation of the French. The spread of computers offers hope of a restoration. Since their technology is largely of American origin their settings tend to be referred to by the American term, i.e. **program**. This spelling is of course consistent with *anagram/diagram/telegram* and should never have been lost.

Another technological effect on **program** is the new sense given to it by television. The traditional sense of the word is of a prospectus of events, as in *What's on tonight's program?*. What is meant by a *TV program* however is a show, i.e. one of the individual events rather than the whole series.

progressive As used in political controversy, this is a modern hooray word denoting the user's approval of whatever he applies it to. It is limited to the figurative sense of the verb *to progress* = advance/ change for the better. A **progressive** idea/cause/policy is thus one promoting change for the better, and a **progressive** (noun) is a person devoted to such. Betterment, though, is the purpose of all deliberate change, from the point of view of whoever is responsible for initiating it – otherwise there would be no point in changing. So **progressive** is essentially a vague word, and this is part of its appeal. In controversy it provides a convenient opposite to "conservative" without implying "liberal" and without specifying any particular degree of leftism. In leftist jargon it belongs on a graduated scale this side of "fellow traveller" and "communist".

prohibit/prohibition etc The *h* is silent in the noun **prohibition** but sounded in the verb **prohibit** and its other forms (*prohibited/ prohibiting/prohibits*).

project/projectile When **project** is a noun (= a plan) it is stressed like *object*, on the first syllable, hence *projekt*. This stress remains unchanged in the noun **projectile** (*projektII*). But again like *object*, **project** changes stress when it is a verb, as in *Use these data to project the rate of development*. Here the stress is on *ject* (prəjekt), and it remains so in *projected/projecting/projection*.

promenade Though many words of French origin ending in *ade* have been anglicized to rhyme with "aid" (*fusillade*/*renegade*), **promenade** is among the exceptions. The last syllable is ahd. The pronunciation promen*Ad* is peculiar to callers in country dancing.

promote *Promoted to manager*/*foreman*/*captain*/*Secretary of State* etc is a wrong idiom. No *to* is necessary, except in the form *promoted to the rank*/*office* etc *of manager* etc. Otherwise the idiom is simply as in *He was promoted manager*/*You are promoted captain*/*He has been promoted Secretary of State*. As this idiom saves a word it is amazing that headline-writers, usually dedicated to economy, so often get it wrong.

proof/prove The expression *The exception proves the rule* is often taken to be a waggish use of the verb *proves*. In fact it is a use of the word in its only proper sense. **To prove** = to put to the test. It does not mean, as it is widely assumed to mean, to establish as incontrovertibly true for all time – no word in the language means that, including "demonstrate". **To prove** is only to find out by testing, hence such terms as *a printer's proof* (a trial sheet)/*proofing shots* (shots fired to test a gun)/*proof strength* (alcoholic content as tested chemically)/*waterproof, fireproof* etc (tested for impenetrability). A **proof** is a successful test. *The exception proves the rule* = . . . *tests the validity of the rule*, not "establishes that the rule is true". (See also NOT PROVEN.)

proposal/proposition A **proposal** is a suggestion for action, as in *a proposal of marriage*. A **proposition** is a theorem about to be tested or demonstrated, as in geometry. But confusion has led to encroachment by **proposition**, which now carries some of the senses of **proposal**, in particular those of a business proposal or a sexual proposal (*She hoped he was going to propose to her, but instead he propositioned her*).

protagonist This word is probably past saving in its distinctive sense. It means the principal in a drama or, by extension, in a story or cause. The protagonist of monetarism is Dr Milton Friedman and the protagonist of Watergate was President Nixon. **Protagonist** does not mean anyone prominent or just a proponent, though it is commonly misused in those senses. Hence "a chief protagonist", which is like talking about a round circle. But when a recent dictionary can offer "one of the chief protagonists" as a specimen of approved usage (first choice, in fact) there seems little hope of a rescue. *Proponent/advocate/champion/defender/leader* seem enough to choose from, though. (See also ANTAGONIST.)

protest (at)   The age of protest has brought to British television screens many scenes of transatlantic marchers with slogans such as *Mothers protest vice/Veterans protest war/Workers protest conditions.* This phenomenon, grammatically at least, is purely American. Idiom allows protests *at/about/against* sin, but not "We protest sin".

Protest only takes a direct object where this describes an attribute of the protester, as in *She protested her innocence* (or *fear/ignorance/hope* etc). Here of course the sense is of "declare" rather than "complain".

Pronunciation: **protest** varies its stress according to whether it is a noun or a verb. In all the verb forms (*protests/protested/protesting*) the stress is on *test*. In the noun it is on the first syllable, *prO*test.

proverbial   Proverbs are not much invoked these days except in mistaken use of **proverbial/proverbially**, as in specimens like *She tripped over the proverbial mat/Journalists are proverbially rushed/And so he went home to his proverbial bed.* **Proverbial/proverbially** mean "to do with a proverb" and are therefore pointless in those examples, since there is no proverb about tripping over a mat/rushed journalists/going home to bed. The motive is to dress up a stale phrase, but a proper use of **proverbial** is as follows: *He was full of talk about how he'd spend the money he expected to make – counting his proverbial chickens.* This is an obvious reference to the well-known proverb *Don't count your chickens before they're hatched*, but avoids quoting it in full. Whether the familiar is worth invoking in this way is something that must be left to the writer's judgement. It may not stimulate the reader but at least it does not baffle. Misuses like *He stood at the door like the proverbial avenger* set the reader trying to think of a proverb about an avenger, and there is no such thing. A similar misuse is suffered by *legendary* (q.v.).

provided/providing   These participles of the verb *to provide* both lead an independent existence as conjunctions, an idiom shared by *assuming/supposing* (= if) and *considering*. The role frees **provid-**

ing from the need for a specified subject, while **provided** can be regarded as an ellipsis of *it being provided that*. (The same liberty is allowed to *granted*.)

The two roles of **providing** are illustrated in the following examples. [1] Normal present participle, correctly related to the subject of the sentence: *Providing a reliable supply of commodities, the village store is essential to the community*. Clearly it is the village store that does the providing. [2] Conjunction equivalent to *if*: *Providing you do as I told you, we can't go wrong*. Here the subject of the main sentence is *we* but obviously neither *we* nor anybody else is doing any providing. Instead *providing* is linking the two sentences *you do as I told you* and *we can't go wrong*. **Providing/provided** are interchangeable here.

The same thing occurs in *Supposing your train is late, how will your husband know?/Assuming there's a telephone, you could call him*. These are venerable and everyday constructions but they still trouble punctilious writers, wary of unrelated participles. One solution is to use the imperative, as in *Suppose your train is late . . ./Assume there's a telephone . . . .*

provision See FURNISH for shades of meaning of similar words.

provost As a title for heads of colleges, religious communities, Scottish municipalities etc, **provost** is pronounced *provəst*. As a military term for soldiers on regimental police duty or for members of the military police corps (as in *Provost Marshal* etc), **provost** is pronounced *provO*.

prowess The word is often used in contexts suggesting the user believes it means "skill"/"mastery" (*He was showing off his prowess at darts*). What it actually means is valour or daring, traditionally of a manly kind.

pseud Fashionable substitute for *phony/faker/bluffer*, derived from the Greek for "false" and popularized by the British scandal review *Private Eye*. With its implied pretension to culture it makes a genuine improvement on its predecessors.

psychic/psychiatric etc If the mind remains largely a mystery it is not for lack of words to describe its functions. **Psyche**, which once meant "the soul" or "life force", has been appropriated by Freud for his notion of the directing mental mechanism. **Psychic**, which once meant "to do with the soul or psyche", has been appropriated by the spiritualists to describe their phenomena (*psychic powers* = ability to communicate with spirits of the dead). **Psychical** is no longer useful because, besides provoking confusion with the previous two, it is also capable of the sense now more often described by *parapsychological*, i.e. to do with phenomena outside physical laws. **Psychiatry**, the branch of medicine dealing with the mind, is often confused with *psychology*, the study of human mental functions (to the annoyance of psychiatrists, who are qualified doctors, while psychologists need not be). *Psychopathy* and *psychosis* are forms of mental illness, once more or less variants of *neurosis*, but now having precise medical definitions – and therefore better not bandied about by laymen unsure of these.

pulverize   The first syllable is pronounced as in "pulp"/"pulse", not as in "pull".

pundit   The usual sense in which **pundit** appears in print now – scholar or teacher – is described in some dictionaries as "jocular". The joke is over though, as not one reader in a hundred has any idea that the word means anything else. A **pundit** is in fact a Hindu authority on Sanskrit, Indian law, religion etc, and the spelling *pandit* is considered a better rendering of the Hindi (hence *Pandit Nehru*). But as this is no longer generally known, if it ever was, writers would do better to keep clear of this unnecessary word and use a natural English alternative like *sage/expert*.

quagmire   This is supposed to be pronounced with its first syllable rhyming with "wag" (*kwag*mlə). But as the sound differs from that of most common words beginning with *qua* (*quaff/quality/quantity/quandary/quarry*) a rhyme with "wog" is heard at least as often. It is not a choice that need detain anyone long – why not settle for *bog*?

question   We discuss the **question of** Nigel's misbehaviour, or the **question whether** Nigel misbehaved, perhaps because someone asked a **question about** Nigel's behaviour. There is no need in any of these constructions to clutter the wording with *as to*, which seems to be a makeshift form for bridging gaps after words like *question/demand* etc when the obvious preposition or adverb is overlooked. (See also AS.)

quite   A treacherous word to use in writing, as it may be taken to mean the opposite of what is intended. In *quite right/quite certain/ Have you quite finished?* **quite** means "completely". In *quite nice/ quite pleased/quite soon* **quite** means "less than completely" ("rather"). So the same word has the conflicting senses of "unreservedly" or "grudgingly", and the distinction relies on the tone of voice. Without such help the sense can be in doubt, and in writing **quite** is best confined to colloquial phrases.

rabbet/rebate   A **rebate** is a discount but the same spelling is widely used for a groove in the edge of a wood surface, which should properly be spelt **rabbet** and pronounced *rabət* instead of *rEbAt*. The tool for cutting such a groove, as do-it-yourselfers discover, is variously called a *rebate plane, rabbet plane* or *rabbeter*. Some carpenters and joiners say "rabbet" for the tool and the action, and "rebate" for the groove. Historically there is no doubt that **rabbet** is the right form for both and that **rebate** is a corruption, but **rebate** is already the commoner of the two and seems likely to take over.

rabbit   For the Welsh kind see RAREBIT, a corruption.

rack   Not to be confused with WRACK (q.v.).

racket/racquet   Every sense of the word, from bat to extortion, is covered by the spelling **racket**, but tennis enthusiasts, and players of the game of **racquets**, remain attached to the quainter (though not older) spelling.

railway etc   British usage is **railway**, American **railroad**, though this has not always been so. George Stephenson's pioneer line was called the Stockton & Darlington Railroad. The shortened form **rail**, found in phrases like *go by rail/road and rail*, has not displaced the full word, except in the official title of the British nationalized system, British Rail, adopted during one of many desperate reorganizations.

raise/rise   In the sense of an increase in wages, **rise** is the British term, **raise** the American, though in either instance the wages are *raised*. As verbs **raise/rise** differ in that **raise** is transitive and **rise** intransitive. They also have different derivatives: *raise/raised/raising, rise/ rose/risen/rising*.

rarebit/rabbit   Caterers are never going to be persuaded that their dish of toasted cheese is correctly called a *Welsh rabbit* and not, as they prefer to style it, a "Welsh rarebit". But it is so. The "rarebit" fantasy took hold long ago, and now that rabbits are associated with myxomatosis there is no going back.

re/regarding etc   The Latin phrase *in re* (= in the matter of) is the original of **re** (rhymes with "spree") and is still current in legal use. It is a coincidence that *regarding/referring to* have the same sense, but a supposition that **re** is an abbreviation for one or other of these probably accounts for its widespread popular and business use today (*We must have a word re holidays soon/Re your letter of the 10th. . .*). Admittedly not quite so short, but just as practical and untainted by jargon, is *about*. (See also REGARD.)

real   In the game of real tennis **real** does not mean "genuine" but is the Old French form of *royal*. Hence Montreal = Mount Royal. The same word survives in Spanish (Real Madrid = Royal Madrid). Various historic gold coins, especially Spanish, have also been so called, sometimes with the spelling *rial*.

reason (why/that/for)   Tennyson's *Theirs not to reason why/Theirs but to do and die* has so caught the popular imagination that **why** often seems the normal construction after **reason**. Tennyson clearly meant *question why*. We also *wonder why/ask why/explain why*, but we **reason that** and talk of **the reason that/a reason for** etc: *I'll tell you the reason (that) I did it/The reason (that) they're late is the weather/He reasons (that) there must be a market*. In these examples advantage would normally be taken of *that*'s convenience in being allowed to be left out. Popular song, so often a guide to idiom, offers a confirmation in *Tell me what's the reason/I'm not pleasin'/You.*

   Why not only tends to be the wrong choice but is sometimes repetitive, as in *I'd like to know the reason why* – which is a wordy version of *I'd like to know why/I'd like to know the reason.*

   In negatives like *There's no reason why I shouldn't go* **why** has come to seem acceptable, but the construction itself is a poor choice. A more direct phrasing is possible with **reason for**, e.g. *There's no reason for me not to go.*

   Note that **reason for**, the normal choice when followed by nouns etc (*the reason for the delay/his reason for going*), is liable to muddled use with *because/due to* etc, which repeat the sense. So all the following specimens are wrong: *The reason for his success was because he had persevered/. . . was due to his hard work/. . . was on account of his devoted helpers.* The required substitute for *because* is again **that**. In the last two examples the phrases *due to/on account of* are just superfluous.

The appeal of **reason why** may owe something to *the place where,* but this is an unreliable model of limited scope. *Where* may need replacing by *that* too, e.g. you could not say *the place where I told you about.*

rebate Sometimes a corruption of RABBET (q.v.).

rebound/redound/redundant When something works out favourably for you it may be said to *redound to your advantage/credit* etc. (Also possible is *redound to your discredit,* though the unfavourable sense is hardly ever used.) **Redound** is not a misprint or a variant of **rebound**, though the confusion is understandable. **Redound/redounded/redounding**, with the sense of "accruing", are all that remain of an ancient verb that once meant "overflow". The earlier meaning survives in **redundant/redundancy** (= superfluous). Of course many acts could also **rebound** to one's credit etc, but this is not what is meant by the traditional phrases. So, to those in the know, **rebound** will suggest ignorance rather than a different image. Not that either **rebound** or **redound** is worth bothering with when there are so many clearer ways of putting it.

recce Deserves to be recognized as a word in its own right, sparing us the syllables of *reconnaissance* (noun) and *reconnoitre* (verb). **To recce** or *to make a recce* (rhymes with "wreck-y") covers both forms and avoids pronunciation problems. A *recce plane* is much more in the spirit of English than the RAF's formal "reconnaissance aircraft". Probably it is only a matter of time before what soldiers and airmen already say becomes generally accepted. Why any of these terms was ever needed when *scout* was there is another matter.

receipt/recipe Recipe (*res*ipi) now means only "food formula" (it once meant a medical prescription too), and in U.S. usage it does not even mean that – **receipt** is the American term. But in both countries the main senses of **receipt** (ri*sEt*) are reception of money or goods and proof of such reception, as in *On receipt of your payment the goods will be sent/Please give me a receipt for this payment.*

reciprocal   For shade of meaning see MUTUAL.

record   The noun is stressed like "concord"/"discord" (*rek*awd). The verb **to record** is ri*kawd*. The word *accord* varies similarly.

redound/redundant   Confused with REBOUND (q.v.).

refectory   Rhymes with "directory".

reflection/reflexion   See CONNECTION.

refute/deny   Refute is suddenly the public speaker's favourite when what is meant is **deny**. The words are not synonyms. **To deny** is to contradict or repudiate, but the denial need not be effective. **To refute** is to disprove, i.e. to deny unanswerably. This is no doubt the effect public speakers would like all their denials to have, but they cannot ensure it just by abusing **refute**. (See also IRREFUTABLE.)

regard   There is no difference in sense between this verb and *consider* but they require different constructions:

> *We consider your approval essential*
> *We regard your approval **as** essential*
> *It is considered essential to have your approval*
> *It is regarded **as** essential to have your approval*
> *It is considered **that** your approval is essential*
> (No equivalent for *regard*).

In *as regards your insurance problem. . .* **regards** is part of the prepositional phrase *as regards*, other variants of which are *with regard to*/*regarding* – all of course meaning "about".

Note the difference between the phrases *have regard to* (= take into consideration) and *have regard for* (=hold in esteem). (See also CONSIDERING and RE.)

register office/registrar   etc   The place where a ceremony of civil marriage is conducted and registered in Great Britain is called a **register office**. For some reason it is considered an error to refer to it as a "registry office" or "registrar's office". Young journalists have this drummed into them at a time when they might be mastering tricky spellings and idiomatic constructions. As there is no question that a **register office** *is* an office of registry and also the registrar's office, it seems pedantic to insist on its formal title, especially as everybody knows what is meant.

relation/relatives etc   In the sense of "to narrate" or "a narrative" **relate/relation** are normally restricted to writing, and even there they seem formal. This at least reduces confusion about the various senses of **relation** and its offshoots.

In the sense of a person to whom one is related by family, **relation/relative** are interchangeable nouns. But only **relation** can refer to social connection, as in *How are your relations with the boss?/I have very good relations with my cousins*. In such contexts the word **relationship** is often substituted, though it has been traditionally reserved for degrees of relation, i.e. *relationship to* (rather than *relationship with*), as in *What's Jim's relationship to Lavinia? (She's his sister-in-law)*. This sense, which is correct, is clearly different from *What's Jim's relationship with Lavinia like? (They don't get on at all well)*. The traditional version of the last would be *What are Jim's relations like with Lavinia?*, but this is open to ambiguity.

Relative/relatively (adjective and adverb) are treasured by bad writers along with *comparative/comparatively* as a weighty change from "rather": *I thought he did relatively well* (relatively to what?)/*It was a relative success* (relative to what?).

renegade/renege   The noun **renegade**, meaning "turncoat"/"deserter"/"apostate", is an old word enjoying a vogue in the vocabulary of treachery, where it seems to rank first in insult value. It also functions conveniently as an adjective, as in *a renegade priest/a renegade lawyer*. Its popularity may account for the rise of the related verb **renege**, another old word, now settled with the sense of "break faith"/"go back on a promise". The spelling should have stayed as *renegue*, which points to the pronunciation (rhymes with "league", not with "vague" or "edge"). But the current **renege** (*reneges/reneged/reneging*) is a revival of one of the earliest versions, even if it does make for irregularity.

replica/replicate   Pronounced *rep*likə (not re*plik*ə)/*rep*likAt. A **replica** is a duplicate or facsimile and to **replicate** is to duplicate. *Duplicate* seems the more practical word to use.

reportage   Rhymes with "camouflage"/"massage"/"entourage", not with "damage"/"encourage"/"portage". (See also GARAGE.)

respite   Rhymes with "cesspit", not with "despite".

restaurant/restaurateur   In its anglicized form **restaurant** is pronounced *res*trawn or sometimes *res*tərawn. Either way the final *t*
remains silent, even when followed by a word beginning with a
vowel. There is no *n* in **restaurateur** and if the word must be used
in preference to *restaurant owner* etc it should be pronounced
*res*tawrətə.

retch   Rhymes with "reach", not "wretch".

restrospective   Means "looking back", as does *in retrospect*. The
required word in such phrases as *retrospective legislation/with
retrospective effect* is not "retrospective" but *retroactive* (= *acting
backwards*). This distinction is rarely made, perhaps because *in
retrospect* is such a common phrase (with no equivalent *retroact*
form) that it suggests *retrospective*. Any indignation about the
confusion had better be saved for retrospective legislation, a political cooking of the statute book to pretend that laws were in force
when they were not.

reveille   Waking-up time in the Forces or other institutions. Also the
bugle call announcing this. As followers of Sergeant Bilko will have
noted, Americans say it "revel-y". The British version rhymes with
"the valley". Either rendering does equal injury to the French
original, so there's no choice on that score.

reverend/the Rev.   Along with losing many of its flock the Church of
England can no longer count on correct references to its clergy.
Below the rank of dean, clergymen are referred to as **the Rev.**
followed by initial or first name, and by surname. When only the
surname is known *Mr* must be inserted before it (*The Rev. Ian
Goodfellow/The Rev. I. Goodfellow/The Rev. Mr Goodfellow*).
Rev. is short for **reverend** (= deserving reverence), which is not
interchangeable with *reverent* (= displaying or feeling reverence).

revolution   Ignored as model for EVOLUTION (q.v.).

rhythm/rhythmic etc   The adjective can be either **rhythmic** or **rhyth-
mical** without affecting the sense, but the adverb can only be
rhythmically (usually pronounced as though it were "rhythmicly").

ribbon/riband   Ribbon, which was how Shakespeare spelt the word, is right. **Riband**, now rare, is a corruption suggested perhaps by the similarity of shape between a ribbon and a band. It was kept before the public by the so-called Blue Riband of the Atlantic, an award abandoned with the passing of ocean liners (it was held by the fastest). The spelling has gone with them. The nautical use may have been a confusion with *ribband*, a length of wood used to position a ship's ribs during construction.

ricochet   Its forms are *ricochet* (rikəshA), *ricocheted* (rikəshAd), *ricocheting* (rikəshAing), *ricochets* (rikəshAs). The word *crochet* (q.v.) has similar forms but is pronounced *krO*shi etc.

right/rightly   Both are adverbial forms, but they are rarely inter-changeable. **Right** in many phrases is the only idiomatic choice: *Serves you right/He's not doing it right/Is the car running right/No it's not working right/I guessed right, then/All I want is to do right by her*. Note that **right** as adverb always goes after the verb.

Comparable uses of **rightly** in the same sense of "correctly": *He was rightly doing it fast/He rightly held that the car was faulty/You rightly guessed the outcome*. Only **rightly** is possible in contexts like *Rightly believing the rescuers would spot the wreck, he stayed close to it/She is rightly complaining to the authorities/She has rightly objected/She rightly objects*.

rise   See RAISE for sense of financial increase.

Romania/Romansh/Romany   The first two and their variants are derived from *Roman*, but **Romany** is traced to *Rom*, a word for "gypsy" in the gypsy language. **Romania** is the preferred spelling for the name of the country, earlier more often spelt *Roumania/Rumania*. **Romansh** is the Latin-derived language spoken in an eastern pocket of Switzerland, also rendered as *Roumansh/Rumansch* etc. (See also GYPSY.)

rough/roughen   *Roughen* has the sense of "to become rough" or "to make rough" as in *She watched the sea roughen/Roughen the surface of the wood with a rasp*.

Rough, escorted by *in*, *out*, or *up*, has the sense of to treat roughly or to work to approximate limits, as in *He wasn't hurt – just roughed up a bit/Can you rough out your proposals?/Let me rough in the lettering*.

round   For idiomatic choices see AROUND.

rouse/arouse etc   Comparison with *wake/awake* is irresistible but any distinction between **rouse/arouse** is more limited. By far the commoner form is **rouse**. Only **arouse**, though, has a noun for the state of being roused: **arousal**. Sexual permissiveness has brought this noun into much wider use since the 1960s, and the verb **to arouse** with it. These forms have become standard in the sense of sexual excitement. But **rouse** is still capable of carrying that sense too, along with every other available sense.

route   Rhymes with "root". In military usage (*route march/column of route* etc) it is sometimes rhymed with "shout", probably because that is also the pronunciation of *rout* (= to scatter an enemy), which used to mean "a troop".

rugged   The basic sense is "rough/"coarse". The usual American sense, now becoming familiar in Britain, is "robust"/"sturdy", as in *The plane's undercarriage is of rugged construction*. This sense is derived from the association of *rough* and *tough*.

sadism/sadist   Only purists still pronounce these in honour of the Marquis de Sade (sahd). Anglicization has inexorably led to *sAd*izm/ *sAd*ist (but *sə*/*distik*). No offence to the mad marquis, who after all did not invent sadism – it existed centuries before he took to it.

same as etc   In parallel constructions like *We took the same route as you suggested last time* a common confusion is to replace *as* with *that*. But *that* belongs to a different construction without *same*, i.e. *We took the route that you suggested last time*. The sense is unaffected but *same* would be redundant in the second version and *that* would wreck the comparison in the first, as seen when the ellipted words are restored: *We took the same route as (the one) you suggested* .... **Same** ... **as** are the idiomatic pair, not *same* . . . *that*.

save   As an alternative to *except*, **save** is certainly the less obvious and more formal choice but the idea that there is something stylistically objectionable about it seems exaggerated. **Save** has been in use since before Wyclif's time, surely long enough for acceptance, especially as everybody knows what it means.

sceptic/skeptic The spelling **skeptic** is phonetic but purely American. **Sceptic** is the only acceptable form outside America, and as long as nobody confuses it with *septic* (poisoned) there seems to be no reason for changing. Most English words beginning with *sc* are, pronounced sk, though the exceptions include *science/scimitar/ sciatica.*

Scotch/Scots/Scottish etc Sometimes it seems as though every minority feels entitled to an insult to complain about. In the case of the natives of Scotland the alleged offence is to call them **Scotch** instead of **Scots** or **Scottish**. This is a modern grievance, and a contrived one. All three words are merely forms of the same adjective, and none has any claim to greater respectability than the others. In general **Scotch** is now less common than the other forms, particularly in print – perhaps a measure of Sassenach anxiety to please.

As the *Oxford English Dictionary* records, **Scotch** was good enough for the national poet Robert Burns, and for the country's principal novelist, Sir Walter Scott, besides being used officially in *Scotch Education Office.* The word is ineradicable in many established terms, e.g. *Scotch whisky/Scotch egg/Scotch tape/Scotch terrier.* Purists prefer **Scots** (as in *Scots Guards/the Royal Scot/ Flying Scotsman*), especially as a noun (*The Scots are a hardy people/Mary, Queen of Scots*). But the commoner form among those who avoid saying "Scotch" is **Scottish**. This is usual in such terms as *Scottish literature/the Scottish temperament/Scottish history/the Scottish legal tradition* etc.

secret See CLASSIFIED.

secretive The modern pronunciation stressing the first syllable instead of the second makes clear that **secretive** (sEkrətiv) is the adjective of *secret*, and not of *secretion* – which has its own: *secretory/*(sikrEtəri).

seem (to be) Is there any general rule about when **to be** is necessary after the verb **seem**? There does not seem to be. In *They seem to be cousins/The weather seems colder,* **to be** could be omitted from the first and inserted in the second. But **to be** is always inserted between **seem** and a present participle, as in *Everyone seems to be hoping so/Nothing seems to be going well/He seems to be getting better/It seems to be working.*

When a present participle functions as an adjective however, **to**

be can be omitted (*It seems encouraging/The prospect seems daunting*).

Seem can take a complement (*He seemed a crook to me/John seems strange*) without an intervening **to be**. But in constructions with **there seems** it is usual to find **to be** though this cannot be called required: *There seems to be nothing we can do/There seems to be something wrong*.

Past participles capable of functioning as adjectives, like *expected/resented*, can do without **to be**, as in *It seems expected that you'll be there* – unlike *hoped/dreamt/thought* etc (which cannot be used adjectivally without a preposition): *It seems to be hoped that you'll agree*.

But these are pointers only. **Seem**'s awkwardness is shared by *appear* and there are comparable difficulties with *feel/grow/sound/turn out* etc. (See LINKING VERBS in Part II.)

sensual/sensuous etc   As *sense* itself has a dozen or so meanings, several of them in conflict, it is not surprising that its offshoots should confuse. **Sensual** and **sensuous** are best differentiated by reference to *sensualist* (= one who indulges the carnal appetites, a libertine). By contrast **sensuous** relates to taking pleasure in the senses but without any overtone of physical excess or undue sexuality. The frontier here may seem indistinct and is certainly often overstepped by **sensuous**, perhaps because of the word association *sinuous/sexy*.

For a neutral adjective **sensory** provides a technical reference to the five senses (*Sight, smell, taste, touch, and hearing are all sensory experiences*). **Sensitive** means "responsive", and by extension "touchy".

Sensible of course no longer refers to the senses at all. It now means "reasonable"/"practical"/"judicious", and has nothing to do with **sensibility** either (= emotional capacity). *Behave sensibly. Be your usual sensible self and don't make a fuss.*

sergeant/serjeant   The spelling **sergeant** is almost universal, but **serjeant** is still preferred in a few surviving traditional titles (*Serjeant at Arms/H.M. Serjeant Surgeon*) and in a few units of the Army.

serviette   See NAPKIN.

Shakespeare/Shakspere   The standard spelling has always been **Shakespeare**. As Sir Sidney Lee put it in his contribution to the

Dictionary of National Biography (1897), "It is the spelling adopted on the title pages of the majority of contemporary editions of his works". This rather understates the position. It is the spelling found repeatedly in the earliest collection of the plays, the famous 1623 First Folio, which had no mention of "Shakspere", though two of the dedications used the form *Shake-speare*. (This had appeared on earlier publications such as the poems *Venus & Adonis* and *The Rape of Lucrece*.)

The persistence of **Shakspere** as an occasional variant, usually to imply scholarship on the part of the user, is due to a Victorian vogue and its perverse endorsement by the compilers of the *Oxford English Dictionary*. In place of the usual adjective *Shakespearean* they substituted an entry for "Shaksperian". The bizarre explanation offered for this choice was that a long-known copy of Florio's *Montaigne*, alleged to have belonged to the playwright, carried a signature interpreted as "Shakspere" to the satisfaction of the New Shakspere Society. As the authenticity of this signature had already been judged "doubtful" by Lee, the basis for the recommendation was, to say the least, shaky. The best assessment of it is that the spelling has been ignored by all the other dictionaries of the Oxford Press and by its various standard works such as the *Oxford History of England* and the *Oxford Book of English Verse*.

A practical use for **Shakspere** is to distinguish the historical Stratford-on-Avon figure from the author of the Shakespeare works, who may or may not have been one and the same. The man baptized in Stratford on 26 April 1564 was recorded as "William Shaksper". He was buried on 25 April 1616 as "Will. Shaksper(e), gent." No known handwriting of his survives besides a few virtually unreadable signatures, which have been variously interpreted. The inconsistent appearance of these specimens, from a presumed professional writer, is among the evidence cited by supporters of rival claimants to the authorship.

shall/will The way these auxiliary verbs are supposed to be used to express the future is no longer the way people use them. Also what they are supposed to mean is often not what people mean by them. In speech and increasingly in writing people say *I'll/you'll/he'll* etc, unconscious of which verb the contraction stands for. If they use a full version in writing they generally write **will** regardless of context. Even in questions, where contractions are not always possible, **will** encroaches on the traditional preserve of **shall**, so that *When will I hear from you?* is now just as likely as *When shall I hear. . .?*.

These realities are at odds with what has been the grammatical convention, the main point of which is that **shall** should be used with *I/we*, and **will** with *he/she/it/you/they* etc. But even professional writers, including some of the most polished, now ignore this convention. Many have never grasped its basis, let alone its ramifications. Anyway the convention has never been observed in Scotland and Ireland, and if it ever was in North America it has been abandoned there long since.

Some grammarians still keep pointing out alleged valuable distinctions of sense between **shall** and **will**, but nobody seems to have noticed the loss of these advantages. It would be surprising if anyone did, since there is no need for **will** in order to express volition. This is better done by *mean to/intend to* etc (how else are inflected languages supposed to manage, with no *shall/will* to complicate their future tenses?).

One academic view identifies 10 different senses of **shall/will**, as required by convention:

[1] *I shall* – predicts, foretells, surmises etc
[2] *I will* – promises, threatens, warns etc
[3] *You shall* (also *he/she/it/they*) – promises etc
[4] *You will* (also *he/she/it/they*) – predicts etc
[5] *Shall I/we?* – asks for orders
[6] *Will I/we?* – asks for a prediction
[7] *Shall you?* – asks for a prediction (rare, British)
[8] *Will you?* – makes a request
[9] *Shall he?* (also *she/it/they*) – asks for orders
[10] *Will he?* (also *she/it/they*) – asks for a prediction.

Of these **will** is now usual in all except [5] and [9] (*Shall we dance?/Shall she send for the doctor?*). In [3] **shall** still occurs, as in *Applicants shall produce the following documents/Nor shall my sword sleep in my hand*. But as the sense here is held to be equivalent to *It is my/our will that . . .* (i.e. a promise or threat) there seems no reason for not sticking to **will**. Military orders are in fact worded with **will** (*The company will parade at 8.30 hrs*).

The main area of contention is [2], use of **will** in the first person to promise or threaten, i.e. to express volition (will) rather than futurity. Surely nobody can discern volition in *I will see you at the weekend* as opposed to *I shall see you . . . .* Besides, what would most likely be said is *I'll see you . . .* , in which form no distinction of meaning is either intended or understood.

All this leaves out of account whether any practical difference can in fact exist between a statement of futurity concerning the speaker and a statement of his will. When General McArthur abandoned Corregidor he declared: "I shall return". But nobody has ever supposed that this statement of grammatical futurity was not also a statement of will.

To sum up: the different uses of **shall** and **will** are now largely a matter of taste, generally evaded by the neutral *'ll*. This development is a gain for simplicity and uniformity. R. A. Close, author of the influential analysis *English As a Foreign Language*, admits an eccentric usage of his own: he says **shall** when the sound makes a change from **will**. At least that is a proper valuation of the current importance of the choice. In this Guide **shall/will** are used conventionally, but only as a matter of habit. (See also SHOULD/WOULD.)

shot to death   Familiar from television crime serials, this phrase is an American usage. The British form is *shot dead*. This is shorter and so preferable, but the American form has the respectable analogy of *beaten to death/starved to death* etc.

should/would   As with *shall/will* (q.v.) there is a convention with these auxiliaries to use **should** with *I/we* and **would** with all other persons. But the tendency is to ignore the convention and prefer **would** or, wherever either word is unstressed, the contraction *'d* (as in *I knew I'd win*), especially in speech.

Should/would provide equivalents for *shall/will* in future-in-the-past tenses. So they are substituted when direct quotation is turned into reported speech, as in

> "*I* **will** *be there*", *he said/He said he* **would** *be there*
> "*Trespassers* **will** *be prosecuted*", *it stated/It stated that trespassers* **would** *be prosecuted.*

But in addition **should** expresses special senses where it is not limited to use with *I/we*. In most of these it is equivalent to *ought to* but milder, as in

> *You shouldn't behave like that* (= ought not to)
> *They should wait their turn* (= ought to)
> *Things should get better from now on* (= ought to)
> *That's what I should do if I were you* (= what you ought to do).

No substitution of **would** is possible in any of these except the last.

Should is also required in subsentences beginning with *that* after expressions of desire/intention/surprise/regret etc, as in

> *I'm sorry (that) you should take it personally*
> *Their proposal is (that) we should pay half*
> *It's astonishing (that) they should have chosen me.*

Simpler versions of these, like … *you take it personally*, are common now.

In polite conditional expressions **would** is general even where **should** is traditional:

> *We'd be delighted to accept* (or *would be*)
> *I would think what you say is right* (= if you asked me)
> *We would so like to hear your views* (or *we'd*).

shy/shyly   For spelling see DRY.

significant/meaningful etc   The English language has **significant** (= full of meaning) and **meaningless** (= without meaning), but this is not enough for some people. Perhaps the meaning of **significant** is thought to be not immediately obvious, or liable to be taken as the converse of "insignificant" (= unimportant). Anyway we now have the deficiency made good with **meaningful**, a godsend to the imprecise, who find themselves able to talk of *meaningful dialogues* and *meaningful progress* etc without having to commit themselves to what the meaning is.

silicon/silicone   Easily confused, these are two newcomers to the popular scientific vocabulary. **Silicon**, as used in the microchips of electronics, is the main ingredient of sand. **Silicone** is a kind of plastic, a chemical compound of carbon and silicon, used for waterproof lubricants, non-stick pan linings and reconstructive or cosmetic surgery.

sinecure   Rhymes with "mini cure", not with "tiny cure".

sizable   See CONSIDERABLE.

skewer   Rhymes with "skua"/"fewer"/"reviewer", which nobody had ever doubted till *Collins Dictionary of the English Language* singled out the word for its pronunciation key and coupled it with "poor"/"sure". This was evidently a considered view as the same pronunciation is recorded three times (IPA symbol ʊə.) The *Longman Dictionary of Contemporary English*, which also uses the IPA code, confirms the normal pronunciation, as in "skua" (IPA uːə).

ski/skier etc Two doubts occur. [1] Should **ski** be pronounced like "she"? [2] How do you spell the verb in its other forms? Pronunciation: outside Scandinavia, where the word comes from, **ski** should be said the way it nearly always is, i.e. skE. Spelling: the verb forms are spelt normally without awkward hyphening, i.e. **ski/skies/skied/skiing**. The only possible difficulty here is that *skies/skied* might be taken for tenses of *to sky* (= hit a cricket ball skywards). If spoken, however, these would be pronounced sklz/skld, and if written the likelihood of their occurring in a snowbound context is so remote that only cricket maniacs could conceive it.

slander For legal and popular senses see LIBEL.

sled/sledge/sleigh etc Though **sledge** is now obsolescent, **sled** remains current in compounds like *dogsled/bobsled*, especially in the U.S. and Canada. It is also applied to the runners on which the vehicle slides. Otherwise **sleigh** is the usual word both in America and in the British Isles, upheld by phrases like *sleigh bells/sleigh ride/sleigh run*.

sleight Despite its resemblance to *sleigh* (which is of course pronounced as "slay"), **sleight** is pronounced as "slight", not "slate". The word is no longer used in any context but *sleight of hand* = a dexterous feat, particularly of conjuring or juggling.

slow/slowly etc As an adverb **slow** survives in only a few phrases such as *go slow/running slow* (of a watch or train etc). The usual form is **slowly**, though the comparative and superlative are **slower/slowest**.

solder Rhymes with "older", not "odder" (as it once did).

sort of/kind of etc The liberties allowed to these phrases are of long standing, but are still questioned. The basic usage is the straightforward *this kind of apple/a sort of pudding/the type of man*. Here the item specified is usually singular (*apple*, not *apples*) regardless of how many specimens are in question. But already there are exceptions. The thought may have a plural emphasis, as in *They're the type of men you can trust/The sort of apples most British farmers grow*. Here the singular noun becomes plural to match the thought. In practice it is difficult when you are thinking of masses of apples or a lot of men to refer to them in the singular. Theoretically the plural sense is satisfied by the standard plural patterns, *the sorts of apple/the types of man/those kinds of pudding*. But in speech, and increasingly in writing, the plural is repeated on the lines of *the sorts of apples* or even *these sort of apples. These sort of* etc is certainly a grammatical misfit, but it is equally certainly an acknowledged idiom.

What about *I sort of half expected you/She looked kind of upset* etc? These are still uncommon in print but universal in speech. They are equivalent to *rather*, and as they are past the point of no return they have to be tolerated grammatically as just another adverb phrase. The status is shared by parallels like *He's learning carpentry, sort of/He's learning carpentry, really/He's learning carpentry, after a fashion.* Nothing is gained by objecting to usages we all understand and all use.

An American idiom, sometimes heard from British speakers, is **sort of a/kind of a** etc, as in *What kind of a hat is that?/She's that sort of a person*. At least the singular treatment is right, but *a* is redundant after *sort of* etc. It is the concept of *hat/person* etc that is meant in such uses, not an individual specimen.

soupçon   One of those foreign words with no function in English except to exhibit the user's familiarity with a second language. After all, the English equivalent conveys exactly the same meaning. **Soupçon** translates as "suspicion", but is used in the restricted sense of "a suspicion of", i.e. *just a dash of (sugar/Martini/colour/envy* etc).

south/southern etc   See NORTH/NORTHERN.

special etc   For spelling and distinctions see ESPECIAL.

speedometer   For pronunciation see GASOMETER.

spinach   The final sound, despite the spelling, is a *j*, as in *ridge/ tonnage/Greenwich* (spinij).

spite of, in   See DESPITE, the simpler variant.

spry/spryness   See DRY for spelling.

stationary/stationery   One of the commonest spelling confusions in the language. **Stationary** = standing still/not moving in any direction. **Stationery** = materials for writing/materials for office work (*Her Majesty's Stationery Office* = government publications department). Hence a **stationer's** (shop).

stay/stop Using the verb **to stop** in the sense of **to stay** is legitimate when the stay is a stop on a journey, as in *We're driving to the Riviera but we'll be stopping a day or two in Paris.* This is in line with the idiomatic uses *stop off/stop over.* Whether **stop** is generally interchangeable with **stay** is less certain. *Can I stop with you?/ Are you stopping?/We have a room at the Splendide – where are you stopping?/Jim's the fair-haired boy who stops with his auntie down the road.* These are all heard but tend to be regarded as non-U (q.v.) if not downright uneducated. Careful writers would use **stay**.

story/storey In the sense of a floor of a building (*a mansion three storeys high*), only **storey** is recognized in British usage. But as so often with such alternatives, the American form (**story/stories**), though considered wrong in England, is in fact the older. In this instance the British spelling is an upstart, only becoming general during the 20th century.

There is also a divergence in the reckoning of storeys. A building with 12 floors has 12 storeys, but in Europe the ground floor is not numbered as 1. The counting begins with the first floor above ground level. In North America the numbering begins at ground level. Where there are basements these are counted in the total of storeys, but the numbering of floors is unaffected in either place.

strait Not to be confused with *straight*, though it often is. **Strait** means "narrow", not "unswerving"/"direct" etc. Hence *strait-jacket/the Straits of Dover/in dire straits/straitened circumstances* etc.

stringed/strung The adjective is **stringed**, the participle **strung**. So a stringed instrument is an instrument strung with taut strings. This leaves the question of which form *hamstring* is modelled on as a verb. It was once a matter of controversy, but *hamstrung* is now the accepted past tense and past participle. Of course the sense is perverse: a hamstring is a leg tendon, but when it is hamstrung it is cut, not strung.

struck/stricken The past participle of the verb *to strike* is **struck** (*The tree had been struck by lightning*). **Stricken** is an earlier form with surviving but limited uses as an adjective, as in *panic-stricken/ poverty-stricken/the stricken warrior*. Its sense is "injured"/"distressed".

subpoena   As a verb the forms are **subpoena** (səpEnə)/**subpoenaes**/ **subpoenaed**/**subpoenaing**. They may look odd but not so odd as they would with apostrophes to draw attention to unEnglishness (e.g. "subpoena'd"). As apostrophes are used to indicate omission it seems silly to enlist their services when there is nothing omitted. There is no difficulty in saying the words: *I'm going to subpoena him/He has been subpoenaed/We'll see if he subpoenaes you/Will they be subpoenaing him?*

subside/subsidence   Subside is stressed like "decide", but dictionaries differ on **subsidence**, traditionally səbs/dəns. A pronunciation of **subsidence** in imitation of "subsidy" rose in popularity for a time (and is still recommended by the *Oxford Paperback Dictionary*) but now seems to be subsiding.

substitute   The word is not a synonym for "replace"/"replacement". To substitute black for white is to replace white with black. In this exchange the *substitute* is black, black is *substituted* (not white), and the *substitution* is of black for white. (White is replaced, and the replacement is of white by black, but black can also be said to be white's replacement, i.e. substitute).

This difference should not be too taxing for football commentators. What they have to grasp is that neither set of words has a noun to describe the supplanted. Assuming Black and White to be players and Black to be sent on for White, Black is the substitute but there is no noun for White unless he is termed "the replaced". This is inconvenient for commentators, but then so are the rules of the game for players.

sufficient etc   See ENOUGH.

summary/summation etc   A **summary** is not the same as a **summation**, though U.S. officialese (always tempted by the bigger mouthful) confuses the two. **Summary** = epitome/digest. **Summation** = addition. To summarize, **summation** is wrong when "summary" is meant and inappropriate outside mathematical texts.

Misuse of **summation** seems to derive from the two senses of *summing up*, which can mean either "adding up" or "summarizing". A judge's summing up is a summary, which is what it ought to be called. The root of the U.S. mix-up may be that **summary** has another legal use, as in *summary jurisdiction/summary proceedings*, i.e. quick processes of law in which only the main formalities are observed.

summon/summons A **summons** is a call summoning the recipient to attend, usually a formal call to attend court and answer a charge. To issue a legal call of this kind is **to summons** the recipient. Thus there are two parallel verbs, **to summon** and **to summons** (*summonses/summonsed* etc). Both have the same general sense but **summons** has a special application. As a noun **summons** serves for either. (*She summoned her sympathizers, who responded loyally to her summons/This is a summons – they're summonsing me for speeding*).

super A prefix in compound words like *supercharge*, **super** also functions independently as a colloquial adjective (*What a super idea/We had a super meal*). It has no meaning not already available in the established words *superb/superlative*, which were presumably overlooked when it received the call. But **super** belongs in the colloquial tradition of *smashing/ripping/terrific* and will probably match them for endurance.

supertax This has not existed in Great Britain for many years, but journalists, unwilling to let go of a good word (or perhaps just not abreast of events), continue to write as though it had never been merged with surtax.

surveillance There is no verb form and a suspect is said to be *put under surveillance* etc. Pronounced sĕv*A*/əns.

sympathy/sympathetic etc We **sympathize with**, and are **in sympathy with**, but we have **sympathy for** and are **sympathetic to**. After all this we are hardly in need of *sympathique*, a French affectation for "likeable".

syndrome For pronunciation see EPITOME.

Tangier Like Algiers this city is on the North African coast, but as the two are separated by more than 200 miles and a frontier the resemblance is not so close that **Tangier** needs the matching *s* often added to it. There is no such place as "Tangiers". There is Tangier in Morocco, and Algiers in Algeria.

Tannoy   See HOOVER.

Terylene   See HOOVER.

that (as adverb)   The word **that** has so many grammatical functions that one more is nothing to get excited about. They include adjective (*that man*), demonstrative pronoun (*that's that*), conjunction (*I know that you will*). A further role, widely used in speech but resisted in writing, is as adverb in phrases like *He won't pay that much/Volunteer? I'm not that silly/She was that confused she couldn't think straight.* The sense is equivalent to *so* (*I'm not so silly* etc) or to *as . . . as that* (*I'm not as silly as that* etc). It is therefore an unnecessary variant, besides being thought too ignorant for writing. On the other hand the idiom is soundly rooted in the sort of phrase everybody uses when demonstrating a measure: *It was about **that big**/There was about **that much.***

that (when to omit)   There are two kinds of context in which **that** need not be stated. It can be left out wherever it has the function of [1] a conjunction, or [2] a conjunctive – or relative – pronoun acting as the object of its subsentence. Such omission is normal in speech and usual in writing except the formal kind.

[1]   **that** as conjunction:

> *I can't believe (that) you're serious*
> *It is lucky (that) you agree*
> *He wants a bicycle so (that) he can ride to school.*

In these examples the word is a piece of grammatical carpentry with no intrinsic meaning. It is not missed. (In *so that*, though the phrase can be regarded as a conjunction, only the word *that* can be omitted.)

Sometimes **that** acts as a conjunction equivalent in sense to *when* or *at which* (i.e. expressing time). Here too it can be left out, as in

> *The last time (that) I saw Paris*
> *Remember the day (that) war broke out?*

There are some exceptions where **that** as a conjunction is usually retained, particularly in writing. These include the constructions *the fact that/with the result that* (see STYLE in Part II), as in

*The fact **that** you agree is lucky*
*The car broke down, with the result **that** we were late.*

Another instance is where other words interrupt a phrase introduced by **that**, as in

*He threatened **that**, if we were late, he wouldn't wait.*

[2] **that** as conjunctive or relative pronoun ("relative" is the usual term, though "conjunctive" describes the function better). It can be omitted in contexts like

*The girl (**that**) I marry*
*You're the one (**that**) I want.*

In this pronoun role **that** occurs as either the object of the subsentence it introduces (as above) or as its subject. It must be retained when it is the subject, as in

*The one **that** got away*
*The tribe **that** lost its head.*

(See also THAT/WHICH for omission and/or substitution of *who/whom*.)
    One exception to the rule of retaining **that** when it functions as a subject occurs in sentences with *There is . . .* , as in

*There's a bus (**that**) goes every hour.*

This is a colloquial use, heard from educated speakers but probably not spoken consciously. It is not acceptable in print.

that/which etc   A cause of hesitation just as nagging as when to omit **that** (already noted) is when to put it in instead of **which** or instead of **who/whom**. Many inviolable expressions demonstrate the distinction:

All's well that ends well
All that glisters is not gold
The house that Jack built
The dog it was that died
Ships that pass in the night.

In all such contexts **that** has a defining function. It sets apart the noun or pronoun it refers to and identifies it as a particular specimen, e.g. the sense of *all* in *All that glisters is not gold* is narrowed to that of all glistering things. No comma should intrude to separate **that** from its noun, just as no pause occurs between them when such an expression is spoken. By contrast a similar subsentence introduced by **which** is normally marked off by commas and separated with a slight pause, indicating that this is a parenthesis:

The house, which Jack built, still stands.

Here the reader or listener already knows which house is meant, and Jack is mentioned by the way.

The need or lack of need for a comma is a convenient test of whether the sense requires **that** or **which**. If the pronoun can be left out altogether the matter is clinched in favour of **that** (though **that** cannot always be omitted) – see THAT (WHEN TO OMIT):

There's the shop window (that) I told you about.

Who/whom   These are often preferred to *that* where the reference is to persons, as the following alternatives exemplify:

The girl that I marry/The girl whom I marry
You're the one that I want/You're the one whom I want
The one that got away/The one who got away.

Again no comma intrudes and omission follows the rules previously outlined. But *that* is just as acceptable even in personal references.

Which   Though the usages described so far are much the commoner in speech, at least as common in writing, and standard in North America, **which** still has its partisans. A few writers and editors, perhaps finding the distinctions too fussy or inconsistent, avoid *that* altogether in this pronoun function and use only *who/whom/which*. They can point out a context where these alternatives are unavoidable. This occurs owing to the limitations of *that* in the possessive, as seen in *Here's the radio whose switch is broken* or *. . . of which the switch is broken*. These are defining uses typical of *that*, but for lack of a possessive form *that* cannot be called on.

All the same the policy of avoiding *that* is an artificial response. It repudiates idiom. Besides being entrenched in literature *that* is what people generally say. They have good reason. Unlike **which**, *that* has an unstressed form (thət) helpful to the flow of a spoken English sentence. Substitution of **which** holds it up. Compare *the one that I gave you* with *the one which I gave you*.

The point is illustrated even more emphatically by the nursery rhyme about the cow with the crumpled horn:

> . . . *That tossed the dog*
> *That worried the cat*
> *That killed the rat*
> *That ate the malt*
> *That lay in the house that Jack built.*

(See also PRONOUNS [3] in Part II).

them/they For which see I/ME. See also PRONOUNS [1] in Part II.

though Preferable to ALTHOUGH (q.v.).

thrash/thresh These are the same word but the forms are not entirely interchangeable. For the sense of flog only **thrash** (rhymes with "mash") will do. For the sense of beating corn etc to free the grain the usual form is **thresh** (rhymes with "mesh"), though **thrash** is not wrong.

till/until etc **Till** is shorter and the commoner spoken form. That is reason enough for preferring it to **until**, with which it is interchangeable. It also accepts *up* for emphasis, as in *Up till now, I've never thought about it*, though *up to* is the more natural phrase. Both are preferable to the clumsy *up until*, an American-inspired touch that is finding converts. The only reason for the survival of **until** seems to be the help its extra syllable can sometimes give to the rhythm of a sentence.

time, (at this) With the possible exception of *hopefully* (q.v.) no Americanism enrages the British stylist more than **at this time** and its companion *at this moment in time*. As the windbag's circumlocution for *now*, which is their fashionable role, both are indefensible. A respectable use of **at this time** is as in *At this time Christianity was the religion of nearly all Europe* (i.e. at the time we are discussing). (See also PRESENTLY.)

tire/tyre There were **tires** long before there were pneumatic rubber **tyres**, or cars, and the spelling was **tire**. In the U.S. it still is. The spelling **tyre**, now the only one accepted in Great Britain, was a discarded variant revived in late Victorian times as Dunlop's invention began to catch on. In the earliest patent, Thomson's of 1845, the spelling had been **tire**.

tissue See ISSUE.

today/tomorrow/tonight   No hyphen is required in any of these. There is no work for a hyphen to do, and "to-day" etc should be regarded as an affectation.

tortoise   Careful rhyming of the word with "toys" is not an educated pronunciation but an ignorant one. **Tortoise** is pronounced *taw*təs – which, in *tortoiseshell*, nobody doubts. (Note though that the *s* is smothered by the *sh*, hence *taw*təshel.)

toupee   This is an English word, not a French one (theirs is *toupet*), and so requires no accents or special vowels. It rhymes with "loopy"/"droopy", and means a patch of false hair worn to conceal baldness. The same device when worn by women is called a *hairpiece*.

tourniquet   The usual pronunciation is *tour*nikA (*tour* rhyming with "sure").

toward/towards etc   **Towards** is the usual preposition. **Toward** is optional in American usage but only rhetorical in British. **Towards**, formerly pronounced in one syllable (tawdz), is now usually said təwawdz. *Untoward* is not the negative of either word, but of an obsolete adjective meaning "awkward"/"perverse". As such its traditional pronunciation is distinct (un*tO*əd), but this has been generally swamped by a spelling guess (untəwawd).

trade union(s)   In **trade union** the word *trade* functions as an adjective, and the plural of the phrase is formed in the usual way by adding *s* to the noun *union*, i.e. **trade unions**. When such a phrase is itself used as an adjective the singular form is required regardless of whether it refers to one trade union etc or many. Hence a congress of trade unions is a *trade union congress*. Another possible form is the possessive *trade unions' congress*. What is not possible is a *Trades Union Congress*, yet for some reason this is the official title of the trade unions' central body in Great Britain. The injuries inflicted on the language by trade union terminology are too well known to go into here, except to note that they are enshrined at top level.

trait   Some people say this like "tray" and others rhyme it with "strait". "Tray" is more common in Great Britain, but becoming less so, especially under the influence of American usage, in which the *t* is usually sounded. That was also how the word used to be said in Great Britain, till modern French began to be imitated in Victorian times. Any dilemma over this word is best avoided by using *quality*/*characteristic* instead.

trajectory Stress on the first syllable, as with *projectile* (q.v.), has long been usual among those who deal in practical ballistics, i.e. artillery units.

transatlantic Not "trans-Atlantic" (archaic) or "Transatlantic".

transparent etc See APPARENT.

transpire So widely misused that it is hardly a useful word any more. It means "to leak out"/"to become known". What it does not mean is "to happen"/"to turn out" etc. *It transpired that the Queen's curator of paintings was a Russian spy* is a correct use. *I'm dying to hear what transpired in my absence* is almost certainly a wrong use – the speaker probably means *what happened* rather than *what became known*. The root of the confusion seems to be that what becomes known and what turns out are so often the same. *It became known that the Queen's curator was a spy* has the same essential information as *It turned out that the Queen's curator was a spy*. Thus *it transpired* etc often seems to make sense when taken to mean "it turned out". From here is a short step to parading **transpire** as a clever word for "happen", leading to such absurdities as *We shall never know what transpired at that secret meeting*.

transport/transportation World War II reintroduced **transportation** to the British vocabulary, where it is still resented as an American export. In fact it was more of an emigrant's return, **transportation** having been the usual English word till it was abandoned in favour of **transport**. Still, the shorter form was a change for the better and is worth defending.

trauma/traumatic The normal sound of an *au* spelling in English rhymes with "awe" as in "saw"/"taut"/"quart". **Trauma** and its offshoots are no exception, but are often given a rhyme with "cow" – probably under the impression that they are recent arrivals from German, a temptation for those who associate psychological terms with Freud. Actually they were derived centuries ago from Greek, whose *au* syllables are routinely anglicized to "awe". The medical meaning, incidentally, is of an external wound, which is at complete variance with the one for which psychology has appropriated **trauma**, i.e. emotional shock.

traverse   The noun has the same stress as "travel". Recent dictionaries suggest a different model for the verb, "reverse". A change like this is common enough (see STRESS SHIFTS in Part II) but it is not traditional with **traverse**.

treble/triple   Why a *treble twenty* but a *triple alliance*? There is no dependable dividing line between the applications of these adjectives, though **triple** is usual for the sense of "consisting of three parts", as in *the triple crown*, and **treble** for "three times as many", as in *treble chance* (= three chances of winning). In music, only **treble** can be used of a soprano voice, and only **triple** can be used of a beat (*triple time*).

tribute   A **tribute** is a payment in cash or in kind, made to propitiate someone who has the upper hand. Duress is essential to the sense. But as a metaphor – its commonest use nowadays, especially by politicians – all it means is a compliment. When a politician says *I should like to pay tribute to the devoted service of our election helpers* the one certainty is that no money will be changing hands.

troop/troupe   The same word in origin, but **troupe** is now reserved for entertainers, especially acrobats and circus performers. As a noun **troop** has a peculiarity: it is a collective noun in the singular (*a troop of cavalry/artillery* etc, the equivalent of a company) but is also used in the plural in a way suggesting that the singular refers to individuals. Thus in *comforts for the troops/Which officer is in charge of the troops?/There are 400 troops under canvas* etc, **troops** does not mean military units but soldiers. Nor does it mean soldiers of a particular kind (cavalry/artillery etc) but soldiers in general. In the singular, however, **troop** cannot mean an individual soldier, and **trooper** can only mean a particular kind of individual soldier, i.e. belonging to cavalry, artillery or armour. When a professional performer is meant, especially in an approving context, the word is **trouper** (*She's a real trouper*).

trooping the colour   The annual ceremony of the royal household troops on Horse Guards Parade is called **Trooping the Colour**, not "Trooping of the Colour". This is a fact. Is it, however, a blunder –

as it is held to be – to say *A guardsman fainted during the Trooping of the Colour/I enjoyed the Trooping of the Colour on TV?* There is a military misunderstanding here. **Trooping the Colour** is a gerundive construction like *exploring the Amazon/crossing the Sahara.* This does not preclude referring to the action by converting the gerund into a normal noun, e.g. *during the crossing of the Sahara/no more exploring of the Amazon for me.* On the contrary this is normal English, from which even the Trooping the Colour cannot be exempt.

troupe See TROOP.

tsar The preferable spelling is CZAR (q.v.).

twelfth The *f* is always omitted from the spoken word, but its omission from the written word is a common spelling error, severely regarded.

tyre See TIRE for spelling choice.

unaware Not an alternative to OBLIVIOUS (q.v.).

unbeknownst A freak word of uncertain ancestry and inexplicable spelling. As all it means is "unknown", why bother with it at all?

under/below etc **Under** pairs with *over*, and **below** with *above*. The difference in sense is elusive, but the dividing lines of usage are firm in many phrases:

below (above)	*under* (over)
average	*age*
the belt	*under*
sea level	*instruction*
zero	*sail*
expectations	*the sun*
	the rules
go *below* (=downstairs)	go *under* (=sink)

Interchangeable exceptions include *below/under par, below/under £5000 a year* etc, and a rare mixture is *under/above water.* All these are prepositional uses.

Underneath refers only to physical placing and is used for emphasis: *Did you leave that address list by the telephone? / No, underneath.*

Underneath has also appropriated the functions of *beneath*, an obsolescent word surviving only in the phrases *beneath contempt / marry beneath* (i.e. marry someone of lower status) / *beneath me* etc *to do something* (i.e. unworthy of me etc).

under way/under weigh It is sometimes contended that the phrase **under way** (= launched on a journey/in progress) should be "under weigh", an alleged nautical phrase derived from *to weigh anchor*. This sounds plausible, but it is a superstition. There is no such nautical phrase as "under weigh". The correct phrase, nautical in origin but now of general application, is **under way**.

underprivileged See PRIVILEGED.

undiscriminating See INDISCRIMINATE.

unexceptional/unexceptionable The adjective of *exception* is *exceptional*, and its negative is **unexceptional**. The little-used adjective *exceptionable* belongs with the phrase *take exception to* (object to/take offence at) and means "open to objection". **Unexceptionable** is the negative of this, meaning "unobjectionable".

uninterested For a common confusion see DISINTERESTED.

unique etc As there are no degrees of uniqueness a thing cannot be "rather unique"/"very unique" etc and to describe it as "quite unique"/"absolutely unique" is like talking about a "dead corpse". Uniqueness is oneness and anything **unique** is the only one of its kind. There may be things that would be unique barring a small difference, so that *nearly unique/almost unique* cannot be ruled out. But unless the difference is specified the effect of **unique** is inevitably weakened by such qualification, which spoils an absolute by introducing vagueness.

A similar absolute is *perfect*. One thing cannot be more perfect than another etc, nor can it be "so perfect that . . .", though it is often said to be. At least *perfect* has been more successful at fending off corrupters than *necessity/necessary/essential*. These are also absolutes in their strict sense, but have long since succumbed to uses like "very necessary"/"rather essential"/"an absolute necessity".

universal Though *universe*, except in astronomical terms, strictly refers to the whole of creation, its adjective **universal** has never been limited to this sense. Far from being a modern hyperbole, **universal** has always had the sense of everyone or everywhere within a specified or implied category. Hence *universal suffrage* means no more than votes for all in any particular country. Such use of **universal** is unavoidable, as *general* allows of exceptions and there is no other adjective meaning "all-embracing".

unmistakable Not "unmistakeable". When *able* is added to a word ending in *e* like *mistake* the *e* is dropped. Hence *unforgivable/ inescapable/inflatable* etc. An exception is *likeable*.

until A simpler version is TILL (q.v.).

us/we For which and when see I/ME. See also PRONOUNS in Part II.

used (to) etc Despite generally confident usage this word is more complicated than it looks. **Used** has several distinct versions with varying pronunciation. There is **used** the past tense or participle of the regular verb *to use* (rhymes with "yews", i.e. *z*), meaning "to utilize", as in *She used the new soap/She said she had used it*. This is the **used** of *used up/a used car* etc. The *z* sound of its *s* is maintained in the associated noun *usage*, but the other noun *use* (as in *I have a use for that*), and its offshoots *useful/useless* etc, have an s sound (i.e. *use* rhymes with "deuce").

  When **used** is pronounced Ust (rhyming with "reduced") it has two separate functions:

[1] an adjective meaning "accustomed", as in *You'll get used to it/I'm just not used to your weather*. This **used** can be constructed with a present participle, as in *I'm **used to going** to bed early*. Note that it does not take an infinitive – the famous lyric from *My Fair Lady* is unidiomatic: *I've grown so used to hear her say/Good morning every day* (should be *used to hearing her say*).

[2] a past-tense auxiliary verb for referring to a continuous segment of the past, as in *He used to be such fun/We used to long for payday*. In this role, always followed by a full infinitive (i.e. with *to*), **used** is one of the props of the language. It also presents some problems.

  Because **used** is a past tense it does not fit into the normal formula for questions, negatives or emphatic statements. This involves combining a verb with *did*, as in *Did I hear? / I did not hear / I did hear*. But *did* can only take an infinitive, so that *did used* is parallel to "did heard", clearly a grammatical misfit. Some people seek a solution in *did use* (*We did use to enjoy those outings / Did you use to go regularly?*). This assumes the existence however of an infinitive form *use*, rhyming with "deuce", for which there is no other evidence.

The issue cannot be settled, and both forms have passed into use under cover of idiom. Whether people usually say *did used to* or *did use to* cannot be determined as the two sound exactly the same. So do *didn't used to / didn't use to*, but in negatives and questions at least there is an alternative: *Used you to enjoy yourself? / Some of us used not to / Used there to be . . . / Used you not to . . .* etc.

Used can be combined with the contracted form of *not* (*n't*), giving *usedn't*, but the irregular *usen't* is also current. Again the two are pronounced the same.

To achieve emphasis without using *did* a common substitute is *always* (*We always used to enjoy Christmas*). Similarly *never* can sometimes replace *did not* (*We never used to worry*).

valet etc   *Crochet* and *ricochet* (q.v.), despite appearances, are in-appropriate models. The *t* is silent in **valet**, a manservant, but sounded in **valeting**, a service of clothes care offered by hotels, dry-cleaners etc. Hence *valA, valǝting*.

vehement/vehicle   The *h* is silent in both of these. **Vehement**, *vEǝmǝnt*. In **vehicle** the first syllable does not rhyme with the last of "survey". The pronunciation is *vEikl*. Note that the *h* need not stay silent in *vehicular*. It is sounded in American and official British usage.

venison   Pronounced by people who know, as opposed to people who guess, *venzǝn*. But the guessers are in an undoubted majority.

verbal/oral   In the sense of spoken rather than written **oral** is much the safer choice, because **verbal** has two additional senses. These are [1] to do with words in general, [2] to do with verbs in particular. To avoid conflicts, where they can arise, it is best to restrict **verbal** to [1] and to use *verb* adjectivally for [2].

very One of the most overused words in the dictionary, **very** suffers from the universal human urge to load language with more meaning than it can usefully carry. There may be a theoretical difference between, say, *quick* and *very quick*, but it cannot be perceived by the reader or listener unless he is provided with some measure of *quick* to start with. So **very** conveys little but the user's desire to be emphatic, an effect better made in speech by tone of voice. Worse, **very** soon becomes a perfunctory adornment to every attribute, as though the audience might feel short-changed without it: *That was a very good movie/I'm very well, thanks/A very interesting book, this/I'm very pleased to tell you* ... Yet nobody is ever any the wiser for it, as every regular writer soon discovers. Hence the quest for more exotic intensifiers, which has filled the dictionary with terms like *extremely/highly/exceedingly/terribly/exceptionally/awfully/expletive deleted* etc. These may make for variety but are soon found to share a limited value in gingering up other adverbs and adjectives. There is no short cut to vivid expression.

So **very** is usually a candidate for deletion in any prose prepared with care. But there are some instances where it may be required. Verbs cannot accept the adverbs *much/likely* unless these are in turn qualified by *very/rather* etc – e.g. not *We much hope/I'll likely go* but *We very much hope/I'll very likely go* etc. Verbs of course cannot accept **very** alone either (not "I very hope"), though their participles sometimes can, especially those in general use as adjectives (*very worried/very upsetting*).

In its basic sense, equivalent to "veritable", **very** is now uncommon (especially since the rise of *actual*): *the very thought of you* (= sheer)/*the very button I lost* (= true/actual)/*Why, the very idea!* (= sheer).

victuals As the word is no longer used outside the provisions trade (if there) its pronunciation is rarely a problem. But it is said the way it has at times been spelt, "vittles". Similarly with *victualler/victualling*.

vitamin Of the two pronunciations current, vɪtəmin is usual in the U.S., and vītəmin in the British Isles. When the word was coined it was based on *vita* (Latin for "life"), from which English derives *vital/vitality*. As both of these are pronounced vɪt it makes more sense for **vitamin** to follow suit.

wait/await   The usual forms are **wait** (intransitive), as in *Please wait here/There's someone waiting to see you*, and **wait for** (transitive), as in *Wait for me/What are we waiting for?* **Await** is interchangeable with **wait for** in theory, but in fact is never used outside some more or less settled phrases like *await one's fate/await the outcome/await the news anxiously.*

Only **wait** is possible in such phrases as *wait and see/wait at table/wait about/wait up.* **Wait on**, as in *I'm not here to wait on you,* is properly restricted to the sense of "being a servant to", but is colloquially heard as a substitute for **wait for** (*We're waiting on a delivery*).

The construction *wait for the bus to stop/wait for me to catch up* etc is only possible with **wait for**, not **await**. But **wait** on its own is correct in the phrases *wait one's chance/wait your opportunity* etc.

wake/wakeful   See AWAKE.

warranty   For variants see GUARANTEE.

watershed   A geographical concept fatal to writers, who use it for mistaken imagery, and not much help to geographers either. A **watershed** is supposed to be a line or ridge separating the sources feeding a river basin from those feeding another – in other words, the geographical limit of a catchment area. But the term is also used to denote the catchment area itself, which must dilute its scientific value. Undeterred by either abstruseness or imprecision, writers regularly turn to **watershed** for a metaphor, as in *Napoleon sacked Moscow, but he had reached his watershed.* Here the image seems to be of an apogee or turning-point, an inappropriate choice, since rivers neither climb nor reverse. Alternatively **watershed** may be pictured as some sort of source or fertilizer, as in *The discovery of gold in the New World proved to be a watershed for old Europe's stagnant economies.* It is hard to see how understanding can be advanced by likening Moscow or gold to a geographical boundary or catchment area. **Watershed** sounds knowing but will be recognized by careful writers as a model of undesirable metaphor, shedding obscurity rather than light.

we/us   For which and when see I/ME. See also PRONOUNS in Part II.

were/wear   The usual pronunciation of **were** now rhymes with "her"/"sir"/"fur". But the educated pronunciation (first choice in the *Oxford English Dictionary*) was until recently the same as *wear/ware*, rhyming with "where"/"there"/"care". This sound may still be heard, e.g. in U-speech (q.v.), especially when the word is stressed, as when it ends a phrase (*Oh yes we were/As you were/So that's where you were*).

west/western etc   See NORTH/NORTHERN.

whatever/what ever/when ever etc   For when to separate see EVER.

whether (or not)/(as to) whether   Whether is better able to stand on its own than it is given credit for. It hardly ever needs to be introduced by **as to**, and only sometimes needs trailing by **or not**.

[1] **or not**   Whether or not is a shortened form for (e.g.) *whether you do or whether you don't*. The **or not** is required where two possibilities, the positive or the negative, are contemplated. So *Whether or not our careers prosper we can still be happy/She doesn't care whether he calls or not*. An earlier form was *whether or no*, but this is now obsolete.

Often, though, only one possibility is contemplated, and the sense of **whether** is the same as that of *if*, as in

> *I wonder whether we'll win*
> *I'm not sure whether I can get away*
> *Go and ask him whether it matters.*

In all these **or not** is redundant. This remains true in contexts where *if* could not be substituted though the sense is the same, as in

> *Comics can't allow for whether they'll be in a funny mood*
> *I'd like to go but it depends on whether I'm invited.*

[2] **as to**   In the following specimens, which typify its use, as to can and should be deleted:

> *Opinions differ on the question as to whether war was justified*
> *He inquired as to whether breakfast would cost extra*
> *Please inform us as to whether the arrangement is convenient.*

As to is often resorted to to save the trouble of thinking of the right word. The right one is shown in brackets in the following, where every **as to** is the wrong choice:

> *He consulted me as to (on) whether he should apply*

> *No condition was stipulated as to (for) whether he could join*
>
> *Talks as to (about) whether it could be done were resumed.*

The only context where **as to** becomes acceptable is as in

> *As to whether he decided wisely, we cannot go into that issue.*

Even there **as for** is preferable.

which   See THAT.

while/whilst   Prefer *while*. See AMONG/AMONGST.

whisky/whiskey   In the British Isles today **whisky** means the spirit in general and the Scotch product in particular. Irish and bourbon are **whiskey**. Connoisseurs of spirits make much of this distinction but it is only a modern trade custom. In the past **whisky/whiskey** have been used interchangeably. In North America **whiskey** means whisky in general and a distinction is rarely made for Scotch.

who/whom (whoever/whomever)   The pronoun **whom** has the same relation to **who** as has *me* to *I* (see I/ME). But whereas *me* has expanded its empire **whom** is being progressively dispossessed. This is probably because **whom** is not easy to say. In phrases like *Whom were you with last night?/Whom did you ask?/It's you to whom they owe it all* a conscious effort is needed to pronounce the *m*, which at conversational speed is hardly noticed. So **who** takes over, even though each of these examples, not being a subject (nominative) case, requires **whom**.

   In Great Britain, where grammar, along with elocution, has long been neglected in schools, many professional users, including writers and teachers, no longer recognize the difference, and **whom** owes such survival as it has to the attentions of fastidious editors. It may be too late already to save **whom**, and perhaps it is not worth saving. But to those who use it as naturally as *me*, at least in writing, **who** will always look wrong in place of **whom**, whether as the object of a verb (. . . *whom he saw/the woman whom he loved*) or after prepositions as in *For whom the bell tolls*. On the model of *me*, only **whom** is possible in such combinations as *by whom/between whom/about whom/from whom/of whom/than whom/to whom* (See also THAT/WHICH, and PRONOUNS [3] in Part II.)

whose Though **whose** refers primarily to persons it can also be applied to things (*The first column of figures is for houses whose insulation is known to be inadequate*). English has no other suitable possessive, and the alternative is to use *of which* (*. . . houses of which the insulation* etc). This is always more elaborate and in complicated clauses can become artificial. (See also PRONOUNS [1] in Part II.)

wide See BROAD.

will See SHALL.

win out/lose out As *win* has various shades of meaning on the theme of "triumph"/"gain" it has always been helped out by prepositions. Thus *win over* (= to gain the agreement of) and *win through* (= to triumph after overcoming difficulties) are established and useful. But why **win out**? The *out* here is even more unnecessary than in **lose out**, where at least it limits the sense to "fail"/"suffer" (though these would be better). In **win out**, which does not in any way extend the sense of *win*, the extra word seems to have no function but to provide Americans with multi-syllabic reassurance – a sensation many British seem eager to share.

without The only remaining sense of **without** is as the converse of *with*, i.e. "lacking". It is obsolete as the converse of *within*, i.e. "outside", or by extension "unless".

wool/woolly etc **Woollen** is the normal adjective of **wool** (spelt *woolen* in the U.S.). **Woolly** = like wool/fluffy, i.e. not necessarily made of wool. It is also a term of abuse for somebody else's argument or writing, meaning "muddled"/"unclear".

would For accepted uses today see SHOULD.

wrack Shares many of the senses of "wreck", and is similarly derived. Now survives mainly in the phrase *wrack and ruin* (disaster and ruin). Not to be confused with *rack*, an adjustable tensioning frame for torturing prisoners or stretching fabric. In *nerve-racking* the reference is not to **wrack**, though this spelling is sometimes seen, but to *rack*.

wreak See WROUGHT.

wrought As a verb it exists only in the past tense and as a past participle, but is hardly ever used. As an adjective it survives in such variants as *wrought-iron*/*overwrought*. It means "fashioned"/ "made", but should not be confused with the equally obsolescent *wreak*/*wreaked* (to cause or effect), though sometimes the senses overlap.

wry/wryly For spelling see DRY.

year Rhymes with "hear"/"here", not with "her"/"Fleur", though this corruption is common.

zoology Though *zoo* rhymes with "shoe" as a word on its own, it is spoken in two syllables when it forms part of **zoology** (a compound of *zoo*+*ology*). Hence zOo*lə*ji. *Zoologist* likewise.

Part II

Sentences in General

Sentences in General

Adjective   See PARTS OF SPEECH. See also COMPARATIVES and WORD ORDER.

Adverb   See PARTS OF SPEECH. See also CONJUNCTS / DISJUNCTS, COMPARATIVES and WORD ORDER.

Alliteration   This is the effect of repeated sounds, as in *short sharp shock / mean, moody, magnificent / pass the parcel*. The sounds are usually those of the initial letters of adjacent words. Alliteration is a form of word play with an undeniable appeal to popular taste but it tends to be a distraction in prose unless used sparingly. There must be something to be said though for a device responsible for the endurance of so many stock phrases, like *life and limb / chop and change / meek and mild / hum and haw / pillar to post*. Even in print the matching of initials etc can have a unifying effect on what might otherwise be a loose phrase (*crystal clear / mild-mannered / soft-spoken*).

Some writers and editors deliberately weed out alliteration, surely a policy of overreaction. Alliteration is a fact of language and hence something to be turned to advantage. Not for nothing is it such a regular feature of commercial slogans (*Bargain Basement / service with a smile / builds bonnier babies*). A device proved to make for easier remembering is not something a writer can afford to turn up his nose at.

American English   By far the biggest of all the influences on the development of English today is American English. Through television and cinema it regularly reaches most of the population of the British Isles, making American pronunciations and turns of phrase at least as familiar as those of any British dialect. The advent of American-printed books to the British market is likely to extend the effect to American spellings and constructions. Some specialists believe American English and British English are moving inexorably apart, but this is not a general view. How could separation occur while American idioms are constantly absorbed by British usage?

Anyway the traffic is two-way, though unequal. Exports of British television serials may be small compared with the imports of American, but their effect in taking British expressions across the

Atlantic is eked out by the influence of returning American tourists. Words like *autumn/flat/aerial* are widely understood in the U.S., even if *fall/apartment/antenna* are more used. "Speakers of British and American English", comments Professor Raven I. McDavid jnr* of the University of Chicago, "know far more than before about each other's usage." He adds: "The fact is that the standard varieties of British and American English have never lost touch with each other".

Because American English is such a prominent influence, many of its differences from British English are noted individually in Part I. They occur in grammar (hardly any), spelling (a few), vocabulary (more but not many), and pronunciation (many and variable). A large number of terms regarded in the British Isles as strange consist of original versions from which British English has diverged. The following list shows some of the perennial confusions of vocabulary:

British	American
aubergine	*eggplant*
(baby's) dummy	*pacifier*
braces	*suspenders*
car bonnet	*hood*
car boot	*trunk*
car windscreen	*windshield*
car wing	*fender*
caravan	*trailer*
chemist's	*drugstore/pharmacy*
cotton	*thread*
courgette	*zucchini*
crossroads	*intersection*
cupboard	*closet*
drug	*narcotic*
flyover	*overpass*
greengrocer's	*vegetable market*
grill (verb)	*broil*
ladder (in stocking)	*run*
lorry	*truck*
mackintosh	*raincoat*
mean	*stingy*
nappy	*diaper*

*In *The Britannica Book of English Usage*, published by Doubleday/Britannica Books, Garden City, New York (1980) and Columbus Books, London (1981).

British	American
plain (in looks)	*homely*
plimsolls	*sneakers*
soda water	*seltzer*
spanner	*wrench*
sturdy	*rugged*
tap	*faucet*
torch	*flashlight*
trunk call	*long-distance call*
vest	*undershirt*
waistcoat	*vest.*

Spelling differences are never enough to obscure the meaning of a word. Some of the commonest:

British	American
centre/theatre etc	*center/theater* etc
cheque	*check*
cosy	*cozy*
licence (noun)	*license*
manoeuvre	*maneuver*
mould	*mold*
omelette	*omelet*
plough	*plow*
practise (verb)	*practice*
sanitarium	*sanitarum*
sulphur	*sulfur*
tyre	*tire*
vice (clamp)	*vise.*

American English also spells verbs like *energize/finalize/standardize* with an invariable *z*, rather than the *s* that is usual in British writing. This practice can only be faulted when it is extended (as it usually is) to words like *analyse/paralyse/advertise*, which are formed differently (see SPELLING/ENDINGS). Other characteristic differences are omissions of *u* in words like *colour* (see CLAMOUR in Part I) and of doubled consonants in a few verbs like *combated/traveled/worshiping* (instead of *combatted/travelled/worshipping* etc).

A few different verb forms are found in past tenses, notably the well-known *gotten*, and also *fit/spit/dove* (as in *He spit at me*, instead of *spat*, and *The airliner dove*, instead of *dived*). (See IRREGULAR VERBS.)

Pronunciation The characteristics usually associated with an "American accent" in the U.K. can be summarized as: *r* sounded in words like *water/important/sheltered*, drawled *a* in words like *bath/transform/past*, *t* sounded as *d* in words like *created/butter/atom*, and *o* pronounced as in *whole* rather than as in *holy* in words like *go/phone/hallo*. These characteristics are not in fact essentially American. They are not general in American speech; and anyway they all occur in various British dialects.

Numerous factors go to make the effect identified by Europeans as American. Besides changes of vowel and consonant values they include unfamiliar stresses and differences of intonation (pitch). But as there is no single American accent it is not practical to set out such subtleties here. Four main regional types of American speech are recognized, each with subregional, ethnic and social varieties. In addition population shifts have confused the scene, so that cities – where immigrants tend to congregate – often have speech patterns that differ from those of the surrounding countryside.

Some words have typical pronunciations peculiar to America, e.g. *clerk* (klərk, British klahk), *laboratory* (labərətri, British laborətri), *aristocrat* (əristəkrat, British aristəkrat), *strawberry* (strawberi, British strawbri), *anti* as in "anti-war" (antī, English anti).

Idiom   *Mathematics* is abbreviated as *math* (English *maths*), and numbers like 250 are spoken as *two hundred fifty* (English *two hundred and fifty*). What the British refer to as *riding* is termed *horseback riding* by Americans. *Accommodation*, always a singular collective noun (in the sense of shelter) in British English, occurs as *accommodations* in American English, and so on.

American idiom also prefers the simple past tense to the perfect, e.g. *What took you so long* instead of *What has taken you so long?/The best that ever lived* instead of *The best that has ever lived*. Adverbs are typically placed before the auxiliary verb, instead of after (the British norm): *You never can tell* instead of *You can never tell/I always have thought* instead of *I have always thought*.

Many American usages are word savers, like *through* (sometimes "thru") in *Monday through Friday* etc, instead of "from Monday to Friday inclusive". Similarly there is *effective today etc* instead of "with effect from today". *Like* is more widely used as a conjunction (*like there was no tomorrow*) and *different than* also cuts corners (see LIKE and DIFFERENT in Part I). Unfortunately a flair for the pithy and vivid phrase, such as H. L. Mencken gloried in in his study *The American Language*, is balanced by a latter-day addiction to indigestible jargon, especially in formal uses.

But though American speech can sound strikingly different from British the effect turns out to be produced by quite small differences. American dictionaries ignore the tendency to sound *t* as *d*, and use only one extra symbol to convey American vowels. This is the distinctive *ah* shared by *father/bother/cot/modern* etc and lying somewhere between standard British "father" and standard British "bother".

Analysis   In theory the arrangement of words in any grammatical sentence can be separated into connected steps of meaning. This process is called analysis. It uncovers the patterns of construction necessary to logical expression. A sentence can be likened to an appliance and said to consist of an assembly of components. These in turn are subassemblies of nouns, prepositions, adverbs etc (the so-called PARTS OF SPEECH, q.v.), just as the components of an appliance are assembled from screws, mouldings, wiring etc. The idea can be seen in a simple sentence like

A man with a calculator worked out the total cost.

A	(article)	
man	(noun)	
with	(preposition)	subject
a	(article)	
calculator	(noun)	
worked	(verb)	verb
out	(adverb)	
the	(article)	
total	(adjective)	direct object
cost	(noun)	

The essentials of nearly every sentence are the subject (namely what it is about), plus what is said about the subject. The subject consists of a noun or equivalent (what is now called a noun phrase), and the rest consists of a verb, plus any elaboration of the verb's action (e.g. direct object etc). No matter how long the sentence or how many parts of speech it contains, all the words in it are found to fit into a handful of components of meaning. The most persuasive modern account, that of the four professors responsible for

A Grammar of Contemporary English,* reckons the number of possible components at only six:

> subject
> verb
> direct object
> indirect object
> complement
> adverbial.

Every English sentence, or so it is contended, can be explained as a grouping of some of these.

This is such a striking feat of classification that the ordinary writer, on the lookout for a literary equivalent of a ready reckoner, may feel a tug of hope. So it must be said at once that grammatical analysis is no formula for composing sentences. Like every other kind of analysis it tells you what happened, not how to make it happen. At best it is a key to understanding sentences. For language enthusiasts it can even be fun. As a practical guide though, it is a delusion – if only because sentences that look simple often turn out to be complex, and even in simple ones the components can be hard to identify with confidence. Fortunately it is no more necessary to grasp analysis so as to write clearly than to grasp musical theory so as to hum in tune.

What follows is a simplified explanation of the components already named (for an outline of the sentence patterns they form see SENTENCE PATTERNS):

Subject An obvious enough concept, this usually starts a statement and identifies what is going to be spoken about. As seen, it can consist of one word (*I/he*) or several (*Everybody I know . . .*).

Verb Equally obvious, this names what the subject does, its actions (*He **eats***). This too may consist of several words (*will be eating* etc). The verb normally follows right after the subject.

Subject and verb are already enough for making simple statements (*He eats*). Any additional components can be regarded as elaborations of what these two express. So *He eats **noodles***, which has an added *direct object*, extends the sense. *He eats noodles **at home***, which has an added *adverbial*, extends it further.

---

*Drs R. Quirk, S. Greenbaum, G. Leach, and J. Svartvik. Published by Longman Group, London (1972 & 1979).

Direct object This is the object or recipient of the verb's action. Like the subject it is always a noun phrase.

Indirect object Another noun phrase, secondary to the direct object and not found in sentences without this. In *She baked me a cake* the indirect object is *me*, because what was baked was clearly *a cake* (the direct object), not *me*. Another way of putting it would be *She baked a cake for me*, and the sense of *to/for* is implied by an indirect object, e.g. *He wrote (to) her a letter of thanks*. Any indirect object has to precede a direct object.

Complement Word or phrase complementing the sense of either the direct object or the subject. A complement* normally follows the verb or the direct object. So in *Knitting makes me irritable* the adjective *irritable* is the complement of the direct object *me*. Subject complements occur with verbs like *to be/become* (see LINKING VERBS), which denote no action and so cannot take a direct object. So in *You're so touchy/He's such a fusser* the phrases *so touchy/such a fusser* are the complements of the subjects *You/He*.

Adverbial This component is an adverb or equivalent, i.e. any phrase with an adverb function. Examples in bold: *We eat **regularly**/ We eat **every day**/We eat **whenever we can**/We eat **with relish**/ We eat **to keep healthy**.*

Adverbials are more flexible in positioning than other components. More than one position is often possible, e.g. *We regularly eat/Regularly we eat* (see WORD ORDER). The term *adverbial* is loosely used by some grammarians where a word is not being considered as a sentence component, and what is meant is *adverb* (see PARTS OF SPEECH).

Note: The term *component* is not the usual one in sentence analysis, but it seems more illustrative than the traditional *element*. The idea of an element is something incapable of more unravelling, but a sentence "element", as seen, is commonly made up of several words.

Apostrophe (') This is the same thing as a single inverted comma, but the name apostrophe is used when the sign denotes possession

---

*The term as a sentence component must not be confused with the traditional general use of *complement* to mean any word complementing the sense of another, e.g. in *He could do it*, *do* might be labelled the complement of *could*. In this Guide *complement* is used only for a sentence component.

(*dog's life*), or omission (*it's her*). Apostrophes are among the most misunderstood of punctuation marks, often left out when needed or put in the wrong place. (See under POSSESSIVES and CONTRACTIONS for correct uses in those roles.) The commonest mistake with apostrophes is inserting them in the pronouns *its/hers/theirs* etc, which are possessive forms in their own right.

There is a built-in risk of confusion in a sign standing for concepts as different as omission and possession, which is reason enough for not adding to it. But there are those who want to make apostrophes represent junction too, as in "the 1920's". The feeling seems to be that the transition from figures to letters needs help, which it does not. In such contractions, which are worth while for their convenience, the simplest form is adequate and clearer: *the 1920s/The temperature was in the 70s*. In Britain this style may have been resisted in the past for fear of confusion with shillings (*The price is 70s.*), but decimal currency has cleared away that objection.

Article   See PARTS OF SPEECH.

Auxiliary verbs   These are the words enabling other verbs to produce the variations required for tenses, negatives etc, as in *shall be writing/do not agree/have decided*. An auxiliary is always combined with either an infinitive or a participle. Combinations like *shall be writing* are of course equivalent to inflections (see VERBS). Most auxiliaries have no meaning on their own and even *be/have/do*, which all exist separately as independent verbs (*be* = exist/*have* = possess/*do* = act etc), do not carry their normal meanings when acting as auxiliaries.

The traditional tenses (tabulated under TENSES, q.v.) make use of all forms of the verbs *to be* and *to have*, plus *shall/will* and *should/would*. Questions, negatives and emphasis make use of the verb *to do*, as in *Does she agree?/She did not say/We did ask/Do please relax*. Other common auxiliaries (often called "modal", though grammarians differ on how they apply the word) are:

can/could	(= be able to)
may/might	(= be possible to or permitted to – also used subjunctively as in *in case you might need help*)

must *have to / has to / had to* *have* (etc) *got to*	(= it is necessary that. *Have to / have got to* are considered part-auxiliaries)
ought (*to*)	(= have a duty or obligation to / should)
used (*to*)	(= did formerly)
be (etc) *going to*	(= will / shall)
get / got	(as in *got run over / got reduced to the ranks*)
need *dare*	

Can / could / may / might / must / ought are relics with no other forms. So are *shall / will / should / would*. None of these has an infinitive or participle. Whether *used* (*to*) is also a one-form auxiliary is unsettled. It occurs only in the past tense but there is doubt about its infinitive (see USED (TO) in Part I). *Get* is a full verb *get / got / getting*) but has an auxiliary role in some usages. A large number of other verbs and phrases function partly like auxiliaries, but not thoroughly enough to be generally accepted as auxiliaries. These include:

> *be about to / apt to / sure to* etc
> *had better*
> *tend to*
> *appear to / seem to*
> *keep on / continue to*
> *stop / start to.*

Brackets ( )   There are various kinds of bracket but the everyday kind, as shown, is usually what is meant. Typewriters rarely have the so-called square kind ([]), which are for marking interpolations in direct quotations, especially authors' comments like "my italics". Brackets, like dashes, are signs of parenthesis, a word used to describe both the signs themselves and the words contained between them. Unlike dashes, brackets must always be used in pairs. They enable a comment or additional fact etc to be inserted at any convenient point in a sentence, or even between sentences. The insertion can be a word, a phrase or a complete grammatical sentence of its own, but it only requires a special initial capital and a full stop when the parenthesis occurs in between sentences, as in *Food is so expensive here. (They say the same thing about Belgium.)*

The other day it cost me ...   Some writers regard this as a mistaken usage. It is in fact old-established and useful for a footnote effect without making the reader lose the place – especially after a sentence too long to contain a parenthesis. Other writers avoid brackets altogether, assigning the work to commas, but this can be confusing if another comma occurs within the parenthesis.

Similarly brackets should not be placed inside other brackets. In a long parenthesis though, a short insertion (such as a date) may be permissible if the reader can see both ends at a glance so that there is no doubt about boundaries.

Capital letters   Capitals have no counterpart in speech, such as emphasis or pauses, but they are important to clear and readable prose. They should be used sparingly – though not so sparingly as the American poet e. e. cummings used them, contending that only God merited a capital. A capital signals the start of a new sentence after a full stop, and should not be used to start phrases or sections inside a sentence, except direct quotations. Even then, the quotations need not start with a capital unless they do so in their context.

Capital initials, invariably used for *I* and names of people, flourish in official documents and wherever formal titles are bandied about. There is no need for similar elaboration elsewhere. The Oxford History of England series, which would otherwise be awash with capitals, uses none for government offices like *prime minister/chancellor of the exchequer.* Usually it is enough to use capitals for the first mention and a lower-case form (or abbreviated title) for later mentions, as in *Prizes were donated by the Duke of Redford. Afterwards Mrs Robinson thanked the duke.*

The same system works with institutions like *The British Government ... the government/The Church of Scotland ... the church (or kirk). Royal/royalty* carry traditional capitals in official writing, a style comparable with writing "Holy" with a capital *H* in church documents. There is no need for it in ordinary usage, any more than for "The Lord Debrett" rather than just *Lord Debrett.*

As every community likes to award itself a capital, such styles as *employees of the Company/the Industry/the Movement/the Play-Group* abound, no doubt encouraged by the newspaper habit of always referring to the newspaper industry as "the Press". These airs and graces reflect self-importance, not useful style. Acronyms (abbreviations like *WHO/UNESCO/NASA*) or even straightforward initials like *CIA/FBI/BBC* save a lot of trouble, and they do not need stops. *USSR* is fairly general, but *U.S.* tends to keep its stops, perhaps because it could be misread without them.

Capitals should not be used for emphasis (*The boy must Concentrate more*/*It WAS him* etc). If additional emphasis is required, and it usually is not, underlining or, in print, italic type is less disturbing.

(Capitals are also called "upper case", a printer's term from the days of metal type, when capitals were racked above the small types, called "lower case". *Italic* is the term for print set in a slanting style of letter derived from script, and used nowadays mainly for distinguishing book and play titles etc, and foreign words, and occasionally for emphasis.)

Clichés A cliché is a stale phrase – everybody agrees about that. In the classic example, clichés are phrases to avoid *like the plague* – everybody agrees about that. But are all stale phrases clichés? *I'm hungry*/*Pass the paper*/*What's the time?* are stale phrases, but they are hardly phrases to avoid. Many of the stale phrases listed in Eric Partridge's *Dictionary of Clichés* can also be found in the Oxford University Press manual for foreign learners, *English Idioms & How to Use Them*, only there they are described as "an essential part of the general vocabulary of English". Clearly there is more to a cliché than mere staleness, and everybody does not agree what it is.

What cannot be doubted is that stale phrases do form part of the vocabulary of spontaneous speech. Conversations would be difficult without phrases like *asking for trouble*/*now that you mention it*/*giving the game away*/*six of one and half a dozen of the other*/*if you ask me*. Are these clichés? They are certainly stale phrases but they are still useful phrases. They have become stock phrases by providing a shorthand for senses that repeatedly need expressing. When we talk about *any port in a storm*/*Hobson's choice*/*fools rush in* we all know we are using stock phrases, but should we censor them as clichés? How then should we express the meanings? Are we to devise a new phrase every time or stay silent just because the thought is not a new one?

Obviously stock phrases in general cannot be excommunicated as clichés. As daily experience is full of similar incidents and responses it is only to be expected that languages should be full of familiar phrases for referring to them. The test of a phrase, stale or not, is surely whether it is an effective phrase.

Some clichés suffer from out-of-date imagery, like

in the limelight (limelight has not been used in the theatre
for decades)
wild goose chase (a forgotten and probably illegal pursuit)
pig in a poke (*poke* once meant sack, but not within living
memory)
hiding one's light under a bushel (few town-dwellers have
ever seen a bushel).

Some clichés waste words, like

few and far between (= rare)
take a leaf out of someone's book (= imitate)
not to put too fine a point on it (= frankly).

Some are tautologies, like

essential prerequisite (a prerequisite is intrinsically essential)
closely guarded secret (secrets are by definition guarded, i.e.
kept secret)
taking active steps (taking a step is unavoidably active)
a searching inquiry (inquiries are by definition investigative,
i.e. searching).

Still others are pretentious or facetious, like

ministering to the inner man (= having a meal)
go by Shanks's pony (= go on foot)
consigned to oblivion (= forgotten).

A few of the most overused irritate rather than illuminate, and
have even achieved notoriety, like

unaccustomed as I am to public speaking
last but not least
explore every avenue
leave no stone unturned.

Then there are the unnecessary foreign phrases, particularly
those with exact English equivalents, like

je ne sais quoi (I don't know what)
nous avons changé tout celà (we've changed all that)
savoir faire (know-how)
bête noire (bugbear).

Many English quotations are also used so often that they now
count as clichés, however apt the phrase, or eminent the author.
What all these types have in common is inefficiency. They are

objectionable because they have lost the power to arrest. A cliché is essentially a special effect that no longer comes off. The following specimens should leave no doubt of the kind of thing to be considered outcasts by this definition:

> *a minus quantity*
> *come through with flying colours*
> *can't afford not to afford it* (a false parallel of different senses of "afford")
> *get down to brass tacks* (who uses brass tacks?)
> *hardy annual* (when not referring to plants)
> *imagination runs riot*
> *more in sorrow than in anger*
> *not wisely but too well*
> *shake off the yoke*
> *sleep the sleep of the just*
> *something is rotten in the state of Denmark*
> *too funny for words*
> *wend one's way.*

Such evidence may seem to clinch a conviction, but this depends on the jury. What is a cliché to one person may not be a cliché to another. Phrases the constant reader turns away from in boredom may surprise the infrequent reader as colourful. Unpractised writers are often similarly beguiled – some try to fit in stock phrases to show the range of their literary knowledge, perhaps a measure of popular taste. At least one successful Fleet Street editor, the late John Gordon of the *Sunday Express*, has upheld clichés on the ground that popular newspaper readers are reassured by coming across phrases they recognize. Time and place make all the difference to a cliché.

It has already been noted that clichés are freely used in conversation. In writing with any aspiration to literary rather than commercial merit they are just as certainly out of place. Careful writers draw back from an imminent cliché and reconsider the thought – a process that often yields a different but fresher one. Here again though, it depends on what each writer considers a cliché. Where does he draw the line among stale phrases? Does he banish

> *hitting the nail on the head*
> *failing to see the wood for the trees*
> *falling between two stools*
> *putting all one's eggs in one basket*
> *never setting the Thames on fire?*

Perhaps he does. Or perhaps he recognizes the difficulty of improving on such pithy though antique sayings.

Collective nouns   See PLURAL/SINGULAR PROBLEMS.

Colons (:)   These are the next strongest stop to the full stop. The writer and editor E. B. White, in his excellent edition of Strunk's *Elements of Style** (a minor American classic), limits the colon to heralding "formal quotations cited as documentary evidence". A more reasonable policy, followed by many publications, is to place a colon before any direct quotation occupying the rest of the sentence, as in

    The chairman said: "Let's break for lunch".

If the sentence is to be resumed after the quotation a comma should be used instead:

    The chairman said, "Let's break for lunch", and led the way.

The colon is also the usual herald of lists (*The following are picked for tomorrow's team: Smith, Jones, Brown* etc), explanations (*The reason for his lateness was clear: he had been drinking*), or revelations (*My tip for the Derby: Runaway Boy*).

In all these roles the colon has replaced the older symbol of combined colon and dash (:-). Some writers still see the lone colon as a stronger form of semi-colon, but no practical definition has been forthcoming, and in the writing of those who favour such subtleties no clear distinction can be discerned between colons and semi-colons.

Colons should not be used for abbreviation (*3 doz: eggs*), a usurping of the full stop's territory.

Commas (,)   Commas are the most useful form of stop next to the period itself, but also the most overworked. Superfluous commas are the commonest of punctuation faults, even among professionals. Only the most careful writers use commas sparsely enough to defy pruning. A modern fad is to inject commas in any sequence of attributes, from *the cool, cool, cool of the evening* to *a long, farewell kiss*. Why not *lucky, old you* or *Many, happy*

*Collier MacMillan, publishers, London 1972.

returns? At this rate A. A. Milne's admirably idiomatic *John's got great big waterproof boots on* will need updating to *John's got great, big, waterproof boots on.* This absurd habit breaks up natural phrases and introduces visual breaks where no speaker would pause.

When attributes are arrayed before a noun, as in the following phrases, commas are unnecessary and awkward:

> *She wore a slinky red two-piece outfit*
> *They ran a huge old black supercharged Mercedes*
> *The wobbly wooden mail-order garden shed*
> *. . . a wonderful new long French romantic novel*
> *. . . appalling little overpriced jerry-built modern cottages.*

At least five attributes, or as many as do not make too much of a mouthful, can have an uninterrupted series, as long as they go naturally together. If ill-assorted attributes are to be grouped, as in *Tall unpunctual highly paid team manager John Smith,* a comma or two might come as a relief. The real need, though, is not punctuation but a more logical redeployment of the information.

When attributes are listed without a following noun, commas between them become necessary, unless *and* links each to the next: *Their supercharged Mercedes was huge, old and black* (attributes rearranged to make list more manageable) / *Her two-piece outfit was red, slinky, revealing, expensive, exciting.* Only judgement limits the length of the series. The commas here reflect the pauses, or at least hesitations, found in speech.

Various simple policies have been advocated for avoiding mistakes with commas ("always put one before *and*"), but there are too many exceptions (*you and the night and the music* for one). The usual dilemmas concern where to put the commas in [1] a series of expressions involving *and/or* etc, and [2] sentences containing subsentences.

[1] **and/or** etc Simple pairings need no comma: *George and Margaret/Berlin or bust/bed and breakfast/spaghetti with bolognese sauce* etc. Trios and longer series cause arguments. The trend now is to punctuate as in *ready, willing and able to serve,* instead of the purist *ready, willing, and able, to serve.* The objection to the simpler system is that it tends to make a pair of the last two items, but the sense is unaffected even if the balance is upset. The arrangement applies equally to other conjunctions like *but/while* and to series of subsentences, as in

Take the script away, learn your part and come back on Friday.

[2] **Series of subsentences**   These range from *I told her the news and she was delighted* (comma optional) to miniature paragraphs with *buts* and *ands* and *on-the-other-hands*. The play-safe policy is to put a comma in front of any subsentence introduced by *and* or other conjunction. Hence

I told her the news, and she was delighted
We'll be late, but I don't care.

These too are matters of taste. The commas can usually be dropped without making the slightest difference to the sense in these simple constructions, and so they can in mildly inverted sentences like

At the time, there was nobody at home
Though we'll be late, I don't care
Because you were out, we missed you.

In a long sentence a comma may be desirable just to give the reader time to digest the thought. In dialogue commas may be added or dropped just to imitate speech rather than to clarify sense.

If the sense is ambiguous a dropped comma may have to be restored. In *The clowns fell about, the acrobats balanced on chairbacks and the elephants sat up and begged* the acrobats seem to be balancing on the elephants, and a comma is needed after *chairbacks*. But *sat up and begged* is an integral phrase that should not be interrupted.

Parentheses   Comments, added facts, and similar interruptions of the text should be marked off by punctuation to avoid confusion. This is mostly done with commas, but brackets or dashes have a similar effect. The choice is sometimes a matter of style. Prefer commas for any parenthesis essential to the text, as in

*War, **the author tells us**, is caused more by muddle than ambition*
*Never tangle, **unless you are looking for trouble**, with a proud parent.*

Brackets may be a solution if there are already a lot of commas or more than one parenthesis: *The tribesmen, **to our surprise**, were most helpful and, **contrary to their reputation** (probably dreamed up by travellers who had never met them), not at all menacing.*

Subsentences starting with *which/where/who* or *if/provided/though* etc are usually parentheses:

*The gift, **which we hadn't expected**, was most welcome*
*Paris, **where we spent our honeymoon**, is impossibly*
*   expensive now*
*There's no-one to blame, **if you ask me**, but himself*
*The laundry, **provided it gets away on time**, comes back on*
*   Wednesday.*

All these commas are needed. But *which/where/who* may introduce defining subsentences, as in

The man who came to dinner
Is that the street where you live?.

Always omit commas from defining phrases, or the sense will be affected. See the explanation in Part I under THAT/WHICH.

Adverbs   The kinds of adverb known as conjuncts and disjuncts tend to be automatically marked off, especially when they occur at the start of a sentence, as in ***Fortunately**, there was nothing wrong*. Unless such words can mislead by being read as applying to the next word or phrase no comma is necessary. (See CONJUNCTS/DISJUNCTS.)

Common mistakes with commas   (i) *Failure to complete the punctuation*: If any section of a sentence is to be marked off, except the opening or closing phrase, two commas are needed, marking the section at both ends – i.e. not *The tribesmen(,) to our suprise, were most helpful . . ./War, the author tells us(,) is caused . . . .*

An exception sanctioned in American usage is the style for adding the abbreviated name of an identifying state after that of a town, as in *A fire destroyed a Philadelphia, Pa. store/. . . his Milwaukee Wis. origins . . .* etc. A comma ought to complete the parenthesis of the state, but custom has let it drop.

(ii) *Unnecessary comma in appositions*: In phrases like *My friend Flicka/God the Father/My cousin Rachel/That nuisance Roger* the two nouns are said to be in apposition, both having the same relationship to whatever follows or went before. These are integral phrases and should not be interrupted by commas. In *The Prime Minister, Margaret Thatcher, was here last week* the name is an added fact, not part of an integral phrase, and the commas are needed. A modern style is to title people by their occupations, as in *Historian Arnold Toynbee/Philosopher Sir Karl Popper/Econom-*

ist Milton Friedman. Though the occupations are nouns, they function here as adjectives and so should not be marked off. So *Economist, Milton Friedman said . . .* is a blunder. *Industrialist, Mr Ford . . .* is worse, adding to an intrusive comma an intrusive *Mr.* Occupational titles are normal before titles of rank (as in *Professor Lord Blake / General Sir John More*) but are never coupled with *Mr.*

(iii) *Using commas to join sentences*: A comma is an interruption, not a connection. Do not use it as in *I know it was her, she told me so / Don't do it like that, do it like this / He didn't answer, he didn't need to.* The proper punctuation is a DASH (q.v.), the second sentence in each case being a comment on the first. Alternatively full stops followed by capital letters would do.

(iv) *Using commas for emphasis*: This is not so much wrong as unreliable. *The shop took it back without haggling* is a plain statement. *The shop took it back, without haggling* is meant to convey that the lack of haggling is the point of interest. The comma represents a spoken pause. But will the reader get the message?

Comparatives   *Pretty / prettier / prettiest* and *obnoxious / more obnoxious / most obnoxious* illustrate two systems of forming comparatives and superlatives. There are rules about which adverbs and adjectives use which. People who do not know the rules put *more / most* in front of words that take easily to *er / est*, a waste of idiomatic opportunity.

Adverbs   Only a few are capable of the inflections, and they are mostly words that also function as adjectives, like *early / fast / hard / long / loud / quick.* These vary in the same way as adjectives do, e.g. *loud / louder / loudest* (as in *I can sing anything louder than you / He shouts loudest*). There is a handful of irregular inflections, including *little (less / least), much (more / most), well (better / best).*

A typical adverb ending in *ly* has to follow the pattern of *steadily (more steadily / most steadily).*

Adjectives   All adjectives of one syllable (sense permitting) inflect with *er / est.* So do many of two syllables. Those of three or more syllables have to use *more / most*, as in *beautiful (more beautiful / most beautiful)* – despite their spellings *full / fuller / fullest* are not a model for words ending in *ful.* Irregular exceptions are few and well known: *good (better / best), bad (worse / worst), little (less / least).*

Among adjectives of two syllables, those taking *er / est* are as follows:

[1] those stressed on the final syllable, like *severe / polite*
[2] those ending in *y*, like *heavy*
[3] those ending in *le*, like *simple / gentle*
[4] those ending in *ow*, like *narrow / shallow*
[5] those ending in *er*, like *clever / tender*.

If the adjective's spelling ends with a single consonant after a stressed vowel, the consonant is doubled, as in *sad (sadder / saddest)*. Hence no extra consonant in *stupid / stupider / stupidest*, where the final vowel is not stressed.

If the adjective ends with *e*, this is dropped before acceptance of the suffixes, as in *true (truer / truest), mauve (mauver / mauvest)*.

If the adjective ends with a *y* preceded by a consonant (as in *dry*), *i* is substituted for the *y* before acceptance of the suffixes. Hence *dry (drier / driest), early (earlier / earliest)*. Other eligible adjectives just add *er / est* without any change.

Other comparatives Comparison in what might be termed a downward direction makes use of *less / least*, as in *full (less full / least full)*. Then there is the neutral comparison with *as: as full* etc.

(See also ELLIPSIS.)

Conjunction See PARTS OF SPEECH.

Conjuncts / disjuncts These are useful modern subdivisions of adverbs. The older term *adjunct* may be said to cover any adverb acting in its straightforward role of qualifying or modifying a verb or other word. Many adverbs, though, can affect a sentence in general rather than any of its parts (like *though* in this one). These "sentence adverbs", as they are sometimes termed, tend to occur at the beginning of sentences and they fall into two distinct types: **conjuncts**, those linking the sense to that of a previous sentence, as *accordingly* in *She knew his views on punctuality. Accordingly, she arrived on time*, and **disjuncts**, those commenting on what is said in the sentence, as *frankly / strictly speaking* in *Frankly, you don't qualify / Strictly speaking, you're at fault*.

It is clear that in these examples none of the adverbs cited affects the action of the verb or any other word. The conjunct *accordingly* refers back to the previous sentence, and the disjuncts *frankly / strictly speaking* have an overall effect – *frankly* refers to the frankness of the speaker, not to the behaviour of *he*, and *strictly speaking* is a similar reference to the speaker.

Conjuncts   These should not be confused with conjunctions (*and/ or/but/for* etc – see PARTS OF SPEECH). They were formerly called "conjunctive adverbs" or "relative adverbs", and are words like *however/therefore/moreover/besides/still*.

> *He promised to mend the fuse.* **However,** *he may have forgotten.* (Incidentally there is no basis to the belief that *however* should not start a sentence.)
> *You didn't turn up. We* **therefore** *assumed that you'd lost interest*
> *The restaurant has an ambitious menu. The cooking,* **moreover,** *lives up to it*
> *This cadet's excuse is inadequate.* **Besides,** *he has tried it before*
> *I wouldn't dream of eating your last chocolate. Oh I don't know* **though.**

In all these examples the conjuncts stand apart from what is being said now and keep one foot in what has just been said. The reference back can be to a subsentence rather than a separate sentence, as in

> *The theatre was sold out, and* **anyway** *the seats were too dear.*

Other adverbs often used as conjuncts include *again/hence/ incidentally/instead/likewise/equally/namely/rather/then/thus/ so*. A common colloquial form is *only*, as in *I'd lend you the money. Only, I'm overdrawn myself.* Various prepositional phrases can also act as conjuncts: *in addition/in the same way/in other words/ in consequence/in contrast/in any case/after all/above all/all the same/at the same time.*

A routine use of adverbs as conjuncts is enumeration (*first .../second .../third ...* etc, or *in the first place/to begin with*).

Disjuncts   As with conjuncts these are not limited to adverbs, but can include prepositional phrases etc acting adverbially:

> **With respect,** *the witness's memory is mistaken*
> **In short,** *there were many delays*
> *We missed the bus,* **to cut a long story short**
> *We shall* **no doubt** *hear from her eventually.*

Various positions are possible for disjuncts:

> **Significantly,** *he has not been in touch again*
> *The buffet was shut but* **luckily** *we'd already had a meal*
> *I'm quite relieved it's over,* **confidentially**
> **Seriously,** *do you plan to emigrate?*

Notice the difference between the last example and *Do you seriously plan to emigrate?* (adjunct). The disjunct refers to the speaker's seriousness in asking the question or to the required seriousness of the answer. The adjunct refers to the seriousness of the plan to emigrate. The positioning of the adverb helps to show whether it is intended as an adjunct or disjunct.

A controversial example of this effect is the contemporary use of *hopefully*. This word is traditionally an adjunct, as in

> *To travel hopefully is better than to arrive*
> *Our thoughts dwelt hopefully on the future.*

Here *hopefully* qualifies a verb (*travel / dwelt*) in the ordinary way. But American usage, already widely copied in the British Isles, treats the word as a disjunct too, as in

> *Hopefully, we'll be back next year*
> *Hard works pays off, hopefully.*

No new effect has jarred more on British ears, at least among purists. But British usage provides the model for it with *luckily / mercifully / sadly* and the more recent *arguably*, among others:

> *Mercifully, no-one was injured*
> *Sadly, he died last week*
> *The train was late, luckily.*

Grammatically, *hopefully* as a disjunct has nothing to apologize for.

Punctuation of conjuncts / disjuncts   Conjunct and disjunct functions are often indicated by marking off the adverb etc with commas. This is done more by custom than by forethought, and it cannot be taken as a norm. In these examples commas would never be found, even though the words occur in positions associated with adjuncts:

> *She* **unwisely** *accepted / You* **doubtless** *know / He was* **understandably** *proud* (disjuncts)
> *She needed money and I* **accordingly** *sent some* (conjunct).

Commas are common in instances like **Luckily,** *it was all right*/*It was all right,* **luckily,** but they are not necessary. By putting them in where the word occurs in mid-sentence though, the intention can be clarified:

> *Do you* **seriously** *plan to emigrate?* (adjunct)
> *Do you,* **seriously,** *plan to emigrate?* (disjunct).

There are also instances where marking off is necessary to avoid ambiguity or misreading, as in

> **Confidentially** *(,) talking to her is an effort*
> **In short** *(,) time has run out.*

Otherwise conjuncts/disjuncts are no exception to the rule that punctuation should be as sparing as possible.

Consonant conflicts   When words are run together in speech there is a tendency for unwieldy clumps of consonants to form. This happens because most English words begin or end with consonants. The conflicts of sound that come about are overcome by replacing or omitting one of the consonants, usually from the end of the first word in the collision. The changed sound makes for easier pronunciation and passes unnoticed. So *brand new* becomes "bran new", shedding its *d,* and *light car* may become "like car", swapping *t* for *k.*

The main point about this is that it is a normal speech process. Periodical denunciations as "slovenly" by people who have just noticed it overlook the genuine difficulties that cause it. Some patterns of consonants are surprisingly troublesome to speak clearly at conversational speeds. Some can only be articulated by conscious effort when speaking slowly.

The combinations of sound that cause difficulty, and the changes that tend to modify them, are as follows:

> *d* before
>> *b* as in *red belt* changes to *b* ("reb belt")
>> *g* as in *good god* changes to *g* ("goog god")
>> *k* as in *bold king* changes to *g* ("bolg king")
>> *m* as in *good morning* changes to *b* ("goob morning")
>> *p* as in *crowd pulling* changes to *b* ("crowb pulling")
>> *y* as in *need you* changes to *j* ("neej oo")
>
> *n* before
>> *b* as in *down below* changes to *m* ("dowm below")
>> *k* as in *tin can* changes to *ng* ("ting can")

g as in *ten guns* changes to *ng* ("teng guns")
m as in *own mother* changes to *m* ("owm mother")
p as in *on paper* changes to *m* ("om paper")

t before
b as in *get back* changes to *p* ("gep back")
g as in *quite good* changes to *k* ("quike good")
k as in *bought cake* changes to *k* ("boughk cake")
m as in *goat milk* changes to *p* ("goap milk")
p as in *write properly* changes to *p* ("wripe properly")
y as in *put you* changes to *ch* ("puch oo")

s before
sh as in *horse shows* changes to *sh* ("horsh shows")
y as in *bless you* changes to *sh* ("blesh you")

z before
sh as in *baize shirts* changes to sound like "beige shirts"
y as in *peruse yours* changes to sound like "perouge yours".

Besides these substitutions a number of sounds are liable to be left out of consonant clumps altogether, especially *d*/*t*, which occur frequently as terminal sounds in past tenses (*slept*/*slogged*). Neither of these can be discerned at all when they fall between any two of the following sounds: *b*/*d*/*g*/*j*/*k*/*p*/*t*/*ch*. So it is not surprising that they get left out of word sequences like *grabb(ed) back*/*sack(ed) gardener*/*wrapp(ed) goods*/*jogg(ed) past*/*ac(t) churlishly*. Endings in *md*/*nd* sounds also shed their *d* before some consonants: *a time(d) game*/*steam(ed) noodles*/*cann(ed) beef*/*an(d) more*. The same fate strikes *t* in endings in *ft*/*st*: *sif(t) grain*/*lef(t) nothing*/*daf(t) skit* and *wors(t) day*/*mus(t) fly*/*trus(t) me*.

None of these is a recommended pronunciation but there is no future in objecting to any of them when they occur in rapid speech. Avoiding them and noticing them are of equal difficulty.

Everyone is inclined to deny ever being guilty of such travesties oneself, but the obstacles and the evasions are the same for all. Priding oneself on careful enunciation does not help to get the tongue round *guest star* ("gues star")/*kind thought* ("kine thought") etc. Besides, the same process long ago produced many pronunciations we now take for granted: *grandmother*/*handkerchief*/*ink*/*castle*/*Wednesday*/*raspberry*/*colonel*. The consonant clumps in these have been felt to be too much of a mouthful, so that more manageable sounds have evolved: "granmother"/"hangkerchief"/"ingk"/"Wenzday" etc.

Other common words so affected include *income* ("ingcome") / *length* / *strength* (". . . engkth"). These variants are usual but not universal. Then there are *issue* / *tissue* ("ishoo" / "tishoo"), *appreciate* ("appreshiate") and *associated* ("assoshiated") – there are signs of a comeback for the literal spelling sounds of those. In *soldier* (soljə), *furniture* (. . . itshə), and *question*(. . . stshn) there is no going back.

If English is pronounced with each word uttered as a word on its own the effect, far from being correct or natural, is contrived and theatrical.

Consonant sounds   English has 24 consonant sounds, according to the conventional count in which *w* / *y* are included, though considered semi-vowels. The sound represented by *s* in "vision" and *g* in "beige" has no corresponding alphabet letter, while various other letters represent no predictable sound. Thus *c* may stand for the sound of *s* or *k*, *g* may be hard (*gift*) or soft (*gist*), and *x* stands for *ks* (as in "express") or *gz* ("exact") or *ksh* ("complexion"). Even the combination *th* has two sounds. So the knowledge that the alphabet has 21 consonant letters, probably the only conscious information about consonants that school-leavers take away from English classes, has to be seen as an inadequate introduction to one of the basics of the language.

The following list sets out the 24 consonant sounds. In referring to them this Guide, as with VOWEL SOUNDS (q.v.), avoids the symbols of the International Phonetic Alphabet, though they are much more reliable for consonants than for vowels. The least satisfactory is *t*, discussed later. In this list however IPA symbols are shown for reference along with the usual alphabet letters.

Usual alphabet letter(s)	IPA symbol	Consonant sound as found in words like
b	b	*bee* / *baby* / *baker*
d	d	*did* / *add* / *ado* / *aid*
f	f	*fox* / *offer* / *if* / *photograph*
g	g	*gag* / *ago* / *big* / *vague*
h	h	*her* / *ahoy!* / *who*
j / g	dʒ	*jay* / *jam* / *age* / *dodge* / *hinge* / *gin*
–	ʒ	*beige* / *prestige* / *equation* / *invasion* / *seizure* / *closure*

Usual alphabet letter(s)	IPA symbol	Consonant sound as found in words like
k/c/q	k	*key/quay/queer/okay/elk/arc/cat/act*
l	l	*loll/ale/old/bell*
m	m	*mummy/man/am/aim/omen*
n	n	*nun/noun/on/annoy/into*
ng	ŋ	*angle/ink/tongue/gong/singing/sunk*
p	p	*pea/peep/ape/stop*
r	r	*roaring/arrow/river/rare*
s	s	*sauce/boss/cigar/science/ace*
sh	ʃ	*shoe/shop/sugar/nation/ocean/chute/ session/complexion*
ch	tʃ	*church/catch/ancient/nature/inch*
t	t	*tea/duty/tart/pistol/slept/intimate*
th	ð	*the/then/than/bathe/other/with/father*
th	θ	*thing/earth/author/throttle/forthwith*
v	v	*vain/victor/vote/of/over/have/wave*
w	w	*we/want/when/sweet/queen/one/ acquire*
y	j	*yes/you/due/view/few/neuter/nude/ onion*
z/s	z	*zoo/craze/easy/accuse/dogs/ruse/ muzzle.*

Note: *w* and *y* are termed semi-vowels because their consonant sounds consist of exceptionally fast renderings of the vowel sounds oo and E prefixing other vowels, as in *well* (oo+*el*)/*your* (E+aw). In writing, neither letter necessarily represents its consonant sound. W is often silent, as in *awe/sow/wrong*, and *y* sometimes represents the sound of *I*, as in *type/pyre*, or *i* as in *story/royal*.

Consonant sounds tend to vary according to neighbouring sounds. So the *d* in *mid-morning*, wedged between a vowel and a consonant, is not identical with the *d* in *danger*. The *l* in *love* is not quite the same as the *l* in *ale*. There are many small differences of this kind. They go unrecorded in dictionaries on the basis that native speakers are not even aware of most of them. This is true but at least one difference is noticeable enough to be a point of controversy.

According to the *Encyclopaedia Britannica* (15th edition) "in English there is only one *t* sound distinguished by native speakers". This is plainly an exaggeration. Plenty of native English speakers are aware of the characteristic Cockney *t* sound, which is sometimes described as "swallowing your *ts*". Some of them notice that they make the same or nearly the same sound themselves in certain words but not in others. Is this a mispronunciation, they wonder? Are they speaking carelessly? They will not find an answer in any nonspecialist dictionary.

Phoneticians distinguish at least six different *t* sounds according to the mechanics of utterance. For the layman's purposes though, there may be said to be two. There is [1] the sharp *t* of *rotter*, as found before vowels, and [2] the blunt *t* of *rotten* (*rot*n) as found before consonants. The sharp *t* has a spitting sound, and when it is strongly stressed as in *tea/time/too* the necessary puff of breath gives a fleeting effect of an *h* right after the *t*. By contrast the blunt *t* is less clearcut and lacks the spit effect.

In *rotten* the *t* looks as though it occurs before a vowel, but the second syllable consists of just the *n* sound with a vestige of introductory vowel to make it pronounceable. The *n* is said to be syllabic. This effect is common before *n* or *l*, as in *beaten/button/ cotton/curtain/eaten/gluttony/tighten* and *metal/mettle/rattle/ title/shuttle/battle/petal*. It is possible though not easy to pronounce such words so that the *t* sounds like the one in *rotter*, but the effect is artificial. A blunt *t* is normal in them, and also before other consonants, as in *utmost/nutmeg/batman/nightmare, football/ hatbox, nightcap/suitcase, letdown/outdo, catgut/outgrow, footpath/hotpot, fitful/cutthroat*. The *t* is also blunt where it occurs at the end of a word and is followed by a word beginning with a consonant, as in *that man/not yet/get this*.

If a blunt *t* is overdone the effect is the swallowed *t* of Cockney and Glasgow speech, produced by a glottal stop. Here the *t* is not sounded at all. Instead the airstream from the voicebox is interrupted by a closing of the vocal chords. With a stressed vowel this tends to happen whenever the following consonant is *l/m/n/ r/w/y: for(t)night/mu(tt)on/ou(t)right/ ou(t)landish/no(t) you*. The effect is common among educated mainstream speakers, but probably most of those who use such pronunciations regard them as unintentional lapses.

In dialects such as Cockney the glottal stop is more widespread. It replaces *t* in all except initial positions, even where it seems harder to say. (*My car(t) go(t) caugh(t) in a traffic bo(tt)leneck, righ(t)?*). This sound is variously regarded as indistinct, ugly, idle, or comic, but few concerned with elocution regard it as good English.

Silent consonants   Half the consonants of the alphabet are regularly unsounded in various words:

b	*(doubt)*
c	*(indict)*
g	*(gnaw / reign / sign)*
gh	*(bright / bought / naughty)*
h	*(aghast / exhilarate / rhyme / silhouette)*
k	*(know / knot)*
l	*(talk / would / colonel)*
p	*(psychology / psalm)*
r	*(were / air / morning)*
s	*(aisle / island)*
t	*(rustle / moisten)*
w	*(wrong / wrench / owing)*

The only two of these consonants to cause any general difficulty are *h* and *r*.

On its own *h* (as opposed to combinations like *ch / th / sh / gh*) usually occurs at the beginning of a word. Here it is only silent in exceptional instances. (See PRONUNCIATION: DROPPED AITCH.)

The letter *r* is not pronounced at the end of a word unless the next word begins with a vowel. So it is silent in *poor / poor people* but sounded in *poor enough* (and similarly in *poorest*). But the so-called linking *r* (as sounded between *poor* and *enough*), cannot be relied on. Though never wrong, and still general in singing, it is used only spasmodically in speech. It tends to be sounded lightly when used at all. A mere trace of *r* is normally sounded in a sentence like *There's some water over here* – though there are important regional exceptions to all this, especially in American English.

The linking *r* survives mainly as a lubricant of familiar phrases like *cheer up / fire engine / clear off / under age / for ever and ever*. Its gradual disappearance continues an ancient process, as *r* became silent centuries ago in words like *bird / hurt / important*, where it is followed by a consonant (as also in *beer glass / fur coat / pour down*), and in words like *hare / water / tear* spoken singly. It remains silent in derivatives like *hares / watered / tears*, though it makes its presence heard in present participles like *watering / tearing / cheering*.

Though *r* is so often silent in Standard English, it is sounded in various degrees by most speakers in Scotland, Ireland, Lancashire and the West Country. It is also sounded in most – but not all – forms of regional speech in North America. (See also PRONUNCIATION: INTRUSIVE R.)

When s is z   The consonant *s* in writing often represents the sound of *z*. This occurs notably to distinguish *use/abuse/misuse* as nouns (*s*) from the same forms as verbs (*z*). (See also USED (TO) in Part I.) But there is no significance in the variation found when *s* is a plural or possessive ending. Here only the preceding sound determines how the *s* is pronounced. If the *s* follows *f/k/p/t* or *th* as in "moth" it is pronounced as *s*. Hence *cats/hooks/caps/cuffs/skirts, Jack's/ chap's/sheriff's/goat's*. Other endings in *s* are pronounced *z*. If the preceding sound is also *s* or *sh/ch/ge(j)*, as in *gases/wishes/ coaches/rouges, James's/church's/George's*, the ending is pronounced as a separate syllable, iz.

The same rules apply to the pronunciation of *'s* as a contraction of *is/has*. (See CONTRACTIONS.)

Contractions   The shortening and telescoping of words as in *I'd* (= I would/I had), *don't* (= do not), *they've* (= they have) is general in speech but sporadic in writing. Some writers restrict contractions to quoted speech, some use an arbitrary selection, and others bar them altogether. Few use contractions routinely, and even those who do so fail to exploit every possible form. Thus *have* is commonly contracted to *'ve* when combined with pronouns, as in *they've/ we've/you've*, but not when combined with auxiliaries. The following forms are rarely seen:

can've	might've
could've	should've
may've	will've
must've	would've

Also uncommon in print are *there've/where're* (= where are)/ *what're*.

There is a tendency to write *'s* only when it stands for *is* and not when it stands for *has*, though the contraction is freely used for both in speech – as is *'d* for *would* and *had*.

Apart from *let's* (= let us) and a few combinations with adverbs, as in *here's* (= here is)/*how'll* (= how will)/*where'd* (= where had), standard spoken contractions involve auxiliary verbs telescoped with each other, with pronouns or with *not*. The following basics yield more than 50:

'm (am)	*'ll* (will/shall)	*'d* (had)
're (are)	*'ve* (have)	*'d* (would)
's (is)	*'s* (has)	*n't* (not).

The negative *n't* cannot be tacked on to an ordinary verb, e.g. *I hope not* (never "I hopen't"), but the verbs *'s / 'll* can be tacked on to any convenient noun, as in *Dinner's ready / The train'll be late*. But forms like these, though normal in speech, are still generally regarded as too informal for writing.

Note the irregular contractions

aren't (when it stands for "am not" – see entry in Part I)
shan't (= shall not)
won't (= will not).

All the other telescopings with *n't* keep the full spelling of the verb, e.g. *haven't* not "havn't". Negative contractions can end a sentence, but the others cannot, except those that make two syllables, like *should've*. So *Oh no you won't*, but not "Oh yes I'll" (*Oh yes I will*). The lyricist (Ira Gershwin) who wrote *I'm biding my time / 'Cos that's the kind of guy I'm . . .*   was invoking poetic licence.

To contract or not to contract?   In the writing of this Guide the view has been taken that a general use of contractions, which is so widely questioned and resisted, would prove distracting to the reader. So contractions will only be found in examples of speech.

This is not intended as a recommendation though. It is surely unrealistic to hold out for written wording that systematically differs from what is actually said, especially when what is said is as natural to the educated as to the illiterate. After all, writing is primarily a record of what is said, not a script for it. The idea that because the ears are not involved in written communication different conventions are desirable is not calculated to advance human understanding.

Writing contractions out in full is a misrepresentation of sound if not of meaning. It falsifies both the individual sounds and the rhythm of the sentence. It puts in syllables that are not spoken, as with *we have* (two syllables) for *we've* (one syllable), or *will not* (two) for *won't* (one).* It shifts the spoken stress (compare *there isn't* with *there is **not***). Reading aloud from conventional text produces a sound never heard from natural speech, unless the reader makes a point of telescoping the appropriate word pairs.

So there is no logic to the idea that there is something slangy about writing down the contractions everybody speaks. Contractions are part of the language and there is nothing wrong or lazy or

---

*Contractions are essential to many phrases, as instanced by Lewis Carroll's verse *Will you, won't you, will you, won't you, will you join the dance?*.

uneducated about them. It is surprising that they have not yet become the norm in writing.

Logic, however, is not all on one side. It can be countered that the sound of many English words is habitually misrepresented by their spelling. If contractions are to be advocated as standard spellings, should not all the other words spoken with silent syllables be regularized too? Why not *develop'd/delib'rat'ly/armam'nts/ gen'ral*? Why not a revision of all deceiving vowels and posturing consonants? And if a thorough reform of English spelling is too ambitious, why make a fuss about recording, say, *can't* as *cannot* when virtually every English sentence contains spellings just as far removed from the sounds uttered?

It is an emotional issue. Written languages rarely correspond precisely with the spoken. To lovers of English the familiar look of the words, functional or not, is part of the literary appeal. Habits of writing are cherished as personal, like habits of dress. They are not likely to be changed by argument.

Writers who want to use contractions can reasonably contend that there is no need to keep English spelling more inaccurate than it has to be. Things are going their way, and the discovery is being made that contractions need be no bar to dignified style. Writers who hold out for formality can at least compromise by accepting contractions in direct speech and in standard phrases – as most of them do.

Constructions Many entries in Part II touch on this subject – in particular see STYLE/SENTENCE PATTERNS/VERB PATTERNS/INFINITIVE CONSTRUCTIONS.

Dashes (–) Dashes are of two kinds, single and double. The single dash is used for a parenthesis at the end of a sentence, as in *This is Higgins' report on the confidential matter we discussed a few days ago – you will know what I mean*. The dash signals an abrupt break. A comma would not do, as noted under COMMAS. Brackets would pass. A semi-colon would also be possible. But the single dash is essentially for an afterthought:

> *She brought home all her schoolfriends for a snack – there were nine of them*
> *He accepted the job but never arrived for work – just as well, as it turns out.*

Double dashes are also used for parenthesis but their role is less settled. Grammatically brackets are always interchangeable with them, but some writers find brackets too enclosing. Double dashes are for the writer who wants you to notice his parenthesis. He would have used commas if they could contain an independent sentence:

> *If the number of crimes committed has increased, so has the number – the statistics prove this – of young males, the section of the population mainly responsible for crime*
> *We live in a society bored by work – perhaps a new word for it is needed – and obsessed by entertainers.*

Double dashes are confusing if used more than once in the same sentence. Unlike brackets they do not point in either direction, so that with two pairs the middle dashes are easily misread as a pair. For the same reason a sentence should not contain double dashes and a single dash.

Ellipse (. . .)   The term for words left out is ELLIPSIS (q.v.) but the sign for an omission is usually called an *ellipse*. It consists of a series of full stops (periods). Many dictionaries mentioning the condition fail to give a name for the symbol, and *Webster's* calls both "ellipsis". The Fowlers treated the condition in their manuals without differentiating. They called it "ellipse" in one and "ellipsis" in the other, never naming the symbol though using it frequently. This background may help to explain why so many writers use the ellipse vaguely, putting in as many stops as they feel like or trying to make them convey impenetrable meaning.

The number of stops in an ellipse should not be indefinite or left to printers, but should follow the simple rule of as many as are necessary but as few as possible, i.e. three. Two stops, which look like a mistake, are not enough. When the ellipse falls at the end of a sentence a final stop should be added to it in the ordinary way. Examples:

> *How does that line go, "When to the . . . of sweet silent thought"?*
> *The Revd Mother's letter stated that he told her to ". . . off".*
> *He shouted "God for Harry, England and . . .", but could not remember the rest.*
> *Complete the phrase, "Atcheson, Topeka and . . .".*

As these examples suggest, ellipses are mostly used to show where words or sentences are missing from direct quotation. When a quoted extract begins in mid-sentence, or anywhere later than the beginning of the speech/communiqué/poem etc, an ellipse is placed in front of it (just inside the openers if inverted commas are used).

An additional use for ellipses – for want of any other suitable sign – is to suggest suspense or a pause in speech:

Next, the star of our show . . . in person . . . Elvis Presley!
Among the book's fascinating topics are thought-reading . . .
*   levitation . . . psychic surgery . . .*
"Wait for it . . .", he said, "Not yet . . .".

What an ellipse should not be used for is to suggest something the writer leaves to the reader's imagination – a dodge for implying greater depth of thought than the author can communicate:

It was a fascinating discussion, and afterwards he went
*   home wondering . . .*
She hated everything about the place – the noise . . . , the
*   crush . . . , the people . . .*
The consequences can well be imagined . . . .

Similarly ellipses should not be added to questions in which the sense is already complete:

"You wouldn't do it", she said. "What if I did . . . ?", he
*   replied.*

Dashes and hyphens are sometimes still used to denote ellipsis (a dash was at one time called an ellipse), particularly of names. But these are unneeded variants.

Ellipsis   Ellipsis is the omission of words to avoid repetition or to abbreviate. The omitted words are said to be ellipted. Everyday examples of ellipsis for abbreviation:

*(**I'll**) See you later*
*(**Do you**) Want a drink?*
*(**Is**) Anything the matter?*
*That's the way (**in which**) to do it.*

Examples of ellipsis to avoid repetition:

*My father came round and (**my father**) helped me*
*We'll go to the meeting if you will (**go to the meeting**)*

> *They can (**hold out for compensation**) and should hold out for compensation.*

These are all simple short cuts, in which the sense of the missing words is obvious to reader or hearer. If the sense is open to doubt the device is abused.

Note: Ellipsis should not be confused with substitution, though this is sometimes an alternative way of avoiding repetition (see PROFORMS). Nor is ellipsis the same thing as an ELLIPSE (q.v.).

Some of the commonest instances of ellipsis are of verbs made up with auxiliaries, of *that* as a conjunction, and of *that/which/ who* as conjunctive pronouns (see THAT/WHICH in Part I). Ellipsis is also common after determiners, as in *many/most (**of the**) lights failed* (see PRONOUNS/INDEFINITES).

Time phrases   Time phrases are common with ellipsis of *for/on*, as in *I'll be away (**for**) a fortnight/It lasts (**for**) an hour/(**For**) Three years he persevered/Are you doing anything (**on**) Saturday?/(**On**) Tuesday I'll be in Brussels.*

It is worth noticing that *today/tomorrow/yesterday* never take a preposition in a sentence like the last, e.g. *Where were you yesterday?/Are you free a week tomorrow?*. On this model ellipses may be on the way to becoming standard in sentences specifying days by name. At present *on* is still usual in formal writing, though ellipted in speech.

Time phrases introduced by *in*, as in *I'll be home **in** a week/ He'd finished **in** half an hour*, cannot be ellipted. Nor can *for* be dropped if the period of time starts with *the* – hence *She's here **for** the summer* but *She'll be gone (**for**) a year.*

With verbs   Typical ellipses of verbs, used to avoid repetition, include:

> *He said he'd write at once and he has (**written at once**)*
> *You could have sent word and (**you could have**) told me*
> *We must eat and when we get there we will (**eat**)*

Ellipsis does not require the words left out to be exact repetitions of words left in, but it does have limitations. They include mixing the same verb (i.e. *be/have/do*) as auxiliary and as independent verb. They also include changing of voice from active to passive and vice versa:

> *She **has** a son and (**has**) **brought** him with her* (the second *has* is part of a different verb and cannot be left out)

*You have not applied your mind to the task, and it should be (**applied to the task**)* (apart from the confusion about what *it* means, ellipsis is not acceptable where the verb changes from the active *have not (applied)* to the passive *should be (applied)*.

With comparatives In comparative sentences ellipsis risks changing the sense when overdone. There is no confusion in the following:

*Men are more likely to take to crime than women are (**likely to take to crime**)*.

But with *are* left out too the sentence could be understood as

*Men are more likely to take to crime than (**they are likely to take to**) women*.

Ambiguity after *than* etc is a well known hazard with *me/her/him* etc, as in *Waiting about irritates you more than me*. This could be understood either as *... more than it irritates me* or as *... more than I irritate you*. For the first sense the safest way is substitution (see PROFORMS), not ellipsis, i.e. *... more than it does me*.

Between sentences Words left out of a sentence may be implied by the previous sentence. An extreme example is the story of the trainee journalist told to write an account of a man's accidental death without wasting words. He wrote: "John Smith opened the lift door to see if the lift was coming. It was. Aged 39". Here a lot more is left out after *it was* than *coming*.

The idea that a semi-colon should be used between sentences linked by ellipsis is unfounded. Ellipsis is often implied between sentences spoken by two different people, let alone in two separate sentences:

*I've borrowed your book/I know (**you've borrowed my book**)*.

In subsentences Ellipsis greatly simplifies several kinds of subsentence:

*When (she was) **busy** she was irritable*
*Steak is still popular though (it is) **expensive***
*The precautions (that were) **ordered by headquarters** have not been taken*
*The official (who is) **guilty of this oversight** should be disciplined*.

Exclamation marks (!) The hard-pressed writer, reaching for one of these to enliven a dull patch, deserves sympathy, but the exclamation mark is not an all-purpose stimulant. The frequency of its use is inclined to vary inversely with the quality of the composition. Certainly there is never any reason for using more than one exclamation mark at a time and often no reason for using one at all. For once, the grammatical name accurately describes function, and use of the exclamation mark depends on what is understood by an exclamation. This excludes statements in general, even those the writer regards as arresting, but it covers more than what grammar calls interjections, e.g. *Oh!/phew!/ugh!* etc.

The main qualifying categories are:

> oaths (*Blimey!/Hell!/Well, I'll be damned!/Goodness gracious me!*)
> alarms and warnings (*Help!/Look out!/Fire!*)
> commands (*Halt!/Quick march!/Fire!/Charge!*)
> insults (*You humbug!/Drop dead!/Murderer!*)
> miscellaneous expletives (*Jeez!/Well!/So there!*)
> inverted exclamations (*What fun!/How we ran!/What a shame about Mame!*)

But the essential qualifications are not so much the category as [1] brevity, and [2] exclamatory tone of utterance. There is an obvious difference of expression between *"Oh!", she said, startled* and *"Oh, all right", she said.* Similarly not every command is exclaimed (*Wait for me here*), nor is every inverted comment (*What an interesting book that seems*) or oath (*Hell, I'll be late*). Exclamation marks should be reserved for instances where a sharp manner of utterance needs indicating. These might include greetings (*Hallo!*), congratulations (*Well done!*), incomplete reflections (*If only you were here!*) etc.

Exclamation marks compare in force with QUESTION MARKS (q.v.). They function like full stops at the ends of sentences, but may occur like commas inside sentences.

Full stop/Full point/Period (.) The usual term in the British Isles is *full stop. Full point* is a technician's term. *Period*, regarded as an American peculiarity, is a much older term than either, with origins in Greek grammar. Under whatever name, this stop denotes [1] the end of a sentence, or [2] that the form of letters preceding it is an abbreviation.

Premature stops Unless done for a considered literary effect, which requires a skilled touch, periods should not be used to turn subsentences into independent sentences (not *They offered him wine. Which he took. Drinking it with relish*, but . . . *wine, which he took, drinking it with relish*).

It is sometimes held that full stops, except for abbreviations, should never be used before *and* and *but*, a precept that would outlaw the Bible. The objection is not to using such words as conjuncts but to setting apart grammatically incomplete subsentences, as in *It was not till dusk that Samantha, peering anxiously through the window, spotted the lost child coming up the garden path. And cried for joy*. The words *And cried for joy* are not an independent sentence, their subject being part of the previous sentence. Instead of using a full stop the passage could be punctuated in any of these ways: . . . *path – and cried for joy*/ . . . *path, and cried for joy*/ . . . *path. She cried for joy*. Again, a liberty may be taken when intended for literary effect.

Abbreviations The simplest style is to use a period only when the last letter of the abbreviation differs from that of the full word, as in *Gen.* (General)/*Sept.* (September)/*oz.* (ounces)/*reg.* (regulation)/ *Geo.* (George)/*encyc.* (encyclopaedia). Abbreviations ending with the same letter as their full form are more easily recognized and do not need a stop, e.g. *Dr* (Doctor)/*Mr* (Mister)/*Apl* (April)/*wt* (weight)/*regd* (registered)/*Thos* (Thomas)/*bk* (book).

A disputed form is *per cent* (q.v. in Part I). Several terms now better known as abbreviations than in their full forms are used increasingly without stops (*etc*/*viz*/*lbs*), sometimes with a space instead (*e g*/*i e*/*m p h*). This is a predictable development, not likely to be slowed.

(For use of periods to denote ellipsis see ELLIPSE.)

Future idioms The orthodox future verb forms, as set out under TENSES (q.v.), are among several ways of expressing future action in English. The alternative devices that are available occur in all kinds of speech and writing, and are in no sense second choices. They are just as readily used as the notional future simple. This consists of the auxiliary forms *'ll*/*will*/*shall* (according to choice) plus an infinitive, as in

> *I'll see you soon*
> *The doctor **will** see you soon.*

But another way of putting it uses the present imperfect of *to go* as the auxiliary:

> *The doctor **is going to see** you soon.*

Also possible is

> *The doctor **is seeing** you soon.*

This is a common idiom and not restricted, as the example might suggest, to the immediate future:

> *The doctor is seeing me the week after next*
> *When is the doctor seeing me – next month?.*

Use of an auxiliary verb is avoided altogether by the simple present, as in

> *He sees me next week/next month/next winter.*

Present tenses are of course widely used to express the future, as in

> *When do you leave?/We are off tomorrow.*

All these are straightforward expressions of future action. So is

> *He's **to see** the doctor next week.*

More of a borderline case is

> *He's **about to see** the doctor,*

but though this looks like a description of the present the sense is indistinguishable from that of *He's going to see* etc.

The idioms are not always interchangeable. You could not say, instead of *I'll wait for you*, any of the following: *I wait for you/I'm waiting for you/I'm to wait for you.* It would change the sense. Only the non-native speaker ever stumbles over these subtleties though. Nobody else finds anything confusing about a jumble like: *We **have** a busy schedule next week. We're **going to see** the Browns on Tuesday. Then we **fetch** Dirk from college and we're all **driving** over to Stratford, where we're **to see** "Twelfth Night". We're **staying** at the Shakespeare Arms and we **come back** on Friday.* This is perfectly normal English about events entirely in the future, and not once does it use an orthodox future tense. But such a tense could be interchanged for any of the verb forms, which are in turn interchangeable here.

Gerunds   See INFINITIVE CONSTRUCTIONS.

Hyphens (-)   The hyphen, consisting of half a dash, aids clarity by linking adjacent words or bits of words, either permanently or temporarily. English suffers from a reluctance to use hyphens as a temporary aid and an equal reluctance to get rid of them when they have long since made a whole of the linked parts, as in *sit-in/ build-up/post-operative/non-combatant*. Once hyphened terms have been in general circulation long enough to be familiar they can manage without hyphens and ought to be spelt as uninterrupted words, like *layout/overdo/postscript/nonconformist*. That is, providing they do not become unwieldy or hard to recognize, as might *stick-in-the-mud/will-'o-the-wisp/do-it-yourself*.

Hyphens are permanent in names (*Westcliff-on-Sea/Rolls-Royce/Mason-Dixon line*) and wherever pronunciation or meaning might be in doubt without them, as in *drive-in* (?drivein)/ *re-cover* (as distinct from *recover*). They are temporary in joining words to show a combined sense in a particular sentence:

> *You pay as you earn* but *a pay-as-you-earn plan*
> *The polka dots of her bikini are yellow* but *her yellow polka-dot bikini*
> *It happens once in a lifetime* but *a once-in-a-lifetime experience*
> *He drove hell-for-leather.*

Hyphens are also temporary of course in joining broken words at the ends of lines. When such a break is needed it should be made where the word divides naturally, i.e. between syllables (which are shown in many dictionaries). The hyphen should obviously not interrupt letters representing clumps of sound, as *tch* in *catching*, *st* in *disaster*, or *gr* in *photograph*. Nor is it acceptable in figures like 1,000,000, though this is common in U.S. usage.

In hyphened adjectival phrases to do with age, weight, size, or duration English idiom requires a singular form for the measuring term:

> *She was 15 years old* but *a 15-year-old girl*
> *A postponement of six months* but *a six-month postponement*
> *The box is six feet long* but *a six-foot-long box*
> *It weighs three tons* but *a three-ton weight.*

The hyphens are equally essential in noun-phrases like *She's a 10-year-old/He's tall, a six-footer/The lorry is a three-tonner*. Neglect of hyphens in such uses makes for harder reading. Why should the reader be expected to work out his own links in compounds like *an ice-cold drink / a razor-sharp mind / a rose-red city half as old as time?*

With multi-word titles, however, the capital initials make it obvious that the words form a single term. Hence it is unreasonable to demand hyphens in phrases like *the Buckingham Palace staff / House of Commons catering arrangements / Department of Trade policies*, though all three titles are adjectives here. It is also silly to object to hyphening a prefix to the first word of such terms (*ex-White House lawyer*). The custom saves time and space and, since titles are evident compounds, there is no reason to avoid *pre-World War II films / anti-Atlantic Alliance sentiment* etc. Even *ex-Tory mayor*, which could mean a turncoat Tory, is readily understood as meaning a former mayor, though this sense strictly demands an extra hyphen (*ex-Tory-mayor*).

When familiar short terms like *first class / trade union / high street* are used adjectivally a helpful hyphen signals to the reader that the expected noun is yet to come. But familiarity already binds them, so that it is less important to insist on forms like *first-class degree / trade-union leader / high-street traffic*, ideal though these would be. In less familiar and longer expressions, used generally as adjectives, clarity can only gain from extra hyphens.

Where hyphens are particularly needed is in clarifying the genuine confusions found in verbless strings of nouns, a habit copied from headlines, e.g. *Party leader patronage powers reform demand*. Uncertainty about which noun does what makes a second reading inevitable. Hyphens hack a way through such thickets, and even through denser ones like this (from a Cadillac workshop manual): *Remove rear guide upper bracket to inner panel and guide assembly attaching screws and remove guide bracket from door.* Hyphens to the rescue! *Remove rear guide upper-bracket-to-inner-panel and guide-assembly attaching screws, and remove* etc.

Hyphens used to be common between adverbs and participles functioning as adjectives, as in *a well-known example / a fast-disappearing skill / a slow-burning gasring*. While these cannot be called essential they are often helpful in avoiding ambiguity.

Idiom   Idiom is loosely any expression or way of phrasing peculiar to a language. Thus the expression *take to drink* is an idiom for "become a drunkard". Similarly the phrasing *She does not drink* etc is the idiom for expressing a negative – whereas the expected form would be "She drinks not". This is a general sense of the term. In a narrower sense, one often meant in this Guide, idiom is an odd, even illogical, way of putting it that happens to be the accepted way. Examples:

that temper of his (instead of ... *of him*)
couldn't help it (instead of ... *avoid/prevent it*)
a sought-after vintage (instead of just *a sought vintage*)
had better hurry (instead of *ought to hurry/should ...*).

The baffling *can't help* idiom, entrenched in phrases like *you can't help laughing* is presumably derived from "it (i.e. the situation) can't be helped". This made sense but its variants often express the opposite of what is intended, e.g. *I won't be later than I can help*. What is meant of course is "... later than I can't help" (if *I* could help it *I* presumably would). Fortunately these idioms no longer strike anyone as contradictory, as they are too far gone to be put to rights.

The *had better* idiom, which predates Shakespeare, is a rare survival of the subjunctive. As it so often occurs as a contraction (*'d better*) it is now widely believed to be a mistake for "would better", on the lines of *would sooner/would rather*. Uncertainty about this causes many contemporary writers to avoid the phrase except in safe versions like *You'd better not/I thought I'd better*. In speech the *'d* has long tended to be dropped and the commoner spoken forms are *You better not/I thought I better* etc.

Imagery Phrases used for conveying word pictures are either *similes* or *metaphors*. Both are forms of comparison.

Simile: *The aircraft took off **like a rocket.***
Metaphor: *The aircraft **rocketed off.***

In both the take-off is likened to a rocket's, but only the simile signals the comparison by means of *like* (or *as/in the manner of* etc).

As illustration in language relies on comparison it is important to choose effective comparisons. The ordinary person may not often contrive the fresh and vivid comparisons of gifted writers but can at least avoid obscuring meaning with unsound ones. Most of the duds are either stale comparisons, too familiar to register an image in the mind of the reader or listener, or confused comparisons suggesting an impossible image.

Stale images   The language is cluttered with old metaphors and similes in which the image is a superfluous ornament. Consider:

top dog	*deaf as a post*
early bird	*pretty as a picture*
old hat	*bold as brass*
quick off the mark	*hard as nails*

In all these the sense is established by the initial adjective, i.e. in the sentence *These plans are old hat* the meaning is complete at *old* and no more information is conveyed by likening the oldness to that of an old hat. When such phrases were fresh they may have added emphasis but they do so no longer.

Outdated images   Metaphors taken from technology become pointless when the technology is superseded. Nobody any longer recognizes the references. A people accustomed to aeroplanes and electric trains cannot be expected to be enlightened by imagery left over from sailing ships and steam engines (*mainstay / let off steam*). Diamonds are no longer ranked as *of the first water* etc (this metaphor is now so obscure that it is even taken to refer to the first filling of a teapot). Egalitarianism has largely abolished *second class / third class* in travel, substituting euphemisms like "budget" / "coach" / "economy". Objects like a *bad penny* or a *brass farthing* are no longer of everyday concern. In these days of dry copiers / Ozalids etc *blueprints* are industrial antiques. Candlelight still shines but *limelight* is forgotten. *Bigwig*, more than a century after wigs passed out of fashion, has ceased to suggest a bewigged notable. And so on.

The drift of all these phrases is understood of course, but no picture is conveyed by them – which makes the use of metaphor futile.

Confused images   The use of stale or outdated phrases encourages, because their image is not grasped, the mixed metaphor. Here two or more irreconcilable images are combined:

> *The basic language of her design was forged in the local school of art.*

It is perhaps possible to liken a design style to a language, but a language – not being metal – cannot be forged.

> *He went into the exam room keyed up and cleared his fences at a fast clip.*

It is impossible to picture a stringed instrument (*keyed up*) clearing fences, least of all *at a fast clip*, which is an expression derived from an obsolete sense of the verb *to clip* (= to fly, or move fast), now associated with sailing (*clipper*). There would be no conflict in . . . *the exam room keyed up and raced through the questions*, since a stringed instrument is capable of racing through music.

Whenever a metaphor is used close to another metaphor, care is needed to ensure that one picture does not cancel out the other. (See also CLICHÉS.)

Imperatives   The imperative version of a verb, notionally used for commands, is the same in form as the verb's bare infinitive, e.g. *to hurry* (infinitive) / *hurry* (imperative). Sentences with imperative verbs are said to lack a grammatical subject, as in

> *Get out! / Hurry up! / Quick march! / Stop grumbling!*

The implied subject is whoever the speaker is addressing. The omission is not essential though, as seen in

> **B Company**, *stand at ease!*
> *Everybody freeze!*
> *Get a move on,* **all of you!**

So the usual generalization about imperatives lacking a subject is misleading. Moreover the imperative verb itself may be lacking, as in

> *Hands up! / Down, boy! / To heel!*

These are clearly commands as much as *Quick march!* etc, with the missing verb implied: *(Put your) Hands up / (Get) Down, boy / (Come) To heel.*

Milder instructions bordering on invitations may or may not be commands but they certainly share imperative constructions:

> *Help yourself to more wine*
> *Come to dinner tomorrow*
> *Put the kettle on, Polly*
> *Let me call you back.*

Please for politeness or *do* for persuasion can elaborate:

> *Please try to remember*
> *Do hurry home.*

Negative instructions require *do not* or *never*, as in

> *Do not touch the exhibits / Don't you dare*
> *Never give a sucker an even break* / Never you mind.*

---

*W. C. Fields.

It may be mentioned that the inclusion of the subject in an imperative sentence, though no longer the commonest arrangement, has a long history:

Go *and do* **thou** *likewise* (the Bible)
Go **you** *and enter Harfleur* (Shakespeare).

(For punctuation of imperatives see EXCLAMATION MARKS.)

Infinitive constructions In *I love to climb mountains* there is a typical arrangement of a verb (*love*) followed by the infinitive of a second verb (*to climb*). Another way of saying the same thing is *I love climbing mountains*, which uses a participle (*climbing*) instead of an infinitive. This choice is not always available, because many verbs are limited to only one of the constructions. Further, those limited to an infinitive have no choice of the kind of infinitive – most must take a full infinitive, i.e. *love to climb*. Some of them need a bare infinitive (i.e. no *to*, as in *I do climb*), but these are all auxiliaries.

Verbs requiring bare infinitives:

can/could	*had better*
shall/should	*may/might*
will/would	*do*
	must

Verbs requiring full infinitives (the general construction) include:

ask	*fail*	*laugh*	*think*
agree	*hasten*	*long*	*threaten*
beg	*have*	*ought**	*use**
come	*hesitate*	*promise*	*volunteer*
cry	*hope*	*refuse*	*wish*
expect	*incline*	*tend*	*wait.*

Also verbs in the passive are limited to the full-infinitive construction:

I was required to do
She was chosen to be
We are intended to help.

*If *ought to/used to* are regarded as verb phrases, since they always occur in this form, then they belong with the first list.

Verbs able to accept either a full infinitive or a participle include:

attempt	*hate*	*love*	*prefer*
begin	*intend*	*omit*	*propose*
choose	*like*	*plan*	*write.*

Where such a choice exists the characteristic, though not invariable, American preference is for the infinitive (*She loves to cook fish*), and the British for the participle (*She loves cooking fish*).

In this role the participle is traditionally called a *gerund*, a term supposed to be reserved for the function of "verbal noun". "Gerund" is a convenient shorthand, but it is hard to draw the line where a participle starts being a gerund or turns into a straightforward noun. Infinitives themselves function as verbal nouns (*To eat people is wrong*) but do not need a special name when they do. The so-called gerund is also allegedly a uniquely English advantage, but in fact it creates hazards. With some verbs the gerund construction changes the sense. Compare the following pairs:

Stop looking at that girl (= do not look at her)
Stop to look at that girl (= wait specially to look at her)

Try riding that horse (= see how you like riding it)
Try to ride that horse (= attempt to ride it)

I regret to give you my notice (= sorry, but I'm giving notice)
I regret giving you my notice (= I wish I hadn't done so)

They deserve to eat (= they deserve a meal)
They deserve eating (= they ought to be eaten).

Verbs susceptible to such hazards include:

delay	*hurry*	*require*	*want* (= need,
deserve	*need*	*stop*	with gerund)
forget	*regret*	*try*	

Verbs requiring participles (i.e. gerunds):

abandon	*dismiss*	*put off*
acknowledge	*enjoy*	*recommend*
admit	*finish*	*recall*
advocate	*give up*	*relish*
anticipate	*keep*	*resent*
consider	*merit*	*succeed in/at*
contemplate	*overlook*	*suggest.*
deprecate		

Split infinitives This is an old dispute which should have been settled long ago. The issue is whether a full infinitive such as *to be* should be interrupted (split) by an adverb as in *to suddenly be*. This practice is avoided by many writers under the impression that it is a grammatical offence or at least a stylistic lapse. It is certainly not a grammatical offence.

Perhaps because a confident grasp of grammar is uncommon among native speakers of English – a language that makes few demands for declension and conjugation etc – concern for whatever offences the ordinary person thinks he can recognize is all the more passionate. Split infinitives are one of these. A split infinitive can inflame a businessman who muddles his tenses and upset a politician who is blind to a non sequitur. This concern is the more extraordinary in that objectors can rarely explain why they object. Vague authority may be invoked, but the fact is that 20th-century grammarians from Otto Jespersen onwards have dismissed the aversion as unfounded.

The English infinitive occurs in two forms, full (*to be*) and bare (*be*), though it is doubtful whether many users recognize it except when it has a *to*. Traditional grammar books convey the impression that it usually has, but this is not so. *To quibble* is an obvious infinitive but in *Why must you quibble?/I do not quibble* the word *quibble* by itself is an infinitive. In this form nobody cares what kind of word is placed in front of it, nor that it has lost its *to*. Only lately, in fact, has grammar bothered to find a technical term for its deprived condition (*bare*), having previously made do with "infinitive without *to*". If it is all right to say *Your trouble is that you incorrigibly quibble* (and it is) how can it be objectionable to say *You have a tendency to incorrigibly quibble*? *Quibble* is an infinitive in both instances.

The resistance may survive from the days when Latin was taken as the model for English. Dryden, the scourge of prepositions at the end of sentences, admittedly tested his English by translation into Latin, and Latin of course has neither prepositions at the end of sentences nor splittable infinitives. Explaining English in terms of Latin has been a traditional theme of grammarians. Old English had infinitives with a dative form, as in Latin, and *to* (which is a dative preposition) commemorates this in modern infinitives.

That however is an absurd reason for never separating it, since most English verb forms consist of two or more words, and we split them freely, as in *Scholars **will** always **quibble***. Besides, there is more than one kind of infinitive. *To have asked* is as much an infinitive as *to ask*, yet we split the three words of *to have asked* (*He was wise to have politely asked*) as a matter of routine. So why not the two words of *to ask* or *to have*?

Fowler, in giving guarded approval to splitting, fogged the point with an appeal to "instinctive good taste". Good taste, as Mae West said of goodness in relation to how she came by her big diamond, has nothing to do with it. But clarity has, and so has natural English rhythm. *To really learn a language you have to keep practising* is a clear and natural wording. If reworded as *Really to learn a language . . .* it would be affected. If reworded as *To learn a language really you have . . .* there would be doubt about which half of the sentence *really* was intended to intensify.

Should we all stop and think every time we want to say something like *I am anxious not to unduly burden you*/*He is right to strongly oppose these changes*? Must we then take care to revise the sequence to *. . . anxious not to burden you unduly*/*. . . right to oppose these changes strongly*? To seriously expect any such thing would be far-fetched even if grammar required it – and it does not.

Infinitives in the past   In the simple present and past tenses nobody hesitates over an infinitive construction. The infinitive form is the same for both: *I want to go* (present)/*I wanted to go* (past). But even practised writers tend to stumble when expressing further stages of pastness. Confront them with *I should have wanted . . .* or even *I had wanted . . .* and they are liable to clutch at *to have gone*, ending up with the indigestible *I should have wanted to have gone*/*I had wanted to have gone* etc. The extra degree of remoteness seems to draw attention to the "present" status of the infinitive, provoking an attempted demonstration of familiarity with the full range of infinitive forms. These amount to six:

to go	*to have gone*	*to be gone*
to be going	*to have been going*	*to have been gone.*

But rummaging among them is more likely to produce a wrong tense than a better match. The indefinite present infinitive (e.g. *to go*), the commonest form, is also usually the wanted one.

Specifically, this infinitive remains correct for any point in time concurrent with or later than the time expressed by the preceding verb. Hence *I should have wanted to go*/*I had wanted to go*/*I wanted to go*/*I want to go*. In all these the wanting clearly occurs before or at the same time as the going, and there is no excuse for any fancy infinitive.

Among these combinations is nearly always the appropriate form, since the past infinitive with a past tense is inclined to refer to extremely unlikely circumstances. *I should have liked* **to have gone** would be all right if the intended sense was that the speaker would have liked on Wednesday (say) to have gone the previous Sunday (say), but no longer has that desire today, Friday (say). This is not a thought that often needs expressing. Usually if the speaker would have liked something well enough to recall the emotion the idea will still appeal to him today, and he can put his liking in a present tense: *I should like* to have gone (present conditional). Or, if he has gone off the idea, he can say *I should have liked* to go. Only if he is undergoing psychoanalysis is he likely to need to pinpoint how he felt at some time in the past about something that happened even earlier.

In general, then, it can be said that anything on the lines of *should have wanted* **to have gone**/*would have been hopeless* **to have tried**/*might have been the thing* **to have done** etc is likely to be wrong. The error is due to an excess of zeal. To put it right what is usually needed is to substitute a present infinitive (*to go*/*to try*/*to do* etc).

Verbs often found in such tangles include *dare*/*expect*/*hope*/*seem*/*want*, the sense of which permits pairing with the rarer infinitive forms. Many verbs would be meaningless if so paired, e.g. *fight*/*try*, and others cannot be constructed with infinitives at all. The hazard arises mainly with conditional past tenses (*should have ...*/*would have ...*/*might have ...* etc), which seem to disorient the user.

Interjection   See PARTS OF SPEECH.

Inversion   This is back-to-front word order, as used for questions etc. All it usually amounts to is a repositioning of the subject of the sentence after the verb.

> Normal order: *You are ready.*
> Question inversion: *Are you ready?*
> Negative inversion: *Nor are you ready*/*Not only are you ready*/*Not for the first time are you ready* etc.

Inversion also occurs in conditional sentences such as

Should you decide to come, let me know
Had you told me, I could have helped
Ignorant though he is, he knows that

and in many sentences along the lines of

There goes that new car
Generous I call it
To this total should be added certain expenses.

Various labels have been applied to such instances of inversion, but adjustment of emphasis is the purpose of all of them except questions.

Negative inversion Inversion is not the standard negative construction, but inverted negatives remain common for adjustment of emphasis. There is no grammatical necessity for them, as uninverted alternatives are available:

Inverted	Uninverted
Never again will I risk that sort of journey	*I'll never risk that sort of journey again*
Not a word did he say when I taxed him with it	*He didn't say a word when I taxed him with it*
Nowhere has the rot set in so fast as in personal honesty	*The rot has not set in so fast anywhere as in personal honesty*
Not only did he decide to buy it but he paid cash	*He not only decided to buy it but paid cash*
In no circumstances could we agree to your proposal	*We could not agree to your proposal in any circumstances*
We neither want air conditioning nor can we afford it	*We don't want air conditioning and we can't afford it.*

All these inversions, though legitimate, belong more to writing than to speech. When spoken they risk giving a stilted effect. So do such near-negatives as *Rarely have I seen . . . / Seldom has there been . . . / Scarcely had I finished . . . / Barely had he begun . . . / Little did they know . . .* These too are emphasis devices, and are easily turned round. The point about all such negatives and near-negatives is that they require to be followed by inversion if placed at the start of a sentence. This rule is respected by the contemporary colloquialism *no way*, as in *No way am I going to pay as much as that.*

Inversion and variety   Placing words or phrases in an unexpected position in a sentence tends to draw attention to them. In *Suddenly I heard a noise* emphasis is given to the suddenness by transferring the adverbial *suddenly* from its usual position (*I heard a noise suddenly* or *I suddenly . . .*). But an additional effect is to alter the rhythm of the sentence. This can make for variety in a sequence of similarly constructed sentences, and inversion is also exploited for this purpose.

Much the commonest component to be repositioned for emphatic effect is the adverbial. But complements, direct objects and even verbs are sometimes moved:

That he should offer some concession is the least we can expect (complement – *The least we can expect is **that he should offer some concession***).

She's all right but him I can't stand (direct object – *. . .but I can't stand **him***). A superfluous comma is sometimes placed after the shifted object, as though apologizing for the disturbance.

I don't mind going in their car but drive I will not (verb – *. . . but I will not **drive***). Similarly: *I'll give up some sleep willingly but eat I must.*

Incidentally, the undoubted effectiveness of these shifts confirms how deep-rooted is our acceptance of the standard sequences of sentence components outlined in ANALYSIS.

(See also IMPERATIVES.)

Inverted commas (' '/" ")   Also called quotation marks or quotes, these signs enclose direct speech. The traditional style is to regard double inverted commas as standard, and use the single kind for quotation within direct speech. Hence *"Hurry up," called Mother's voice, "Granny did ask, 'Please don't be late'."*

Also possible is the opposite style, single quotes normal, double quotes for quotation within them – which Fowler termed "the more sensible practice". It is widely used in British books but has never caught on elsewhere – fortunately, as it is not sensible at all. The single form is identical with the APOSTROPHE (q.v.), inviting endless confusion with possessives and contractions – two instances occur in the short example above. As simple quotation is far more common than quotation-within-quotation the more sensible practice is to limit this hazard by treating double inverted commas as normal, which most people sensibly do.

Opinions differ about where to put the stops in inverted commas. The example follows the orthodox style, putting commas and full stops, at the end of direct speech, within the closing inverted commas. But an alternative arrangement is to put such stops outside the quotes, so that sentences end consistently – a style some publishers and printers prefer. Others make a distinction, putting the final stop inside the quotes only when the sentence started with quotes. It is not important – in fact it is difficult to see why phrases like *said Mother* need marking off at all (except when they complete a sentence), since the quotes already set them apart.

Inverted commas are also used for play and book titles etc, especially when italic type is unavailable. They sometimes denote foreign expressions or unfamiliar slang phrases too. Some writers object to them for slang words – E. B. White called the style "putting on airs" – but in fact they reassure the reader that this is an unconventional expression if it puzzles him.

Irregular verbs Most English verbs have predictable forms. Except for *to be* and a few auxiliaries they have the same form for infinitive (e.g. *to look*) and for nearly all the present tense (*I/we/you/they look*). Only the 3rd person singular varies (*he/she/it* **looks**). To form past tense and past participle they nearly all combine the infinitive with *ed* (*looked*). But there are more than 100 verbs, including some of the commonest, with unpredictable forms of past tense and/or past participle: *swim*, for example, yields *swam* and *swum*. It is an unusual writer who has never hesitated over which form to use in such instances. One might expect irregular verbs to be set out for easy reference in dictionaries, as they are in some foreign languages, but this is not part of the English tradition.

The problem only arises with the past tense and the past participle, as the other inflections follow predictably (except with *to be*) from the infinitive. Regular verbs just take an added *d* if they end in *e*, or *ed* if they end in any other letter (*blame/blamed, claim/claimed*) except *y*. With *y*, *hurry* becomes *hurried* (see SPELLING ENDINGS). These rules are variously violated by irregular verbs.

There are many ways of grouping such verbs according to their different characteristics – one system discerns nine groups – but the most practical is the one proposed by R. A. Close. He divides irregular verbs into three groups:

[1] those with the same spelling for infinitive, past tense and past participle, like *shut*

[2] those with the same irregular form for past tense and past participle, like *left*, which differs from the infinitive (*leave*)

[3] those with past tense differing from past participle, like *tear* (*tore/torn*).

This grouping still leaves a few exceptions such as irregular verbs with optional or special forms, like *dreamed/dreamt, clothed/ clad*. These are noted individually. The list is not full but covers the main irregular verbs.

Group 1

Infinitive	Past	Participle
bet	*bet**	*bet*
burst	*burst*	*burst*
cast	*cast*	*cast*
cost	*cost*	*cost*
cut	*cut*	*cut*
hit	*hit*	*hit*
hurt	*hurt*	*hurt*
let	*let*	*let*
put	*put*	*put*
quit	*quit**	*quit*
read	*read*	*read*
rid	*rid*	*rid*
set	*set*	*set*
shed	*shed*	*shed*
shut	*shut*	*shut*
slit	*slit*	*slit*
split	*split*	*split*
spread	*spread*	*spread*
thrust	*thrust*	*thrust*

* betted/quitted are regularized past tense forms in occasional use.

Group 2

Infinitive	Past	Participle
bend	*bent*	*bent*
beseech	*besought*	*besought*
bind	*bound*	*bound*
bleed	*bled*	*bled*
breed	*bred*	*bred*

Infinitive	Past	Participle
bring	brought	brought
build	built	built
burn	burnt/burned	burnt/burned
buy	bought	bought
catch	caught	caught
cling	clung	clung
creep	crept	crept
deal	dealt	dealt
dig	dug	dug
dream	dreamt/dreamed	dreamt/dreamed
feed	fed	fed
feel	felt	felt
fight	fought	fought
find	found	found
flee	fled	fled
fling	flung	flung
get	got	got (U.S. gotten)
grind	ground	ground
have	had	had
hear	heard	heard
hold	held	held
keep	kept	kept
kneel	knelt/kneeled	knelt
lay	laid	laid
lead	led	led
lean	leant/leaned	leant/leaned
leave	left	left
lend	lent	lent
light	lit/lighted*	lit/lighted
lose	lost	lost
mean	meant	meant
meet	met	met
pay	paid	paid
rend	rent	rent
say	said	said
seek	sought	sought
sell	sold	sold
send	sent	sent
shine	shone	shone
shoe	shod	shod
shoot	shot	shot

Infinitive	Past	Participle
sit	sat	sat
sleep	slept	slept
sling	slunk	slunk
smell	smelt/smelled	smelt/smelled
speed	sped	sped/speeded up
spell	spelt/spelled	spelt/spelled
spend	spent	spent
spin	spun	spun
stand	stood	stood
stick	stuck	stuck
sting	stung	stung
strike	struck	struck/stricken*
string	strung	strung
sweep	swept	swept
swing	swung	swung
teach	taught	taught
tell	told	told
think	thought	thought
win	won	won
wind	wound	wound
wring	wrung	wrung

*Where regular alternative endings in *ed* are shown, these are commoner in America. *Lighted/stricken* are used mainly as adjectives (*a lighted candle/the stricken ship*).

Group 3

Infinitive	Past	Participle
arise	arose	arisen
bear	bore	borne/born*
beat	beat	beaten
become	became	become
begin	began	begun
bid	bade/bid	bid/bidden
bite	bit	bitten/bit
blow	blew	blown
break	broke	broken
choose	chose	chosen
come	came	come
do	did	done

*borne = carried; born = given birth.

Infinitive	Past	Participle
draw	drew	drawn
eat	ate	eaten
fall	fell	fallen
fly	flew	flown
forbear	forbore	forborne
forget	forgot	forgotten
forsake	forsook	forsaken
freeze	froze	frozen
give	gave	given
go	went	gone
grow	grew	grown
hew	hewed	hewn/hewed
hide	hid	hidden
know	knew	known
lie	lay	lain
mow	mowed	mown
ride	rode	ridden
rise	rose	risen
ring	rang	rung
run	ran	run
saw	sawed	sawn
see	saw	seen
sew	sewed	sewn/sewed
shake	shook	shaken
show	showed	shown
shrink	shrank	shrunk/shrunken
sing	sang	sung
sink	sank	sunk
slay	slew	slain
slide	slid	slid/slidden
smite	smote	smitten
sow	sowed	sown
speak	spoke	spoken
spring	sprang	sprung
steal	stole	stolen
stink	stank	stunk
stride	strode	stridden
strive	strove	striven
swear	swore	sworn
swim	swam	swum
take	took	taken

Infinitive	Past	Participle
tear	*tore*	*torn*
throw	*threw*	*thrown*
tread	*trod*	*trodden / trod*
wear	*wore*	*worn*
weave	*wove*	*woven*
write	*wrote*	*written*

Several older forms have been supplanted as participles but survive as adjectives, like *shaven / shrunken / sunken / shorn (sheared)* – this was the origin of *molten* and *rotten. Proven* too is mainly an adjective. So is *laden*, which is all that survives in normal speech of *to lade*, except the term "bill of lading". *Spit* (expectorate) can keep the same form for past tense or participle but *spat* is commoner. Similarly *fit* can keep *fit* for either in U.S. usage. *Dive* is a regular verb in British usage, but Americans generally use *dove* (rhymes with "cove") for *dived*.

The archaic verb *beget* offers a choice: *begot / begotten* or *begat / begot*. For the vagaries of *awake / wake* etc see the entry in Part I. *Hang* makes *hung / hung*, but in British usage *hanged* is preferred in the sense of execution by hanging. In general where alternatives are current the tendency is to adopt the more regular form, e.g. *thrived* rather than *throve*.

(See also PHRASAL VERBS.)

Italics   See CAPITAL LETTERS for use as an alternative form of emphasis.

Linking verbs   Though verbs in general denote action, there is a group of important exceptions. The verbs in the following sentences merely record an existing state:

> *You look healthy* (or *feel / sound / appear / seem* etc)
> *She is hopeful*
> *He remains devoted.*

Of the 20 or so verbs that function like this (though not all of them do so in every sense) the most obvious is *to be*. In sentences like *She is hopeful / That man is a fool* this verb is merely a grammatical stopgap, contributing no essential meaning except time reference. *She hopeful / That man fool* are just as informative, and in fact *to be* is often left out of telegrams, newspaper headlines and notetaking (e.g. *Married yesterday/GANDHI DEAD* etc). When it is put in, its grammatical function is mainly to link the subject (*She/That man*) with the complement (*hopeful/a fool*). So verbs like this are called linking verbs or copulas.

Note: *To be* is not always a linking verb. In some contexts it is an AUXILIARY VERB (q.v.) and in others it means "exist", as in *to be or not to be/what must be must be*. Similarly *look/feel* become transitive verbs, i.e. transmitting action to an object, in contexts like *to feel the water/to look at pictures*.

Linking verbs are significant in ANALYSIS (q.v.) because they are not capable of taking an object. In *He is a fool*, for example, *a fool* is not a direct object, though it is a noun phrase and occupies the appropriate position after the verb. It is a complement, completing the meaning of *He* (the subject). The thinking here is that as the idea of being implies no action the verb *to be* cannot transmit. Put another way, being changes nothing, as seen in

> *Adam is the man*
> *God is love*
> *You are wrong,*

where the words on either side of the verbs could swap places without changing the sense. The theoretical sentence patterns yielded by analysis cannot be understood if this point is not grasped.

Other linking verbs (in the senses indicated) include:

> *smell (appetizing)*
> *stand (corrected)*
> *taste (delicious).*

Some of them have an illusion of movement:

> *become (argumentative)*
> *come (true)*
> *get (tired)*
> *go (wrong)*
> *turn (nasty).*

Metaphor   See IMAGERY.

Noun   See PARTS OF SPEECH.

Oblique etc (/) Oblique is only one name for a punctuation sign also variously known as a solidus, slash mark, or virgule. It is the origin of the comma (hence French *virgule* = comma). In everyday punctuation its only uses are for abbreviating *care of* to *c/o*, for the symbol % (= per cent), and for separating alternatives as in *and/or*. But it is part of the standard typewriter keyboard, which may explain the revival it has been having in specialist uses. It can be used for separating items placed next to each other without affecting the punctuation or grammar of the sentence containing them. In these pages obliques separate examples of words or phrases.

Participles The terms "present participle" and "past participle" are misleading, as the words they describe do not necessarily refer to present and past. For example *leaving*, the present participle of *to leave*, refers to three different time periods in

> *I am leaving* (present)
> *Leaving tomorrow, we shall benefit from Summer Time*
>   (future)
> *Leaving home, I said goodbye* (past).

Similarly past participles in present passive tenses refer to the present and in future tenses to the future:

> *I am being asked*
> *He will be asked.*

Additional participle forms, not always recognized as such, are compounds like *having asked/being asked/having been asked/having been asking*.

The function of participles as verb forms is set out under TENSES (q.v.), and their sometime roles as other parts of speech are noticed

	Present participle	Past participle
adjective	*a **tempting** dish*	*a **considered** opinion*
noun	*the **tempting** of Tantalus*	*the **tempted** can't always resist*
conjunction	***Considering** that he promised her, he cannot refuse*	
preposition	*That was quick, **considering** the weather*	*All things **considered**, he could have tried harder*

in such entries as INFINITIVE CONSTRUCTIONS / PARTS OF SPEECH / PREPOSITIONS and in Part I under CONSIDERING and PROVIDED. Specimens from the verbs *to tempt* and *to consider* summarize these roles above.

Unrelated participle   The commonest misuse of a participle is the variously termed hanging, dangling, unattached or unrelated participle. (The tabled examples above of participles acting as prepositions or conjunctions are legitimized versions of this lapse.) The rule is that a phrase introduced by a participle, if it precedes the subject of the sentence, must refer to the subject, as in

Struggling to reach the top he passed the guide.

Here the subject of the sentence is *he*, who was doing the struggling. If the participle phrase goes at the end the sense changes:

He passed the guide struggling to reach the top.

Now the sense is that the guide, not *he*, was struggling. In the following example the participle phrase is unrelated:

Struggling to reach the top his foot slipped.

The literal sense is that *his foot* was struggling, and the sentence requires to be recast. The rule applies equally to past participles (and to other similarly placed descriptive phrases):

Depressed by the news she said no more to him.

If this is rearranged as *She said no more to him, depressed by the news*, there is uncertainty about who was depressed, *she* or *him*. The pitfall of the unrelated participle is further explained under PROVIDED in Part I.

Fused participle   This construction still worries careful writers. It was already common when it was condemned by the Fowler brothers (who coined the term). It is more entrenched than ever today, and reformers cannot seriously expect to prevail against everyday turns of phrase like

Stop him making that noise
The girls don't like him watching them
There's no chance of that happening to us
It's no use him complaining
Excuse me mentioning it
I can't see the firm refunding the money
What's preventing you getting on with the job?
How about us getting married?

Obviously people are not going to stop saying such things or writing them. Most would be amazed to learn that grammar expects of them *Stop his making that noise/Excuse my mentioning it* etc. Their response can be imagined when they learn that they are required to differentiate between [1] *Stop him making that noise* (wrong) and [2] *I heard him making a noise* (correct).

In [2] what was heard was *him*, and *making a noise* is a participle phrase giving additional information about him. In [1] what is to be stopped is not so much *him* as the making of the noise. So here *making* is a gerund (a sort of noun – see INFINITIVE CONSTRUCTIONS) and as such it has no grammatical link with the pronoun *him*, and there is no way of telling which word is meant to be the direct object of the verb *stop*. Replacing *him* by *his* is held to settle this theoretical dilemma.

There is a similar grammatical impasse in sentences where such pairs are rivals for the function of subject, as in *You mentioning it reminds me/Us getting married is going to surprise them*. Which are the subjects here? As both verbs are singular (*reminds/is going*), *You* and *Us* are excluded. This exposes their lack of attachment to the two gerunds *mentioning/getting married* (*Us* is of course already excluded as an accusative instead of nominative form – *we*).

The purist solution, as illustrated earlier, is the use of possessives. This produces *Our getting married/Your mentioning it* etc but it does not always work. It could not help . . . *no chance of that happening to us*, because *that* cannot take a *'s* possessive. Nor is it intelligible in difficult sentences where the two words are placed several words apart, as in *Galloping inflation results in* **savings'** *people have painstakingly accumulated* **buying** *next to nothing*. (This is admittedly the sort of sentence that would be better reworded in any case.) There are also many borderline instances where an ordinary participle construction cannot be clearly distinguished from the fused participle.

These are all side issues. The essential point is that though the grammar may be confused nobody is in doubt about the sense. We think of *me mentioning/him making/that happening* etc as single concepts. In doing so we merely follow the established conventions of the language, in which we use entire sentences as single components of other sentences, or treat a plural group as a collective singular, not to mention using the same word variably as singular or plural according to the concept we have of it at the time. In short this construction is no more aberrant than many others. Not that it would make any difference if it were. It is established idiom.

Parts of speech   The traditional "parts of speech", into which different kinds of word are classified, are as follows (examples in brackets).

   adjective (*every book*/*this book*/*which book?*/*thick book*/*good books*/*your book*/*the book is silly*):   Word used to add meaning to a noun or pronoun.

   adverb (*read now*/*read slowly*/*perhaps read*/*spread thickly*/*behave sillily*/*regret very sincerely*):   Word used to add meaning to a verb, but also to adjectives, prepositions and other adverbs. (See also CONJUNCTS/DISJUNCTS.) Too loose a label for so many roles.

   article (*a book*/*the book*/*an attempt*):   Kind of adjective. *A*/*an* are called indefinite articles, *the* a definite article. Modernists lump them all with some other words such as *this*/*these*, *my*/*your*/*their*, and call them "identifiers".

   conjunction (*fish and chips*/*go but hurry*/*I will if you will*):   Word used for linking two similar parts of speech or two subsentences. Typical conjunctions include *or*/*for*/*as*/*because*/*that*.

   interjection (*oh*/*ah*/*ow*/*ugh* etc):   Short exclamation not included in the grammatical construction of a sentence. Some grammarians extend the term to oaths like *blimey*/*hell*/*well I'll be damned*. Other examples: *alas*/*geewhizz*/*hurrah*/*hallo*.

   noun (*car*/*driver*/*speed*/*Gloria*):   Word for a person, thing or concept. Names of persons, places and institutions etc are called "proper" nouns.

   preposition (*Give it to me*/*It's from Father*/*Wait outside Harrods*):   Word showing relation between its "object" (usually the noun following it) and a preceding word, i.e. between what they denote. The word governed by a preposition (i.e. the object) is always in the objective (accusative) case. This makes no difference to nouns but an important difference to pronouns:

of
to
by
for
from
} etc *me*/*her*/*him*/*us*/*them* (not *I*/*she*/*he*/*we*/*they*).

Stock phrases like *in view of*/*as for*/*by means of* act as prepositions.

   pronoun (*you*/*me*/*they*/*herself* etc):   Kind of noun, used as a substitute for a noun or equivalent, either for brevity or to avoid

repetition. Types include personal pronouns (*I*/*we*/*it* etc), possessives (*mine*/*yours*/*hers*), reflexives (*myself*/*oneself*/*itself*), relatives (*which*/*that*/*who*), and indefinites (*each*/*all*/*any*/*either*). (See
entries on PROFORMS and PRONOUNS.)

verb (*who does what*/*he hit me*/*go home*): Word denoting
action, movement, change etc. Its basic form, the infinitive, is an
action concept (*to do*/*to laugh*/*to ask*/*to think*). (See entry on
VERBS.)

Two kinds of verb inflection, called *participles*, can be regarded
as additional parts of speech:

participle (*we were asked*/*were asking* etc): Verb adjective
occurring as either a present form (*asking*) or a past form (*asked*).
All present types end in *ing*, and nearly all past types have the same
spelling as the verb's past tense (except in IRREGULAR VERBS, q.v.).
Participles combine with auxiliary verbs to form various tenses, but
also act on their own as adjectives (**asking** *price*/**going** *rate*/**left**
luggage) and as nouns (see INFINITIVE CONSTRUCTIONS, and also
PARTICIPLES).

Overlapping uses   All these terms refer to function only, because
most English words do not belong exclusively to a single category.
The same word may change category according to its function in
different sentences. So *love* can be a noun (*my love*), an adjective
(*a love match*), or a verb (*love thy neighbour*). This flexibility makes
analysis hazardous for nonspecialists.

It is a regular feature of English that nouns can be made to serve
as adjectives (*a **floor** plan*) or as verbs (*how to **floor** opponents*), and
also that adjectives are convertible into nouns by putting *the* in
front of them, as in *Only the brave deserves the fair*, and sometimes
adding *s* (*one of **the** greats*). Many short words, including some of
the most used, that are thought of primarily as adjectives function
also as adverbs, e.g. *hard* in *worked hard* (adverb)/*hard work*
(adjective). Others include *fast*/*long*/*deep*/*late*/*near*/*loud*. In
some dialects *good*/*bad* are similarly used as adverbs (*It fits good*).
In good English they are limited to use as adjectives.

Note that though parts of speech are classifications by function
the function is not limited to individual words. The characteristic
use of an adverb is to describe how, when and where, but this can
also be achieved with phrases that function as adverb equivalents
(i.e. adverbials). So in the following examples all the phrases in
brackets have the same effect as the adverb *reluctantly*. They all add
description to the verb *enrolled*:

Mr Smith enrolled reluctantly
> *with misgivings*
> *in Birmingham*
> *on his way to work*
> *because his friend did*
> *at lunchtime*
> *sooner than necessary*
> *last week*
> *for want of something better to do.*

(See also COMPARATIVES, CONJUNCTS/DISJUNCTS and WORD ORDER.)

Similarly the characteristic use of an adjective is to add meaning or description to a noun but various devices besides adjectives can have the same effect:

pretty girl (adjective)
office girl (noun)
daddy's girl (possessive noun)
disgusting girl (participle)
dejected girl (participle)
the girl at the office (prepositional phrase)
an above-average girl (prepositional phrase)

These are all adjectival processes in relation to the noun *girl*.

A comparable noun process without employing a noun is seen in sentences like *To be young was very heaven.* Here the subject of the sentence consists of an infinitive (*to be*) and an adjective (*young*). But it is a noun equivalent when considered as a single concept.

(See also COMPARATIVES and WORD ORDER.)

Phrasal verbs   Many of the commonest verbs in English are phrases like *give in/come by/fall for.* Sometimes their sense differs from that of the one-word verb acting alone, e.g. *come by* (= acquire) differs from *come*. In others the partnership merely adds emphasis to the sense of the one-word verb, e.g. *come on/hurry up* are just stronger ways of saying *come/hurry*. There are also phrases in which the individual words keep their normal senses, e.g. *stay away/jut out*. Settled combinations like all of these are viewed as equivalent to one-word verbs in modern sentence analysis, a realistic interpretation.

There is general agreement about the phenomenon but disagreement about the labelling. Some grammarians call all such verbs "phrasal verbs". Others restrict the term to combinations of verb plus adverb particle* (*give up/turn in*). They make separate categories of "prepositional verbs" (verb + preposition, as in *look for/object to*) and "phrasal-prepositional verbs" (verb + preposition + adverb particle, as in *do away with/look down on*).

A practical distinction that cuts across these labels is the possibility or impossibility of separating the particle from the verb word. In the sentence *She turned down the offer* it is possible to split the phrasal verb *turned down* by repositioning the object (*the offer*): *She turned the offer down*. This arrangement is not only just as acceptable as the other but obligatory where the object is a pronoun: *She turned it down*. Some phrasal verbs though cannot usually be split in this way, e.g. *come by/look at*:

> Look at that statue/That's the one to look at
> How did he come by the document?/I saw the document he had come by.

These two verbs illustrate that some are more splittable than others, e.g. *look at* has the flexibility of *Which statue did you look at?/At which statue did you look? Come by* has only the one possibility: *Which document did he come by?*

When an adverb has to be accommodated splitting is just one of the options. The following are all possible arrangements:

> She **turned down** the offer firmly
> She **turned** the offer **down** firmly
> She **turned** the offer firmly **down**†
> She firmly **turned** the offer **down**.

The first two are likely to be preferred by most writers with a feel for the natural flow of the language.

A similar choice is available with intransitive phrasal verbs, though not with all of them:

> We **pressed on**
> We **pressed on** resolutely
> We **pressed** resolutely **on**
> We resolutely **pressed on**.†

---

*Adverb particle = any short adverb capable of also functioning as a preposition, like *in/out/up/down/by/over*.

†This arrangement is not mentioned in the rules offered by the specialist *Dictionary of English Phrasal Verbs & Their Idioms* (by McArthur and Atkins, Collins 1980), though it is undoubtedly current and cannot be excluded.

Many intransitives however are not normally split at all, e.g. *give in/ break out/come on*. The versions in brackets are thus all impossible:

> *He* **gave in** *quickly* ("He gave quickly in")
> *The captives* **broke out** *suddenly* (". . . broke suddenly out")
> **Come on** *at once* ("Come at once on").

Phrasal verbs are commoner in speech than in writing, probably because they are by nature spontaneous forms, continually developing new combinations. All the same they are not in any sense inferior to the one-word alternatives that are often available, like *seek* (look for)/*abolish* (do away with)/*yield* (give in)/*observe* (look at)/*reject* (turn down) and so on. There is no reason for consciously excluding them from writing, as far as that is possible, and every reason for preferring them to one-word alternatives when these have a formal flavour (like *seek/yield/observe*). It hardly needs pointing out that phrasal verbs, where a choice exists, tend to be the natural expression.

Plural forms   The regular plurals of English nouns are more complicated than just an addition of *s* or *es*. They involve many exceptions and subtleties, both of spelling and pronunciation. A straightforward noun like *house* needs only an added *s* for its plural form *houses*, but in the process it changes pronunciation from hows to howziz. *Cat* and *dog* look regular enough as they each accept an *s*, but while *cats* is pronounced as written *dogs* becomes dogz. Few native speakers notice such differences and fewer still could offer an adequate summary of the process.

Pronunciation   All plural word endings in *es* (except after *o*, as in *heroes*) are sounded iz. Most *s* endings are sounded as *z* rather than *s*, but not those following the sounds of *f/k/p/t* or *th* as in "thing". So *cuffs/licks/gaps/bits/deaths* end in an *s* sound, while *cads/legs/ ribs/buns/tithes* end in a *z*.

Spelling rules   Most nouns become plural with the addition of *s*, unless they already end in *s* or in *x/z/ch/sh*. Such words need *es*, as in *miss (misses)/yes (yeses)/box (boxes)/match (matches)/dash (dashes)*. Nouns ending in *y* like *duty* also change the *y* for *i* (*duties*) but this does not apply where the final *y* is preceded by a vowel, as in *boy/day/key* (*boys/days/keys*).

The choice of *s* or *es* is more or less arbitrary in nouns ending in *o*, some of which accept either form. In general older words take *es*, and newer ones, especially abbreviated forms or those with a technical sense, take just *s*. So the model of *hero* (*heroes*) is followed by *embargoes / goes / echoes / noes / potatoes / tomatoes / vetoes / negroes* while *radio* (*radios*) is followed by *embryos / kilos / photos / memos / provisos / rodeos / studios / videos.*

Endings in f   The regular *s* is normal for many words like *roof/oaf* (*roofs/oafs*) and tends to be replacing the older *ves* version, e.g. *wharf* occurs in the plural as either *wharfs* or *wharves*. But many everyday words offer no choice: *calf (calves)/half (halves)/knife (knives)/leaf (leaves)/life (lives)/loaf (loaves)/self (selves)/thief (thieves)/wife (wives)*. More complicated inflections, as in *man (men)/child (children)/foot (feet)/mouse (mice)*, are in such common use that the native is never bothered by them. Where spelling uncertainties occur it is usually with less familiar irregularities, such as compounds or foreign imports.

Compound plurals   No generalization can shed much light on specimens as inconsistent as the following:

> *lady doctor/lady doctors*
> *woman doctor/women doctors*
> *mother-in-law/mothers-in-law* (but possessive
>   *mother-in-law's*)
> *passer-by/passers-by*
> *stand-by/stand-bys* (defying rule for endings in *y*)
> *take-off/take-offs.*

There is nothing for it but to look up such words in a dictionary and hope that it is one of those that gives plural spellings, even if it is unlikely to give plural pronunciations.

Foreign imports   Though foreign words mostly adopt the regular *s/es* endings the number of exceptions is enough to be a nuisance. These tend to be technical or specialist words. Here is a summary.

Endings in us (Latin):   Words like *bus/genius/circus* form regular plurals (*buses/geniuses/circuses*), but exceptions are *alumnus/ bacillus/genus* (*alumni/bacilli/genera*). A few words are given their Latin plurals by specialists (*cacti/nuclei/fungi*) but regular plurals by laymen (*cactuses/nucleuses/funguses*).

Endings in a (Latin):   Words like *arena/panacea/quota* nearly all have anglicized plurals (*arenas* etc). One exception is *alga*, known to the layman in its Latin plural only (*algae*). Both forms are used for *formula/nebula/vertebra* (*formulas/formulae* etc).

Endings in um (Latin): Again most words like *album/museum/ forum* are regular in the plural, but only the Latin form is used for *addendum/bacterium/erratum* (*addenda* etc). *Memorandums* is about as common as *memoranda*. (See also DATA and MEDIA in Part I.)

Endings in ex (Latin): Words like *index* nearly all take a regular plural in *es*, but *appendixes* is used medically only, the plural of the book kind being *appendices*.

Endings in is (Greek): Words like *analysis/crisis/hypothesis* keep the Greek plural in which the final *is* changes to *es* (*analyses/ crises* etc). An exception is *metropolis* (*metropolises*). This kind of word should not be confused with the French-derived *chassis*, or even *chamois* (q.v.), which remain the same in singular and plural, though the final *s* is sounded (as *z*) in the plural only.

Endings in on (Greek): Only *phenomenon/criterion* give trouble. Their plurals are *phenomena/criteria*, in which form the words are often mistaken for singulars like *arena* (*A strange phenomena!*). *Criterions* (plural) is less of a blunder than *a criteria* (singular), and perhaps encouragement is needed to regularize the plural, a process long ago completed with *electrons* and others.

Endings in o (Italian): These words are mostly to do with music, and the anglicized plural with *s* is now accepted with all of them. Examples: *concertos/contraltos/solos/sopranos/tempos/ virtuosos*. A recent exception is *graffiti*, an Italian word adopted in its plural form, but used for the singular sense too in English.

Endings in eau (French): The commonest of these are *bureau/ trousseau/plateau*. The French plural is an added *x*, which is seen probably almost as often as the anglicized *s*. What seems to happen is that users with any knowledge of French prefer *bureaux* etc but those with little or none follow the regular English pattern and produce *bureaus* etc.

Plurals in numbers There is often doubt about such phrases as *She's five foot eight/a six-week holiday*. Should they not have regular plurals, as in *five feet eight/six-weeks holiday*? The model here is *one hundred/two hundred/three hundred* etc. The *hundred* remains singular even though the number in front of it (*two/three* etc) indicates several hundreds. This is English idiom and it applies consistently to such uses as *three hundred replies/a thousand million people/a few (several/many) dozen mistakes/a six-foot ruler/ another of her five-week holidays*.

The regular plural co-exists of course for uses like *There were thousands of them/Thousands were turned away/The ruler's length was six feet* (but *The ruler was six foot long* is also possible). *Five feet four* is a possible answer to *How tall are you?* but *. . . foot . . .* is likelier. *A five-weeks holiday* is not a possible form, unless repunctuated as *a five weeks' holiday*.

Permanent plurals   It is worth noticing that some nouns are never singular. They include *pants / scissors / thanks / bowels / goods / riches*. Similarly a few that look plural, like *news/measles*, are always singular, as are abstract nouns like *obedience* and mass nouns like *parking/laughter*. Then *cattle/people/the poor* are examples of collective nouns that are always plural.

Plural/singular conflicts   The kind of difficulty meant is illustrated by the following specimens:

> ***Everybody*** *was busy minding* **their** *own business*
> ***Anyone*** *prefers to do that sort of thing for* **themselves**
> ***Motorcycles*** *are* **a menace**
> *There* **is lots** *more to eat.*

In each of these a singular word appears to clash with a plural word. There must be few writers of English who have never paused over such couplings.

[1] **Referring back to every/everyone** etc   In *Everybody was busy minding their own business*, *everybody* is plural in sense but clearly singular in grammar, since it takes the singular verb *was* (instead of *were*). Yet *their* is plural in grammar. Can this contradiction be avoided? Not satisfactorily.

You could repeat *everybody* (*. . . everybody's business*) but this sounds absurd. If the company was mixed you could say *. . . his and her business*, but this is elaborate besides introducing an unwanted sexual element. The masculine *his* has been traditionally accepted as covering females too but is now seen as discriminatory. If the object is a plural noun, as in *. . . his own tasks*, there is a further difficulty because of ambiguity about whether there was one task each or several.

There are meanings that cannot be expressed conveniently in English, and this is one of them. So we have to express them awkwardly, as in the example cited. The difficulty does not occur with things (***Everything*** *was working at* **its** *best*), thanks to *it/its*.

But English is lacking in a singular possessive or pronoun covering male/female without differentiating. So we are stuck with constructions like

> *Every person we invited was surprised they had been chosen*
> *Everyone let themselves go*
> *Everybody expected what they got*
> *Knowing what they knew, everyone was biting their tongues*
> *Everybody blamed themselves for what happened.*

The resort to the plural is unavoidable.

[2] **Referring back to anyone/nobody** etc Much the same difficulty occurs with the pronouns *anyone/anybody/no-one/nobody*. These are singular in sense as well as grammar, but again a lapse into the plural is often the least inconvenient way of referring back to them:

> *Anybody prefers to do that sort of thing for themselves*
> *Nobody likes to see their children in trouble*
> *No-one can be expected to admit everything about their past*
> *Anyone ought to be able to decide for themselves.*

There is always the option of substituting *his/himself* etc in deference to the tradition that the masculine includes the feminine unless the sense of the context excludes it. It is no injury to grammar even if it is a slight to feminists.

If *anyone* is preferred to *anybody*, this opens up solutions with *one/oneself*, as in *Anyone prefers to do it for oneself*. The same possibility exists for *no-one: No-one can be expected to admit . . . one's past*. But *one* is more impersonal than *anyone*, and repeated *ones*, unless carefully deployed, soon become comic. (See ONE/ ONESELF in Part I.) So the plural is the way out that most easily suggests itself, the more so when the pronoun/possessive is well separated from the subject.

[3] **Singular object with plural complement & vice versa** When the verb is *to be*, must the subject of the sentence be singular or plural to match the complement (see LINKING VERBS)? Should *Motorcycles are a menace* be rephrased as *Motorcycles are menaces*? The answer is less obvious in examples like *It is the carollers at the door/Their one hope was the precautions they had taken*. But all that matters is that the verb matches the subject, as it does in all the examples. There is no need for a match with the complement too, as is plain in everyday sentiments like *They shall be one flesh/Children are a blessing*.

Still, there are complications. Consider the sentence *She used to have teacakes in the kitchen, which was what she liked best.* Here a subsentence is introduced by a pronoun of the *which/what/who/ that* variety, as many subsentences are. Such pronouns can be singular or plural, but their verb must match the subject the pronoun represents. So *was* is right in the example only if the meaning is that *having teacakes in the kitchen* was what she liked best. If it was just the teacakes she liked best *were* is necessary. If what she liked best was the kitchen, the wording would need varying to avoid ambiguity, e.g. *. . . which was the room she liked best.*

What if there is more than one subject in a sentence? What happens then depends on whether the subjects are alternatives or compounds. *Doctor and patient/Doctor and patients/Doctors and a patient* are all compounds and all clearly plural. *He or others/ Parents or guardian/Teacher or pupils* are all mixed alternatives, and here the answer is less simple. Normally such alternatives too take a plural verb, but neither choice is ideal. In constructions on the pattern of *there is /are . . .* the verb may match the nearest of the alternative subjects, as in *There's always the teacher or some older pupils.* As with [1] *Referring back to "everyone" etc* English does not always offer a grammatical or logical solution without rephrasing.

[4] **When is *what* singular and when plural?**   This question arises because *what* can mean *that which* or *those which.* Sentences often start along the lines of *What is wanted (is a new effort).* Here the singular verb makes it obvious that *what* must be singular too. So must the next verb (i.e. *What + is wanted + is . . .*), which is unaffected by a subsequent complement in the plural:

> *What is wanted is fewer mistakes* (not *. . . are fewer . . .*).

The confusion is due to the existence of similar sentences such as *What I remember (is the marvellous weather)/. . . (are the many sunny days).* Here *what* may turn out to be plural, depending on the speaker's intention, which does not become known till the second half of the sentence is reached (*. . . is . . . weather* or *. . . are . . . days*). A simple test is to turn the sentence round, as in *Sunny days are what I remember/Marvellous weather is what . . .* But if the speaker is thinking of the sunny days as a collective phenomenon, the singular is also correct. So

> *What I remember is the sunny days*
> *What impressed them was the clean trains*

In establishing whether *what* is singular or plural the test is whether its sense is *that which* (singular) or *those which* (plural). The verb follows suit and the rest is plain sailing:

> *Developers are spoiling what seem to us the loveliest places*
>   (not *seems*)
> *The referee, for what were presumably clear offences,*
>   *awarded two penalties* (not *was*)
> *What worries us is the huge bills* (not *are*).

[5] **Uncertain subject** A common construction, often puzzling, is the kind found in *one of the hardest workers that have ever lived*. It is clear that here the subject of the verb *have lived* is *that*, but uncertainty nags about whether *that* is singular or plural, i.e. does it refer to *one* or *workers*? Writers are sometimes tempted to change the verb to *has*. This unfortunately introduces error where none exists. Consider:

> *He is **one of** the hardest workers that have ever lived*
> *He is **among** the hardest workers that have ever lived.*

The wording in bold is interchangeable, because the sense is the same. Substitution of *has* makes nonsense, which becomes obvious after *among*.

A comparable quicksand is *Those boys – one or other of them have left the door open*. Here the thinking is plural and the presence of *them* attracts the plural verb. So the sentence passes in speech, though it would not do so in careful writing. The subject is *one or other*, a choice of singulars, not a plural. The verb ought to be singular too (*has*).

[6] **Collective nouns** Some nouns denote a collection, like *flock*, which means many birds/many sheep, considered as a group. Similar specimens include *army/crowd/government/herd/jury/ majority/population/party/staff*. All are singular words (*an army/ this crowd* etc) but they do not always have to take a singular verb. Sometimes their sense is more plural than singular, with the emphasis on the parts rather than the whole. Hence

> *The team are all on special diets*
> *The staff are returning to work one by one*
> *The Government are falling out among themselves.*

It may strain grammar but the plural verb is idiomatic in such uses (some grammarians ease the pain by terming the words "nouns of multitude" in this role). Examples of the same words with a singular sense would be:

The team is going to be announced tomorrow
The staff is mainly unskilled
The Government is breaking up.

Often it makes no difference which form is chosen (*Is the jury out?* / *Are the jury out?* are interchangeable). But misuse occurs if a later reference fails to match whichever choice was made, e.g.

The team has been announced by its coach (not *their*)
The staff are returning to their work (not *its*).

It all depends on what the speaker has in mind, as R. A. Close puts it in *English As a Foreign Language* (George Allen & Unwin). But he wisely adds: "In unscripted speech even good speakers change their mental image in the middle of a sentence".

[7] **A lot of / heaps of / a number of** etc   See LOT / A LOT OF in Part I. Such phrases (also *masses of / bags of* etc) are substitutes for *many / much*, whose limitations they avoid. They are capable of being either singular or plural, the choice depending on whether their sense at the time is *much* or *many*. So

There's heaps more to eat (*much*)
There are heaps more presents to open (*many*)
A lot of this is true (*much*)
A lot of these are broken (*many*).

The same rule applies to fractional quantities like *half of / part of / some of*.

Possessives   Not much is required to show possession in English. The convenience of the apostrophe, with or without *s*, is one of the glories of the language. But the rules, simple as they are, are too taxing for many. Hence the omitted apostrophes in examples like *for appearances sake / one of the Smiths children* and the unwanted intrusion in *the car needs it's service* etc.

The general rule is that possession is indicated by

[1] *of* in either singular or plural (*the soldiers of the king / valley of the kings*), or

[2] by an added *'s* in singular words (*the king's soldiers*), or

[3] an added apostrophe (') in plural words ending in *s* (*the kings' tombs*). Plural words not ending in *s* are treated either like

singulars (*children's / phenomena's*), or as though they did end in *s* (*bureaux'*).

Apart from failure to recognize a possessive (or genitive) relationship, as in the examples of omissions noted earlier, the only cause of difficulty is what happens when a singular word ends in *s*. The policy of adding *'s* regardless, on the model of *St James's*, does not match usage. First there are admitted exceptions treated as plurals: *Moses' leadership / Hercules' labours / Jesus' disciples / Dickens' plots*. These are easier to say than the *St James's* (ziz) form and many people prefer to pronounce the possessives of similar names as though they were plurals, e.g. *H. G. Wells' anticipations* rather than *H. G. Wells's* .... Similarly *Harrods' sale / Selfridges' bargains* (businesses often "pluralize" their names like this, i.e. from originals like *Harrod / Selfridge* via *Harrod's / Selfridge's* etc).

The tendency is to avoid adding another *z* sound to words that already end in one. Hence *The Evening News' account / measles' after-effects / Buggins' turn*. But where the terminal sound is *s* there is less resistance to an added *'s* (iz), as seen in *Guy Fawkes's treason / Marx's economics / Mr Watts's fault*. If the following word happens to start with *s* the possessive *'s* is readily sacrificed, as in the traditional *for conscience' sake / for goodness' sake*.

Joint possession   This is indicated by *'s* attached to the last owner mentioned, as in *Jack and Jill's pail*. Similarly in compound terms like *the King of England's throne*. Then there is *someone else's problem* etc. In all these the *'s* is remote from the actual owner, but idiom permits this.

Limitations   *Of / 's* are not always interchangeable but it is hard to generalize about the basis. It does not depend on whether the noun is animate or personal – witness *a ship's captain / Tuesday's child*. Fowler objected to *Austria's farmers* instead of *the farmers of Austria*, holding that it made Austria seem like a person ("incongruous personification"). Nobody could make such a contention today, when *Austria's farmers*, like *London's voters* (not to mention *Dublin's fair city* and *England's green and pleasant land*), is a routine construction.

In a language of irregularities like English it is common sense to regularize convenient wording like the *'s* possessive. The spread of *'s* is owed to newspaper headlines, with their need for compact phrases, and in particular to the influence of the pithy prose style of *Time Magazine*. If only the same form could be applied to the pronouns *this / that / which / those*, which all have to make do with an *of* construction! This development would only bring them into line with *it* and *one*, which both have possessive versions – *its* / *one's*. So you can say of a keyless car *Where's its key?* / *Where's that one's key?*, but not "Where's that's key?" (See IT / IT'S and THAT / WHICH in Part I.)

Ambiguities   In phrases like the following the use of the *'s* possessive can be ambiguous:

> *one of the directors' wives*
> *one of the learners' difficulties.*

The intended sense is presumably *the wife of one of the directors* but the wording could also be construed as *one of the wives of one of the directors* (a Muslim perhaps). In the second example, less hazardous, the usual understanding would be *one of the difficulties of the learners*, but *one of the difficulties of one of the learners* is equally possible. Another possibility, if the phrase is heard rather than read, is *one of the learner's difficulties*, i.e. a difficulty of a typical learner. Such expressions are best rephrased.

Proforms   Sentences become unwieldy or awkward when they contain needless repetition, a problem tackled by leaving out any words that can be taken as understood or putting in shorter ones to stand for the full versions. Leaving out is called ELLIPSIS (q.v.). The putting-in method is illustrated by

> *The head of the department reported that **he** needed more time.*

Here *he* is a pronoun standing for *The head of the department*. PRONOUNS (q.v.) are the obvious example of word substitution and the largest class of their kind. But they are only one device among several. The term modern grammarians use for them all is *proforms* (though they unaccountably spell it with a hyphen).

Proforms substitute not only for nouns but for verbs and entire sentences. Among the commonest examples are *do* / *so* / *then* / *there*:

> *He's a jolly good fellow and **so** say all of us* (i.e. . . . *and all of us say he's a jolly good fellow*)
> *I don't think the boss knows yet, **does he** (the boss know yet)?*
> *Shall I drive to the village and see if they have a Sunday paper left?* / ***Do** (drive to the village* etc)

*If you're at home before lunch I'll look in **then** (before lunch)*
*She says she never goes near the West End but my brother saw her **there** (in the West End).*

Similarly *that* in its pronoun role and *it* can help to save repeating long phrases:

*I asked you to start the washer and turn the lights off and you haven't **done it** (started the washer etc)*
*Hitchhiking across France would be fun, so why don't we try **that**? (hitchhiking etc).*

As/which often represent whole phrases, as in

*The painter says he'll finish tomorrow, **which** is a relief (i.e. that he'll finish tomorrow)*
*They're thinking of emigrating to Australia, **as** I am too (i.e. thinking of emigrating etc).*

Don't/didn't etc save repetition in tag questions:

*I told you I'd be back soon, **didn't** I? (tell you etc)*

The words replaced are not necessarily an exact repetition of words uttered earlier in the sentence, and a degree of guesswork can be left to the reader or listener. There is a narrow strand between enough and too much, overstepped in *I'm longing for a holiday and my wife does too*. Do cannot stand for *is* or any other auxiliary, and the only other grammatical possibility here – ... *does long for one* ... – cannot reasonably be inferred. This kind of confusion is common in American speech. The solution is a simple ellipsis:

*I'm longing for a holiday and my wife **is** (longing etc) too.*

Where *do* is a proform it must of course match the replaced verb in tense and person.

In general there is something wrong with a sentence if the words represented by the proform are not obvious. But more guesswork can be accepted in speech than in writing, because the spoken word need not face a possible second scrutiny.

Preposition See PARTS OF SPEECH.

Pronouns There are many kinds of pronoun but all that can be considered here is some of the commonest difficulties they cause. In what follows each set is headed by typical words and the name they are known by.

[1] **I/you/he/she/it** etc (**personal**) These, unlike nouns, are complicated by grammatical case. The complete system is set out in the table below, where it can be seen that personal pronouns are numbered according to a speaker's viewpoint. Hence *I/we* (the speaker) is 1st person, *you* (the person spoken to) 2nd person, and *he/she/they* (spoken about) 3rd person. *Thou* is omitted as archaic. Its replacement *you* has either a singular or plural sense but is always a grammatical plural (i.e. requires a plural verb).

Case	Singular		
	1st person	2nd person	3rd person
Subjective (nominative)	*I*	*you*	*he/she/it*
Objective (accusative & dative)	*me*	*you*	*him/her/it*
Possessive (*genitive*)	*mine*	*yours*	*his/hers*
	my own	*your own*	*his/her/its own*
	my	*your*	*his/her/its*

Case	Plural		
	1st person	2nd person	3rd person
Subjective (nominative)	*we*	*you*	*they*
Objective (accusative & dative)	*us*	*you*	*them*
Possessive (genitive)	*ours*	*yours*	*theirs*
	our own	*your own*	*their own*
	our	*your*	*their*

Note: The last possessive series (*my/your* etc) consists of what are in effect possessive adjectives (**my** *hat/***your** *fault/***its** *success*) The words cannot stand alone, i.e. we cannot say "That hat is my". But the addition of *own* makes possible a full pronoun use (*my own = mine*) as well as adding emphasis. The first possessive series has no form for *it*, because we cannot say about a door "The handle is its".

Uncertainties about personal pronouns centre on when to use the objective forms. These go after all prepositions, as in *to her/*

from him (never "to she"/"from he"). So there is nothing wrong with *between you and me/from me and her* etc. Nor is there any fault in *She's as rich as him/Nobody but us can go* etc. It is absurd to regard these as ellipted versions of *She's as rich as (he is)* etc.

Of course the objective forms are needed wherever the pronouns are the direct or indirect object of a sentence. Hence *Eve left **him** his supper* (indirect object, equivalent to *for him*), and *Adam left **her** to her spinning* (direct object). But in addition objective forms are usual in many phrases where the pronouns are not objects but complements, following the verb *to be* (see LINKING VERBS).

It's me	*Are those them?*
It's them	*These are them*
It wasn't us	*They aren't them*
That's him	*These will be them*
Is that her?	*That will be her*
That's me	*It won't be me.*

As these are the universal spoken forms and the usual written ones too they cannot be regarded as mistakes for *It is I/That's they* etc. They are simply exceptions. To use versions like *It's I/That's they* is to care more for rules than reality. Only literary writing holds out for sentences as precise as

> *It was she who answered the door*
> *Is it they who live here?*

But then writing is composed after reflection. What comes off the tongue reflects the realities of how we think:

> *It won't be me who benefits*
> *It was her who was blamed*
> *Was it him we saw outside?* etc.

It is worth noting that purist objections seem to be restricted to these simple examples. No-one seems to fret when the objective pronoun follows *can be/might be* etc: *It can't be her/It could be us/It must be them* etc. Even those whose zeal makes them answer *Who's there?* with *It is I* stop short of "It might be I"/"It would be we".

[2] **myself/yourself/themselves/oneself (reflexive)**   Used mainly for emphasis, reflexive pronouns are also essential to a few verbs like *avail/pride (oneself)* and to sentences where subject and object refer to the same person (*She helped herself to sugar*). *Myself* and *oneself* are often forced to masquerade for *I* in a misguided show of

modesty. As the words have an extra syllable they are surely more noticeable. But this does not deter sentences like *Judy and myself plan to go*, instead of the normal *Judy and I* .... Here *myself* becomes the subject, which is permissible as long as it is accompanied by another noun or personal pronoun in the same role (e.g. *Judy*). It is unidiomatic to make *myself/ourselves* etc the subject of a sentence on their own, though they can occupy first position, as in *Myself and two others are going.*

> The full set is:
> *myself*
> *yourself*
> *himself/herself/itself/oneself*
> *ourselves*
> *yourselves*
> *themselves* (not "theirselves").
> *Yourself*, though singular in sense, needs a plural verb.

[3] **who / whom / whose / which / what / that (relative)**   Relative pronouns would be better renamed conjunctive pronouns, since they are the ones that join a subsentence to a noun phrase, as in

> *This is the tool **that** you lost*
> *It was Monday, **which** is always my worst day.*

Some limitations: *Whose*, the possessive, can refer to things as well as people. So can *that*, but *which* can only refer to things. In *Here's someone **that** I'd like you to meet* a replacement for *that* would be *whom*, but not *which* (despite *Our Father which art in Heaven*).

Whom is the objective form of *who*, but during the years when grammar has been virtually abandoned in British schools a generation or more has grown up in ignorance of the difference. See WHO/WHOM in Part I. Sentences like *The clerk to **who** I gave the letter/... **who** I gave it to* are an irritant to those who recognize where to choose *whom*, but the usage is only on a par with *It's me* instead of *It's I*. This, as noted in [1], is universally tolerated.

Which, like *who*, is to some extent interchangeable with *that*. As explained in Part I (see THAT/WHICH), *which* is mainly for introducing supplementary pieces of information, and *that* is for adding defining essentials. Hence *The flowers **that** bloom in the spring* (spring-blooming flowers in particular)/*All **that** I have is thine* (not all, but my all). There is an obvious difference of sense in *The flowers, **which** bloom in the spring, are . . .* , especially when the subsentence is marked off by commas, as it usually is with *which*.

That/whom are often ellipted, but this is only possible when they are not the subject of their subsentence, as in *The girl (that/whom) I love* . . . . In *The spy who loved me* . . . *who* is a subject and ellipsis would destroy the sense.

What is a shorthand for *that which* or *those which*, as in *Remember what I told you* (i.e. . . . *that which I told you*). It can also precede a noun rather like an adjective, as in *Send them what food there is* (i.e. . . . *that food which there is*). All these words except *that* also function as interrogatives, the next category.

[4] **who / whose / whom / which / what (interrogative)** As interrogative pronouns, the kind that asks questions, *which/what* can stand for people as well as things, but *who/whose/whom* can only stand for people. In spoken questions *whom* is even more unusual now than it is as a relative pronoun (see [3]). *Who* is general in questions like *Who are you talking about?/Who did you say you had dinner with last night?*

Which/what/whose can double as adjectives, the kind now called determiners, as in *Which shop do you mean?/What time is it?/Whose baby are you?*

[5] **this / that / these / those (demonstrative)** These too function sometimes as pronouns (*This is our new colleague/That is no way to behave*), sometimes as adjectives (*This young man is our new colleague/That shouting is unladylike*).

[6] **any / each / enough / either / neither / several / some (indefinite)** The numbers *one/two/three* etc are also, oddly, indefinite pronouns. Like previous specimens the indefinites can function as independent pronouns or as adjectives (determiners) – the difference between *We have enough to do* and *There isn't enough time*. When describing a pronoun they have to be followed by *of*, as in *all of them/both of us/each of you*. The indefinites vary greatly in their details of usage, but without causing any particular problems.

Pronunciation There are individual entries in Part I for words prone to mispronunciation. There are also separate entries in Part II covering the following general aspects of pronunciation:

AMERICAN ENGLISH	CONSONANT SOUNDS	VARIABLE VOWELS
CONSONANT CONFLICTS	STRESS SHIFTS	VOWEL SOUNDS.

This entry is introductory, with general notes on Mispronunciations.

The form of spoken English allegedly represented in ordinary dictionaries is what is called Received Pronunciation. This is what English speakers in general would recognize as good English, and what foreigners usually choose to learn. Many native speakers of English do not speak like this themselves, but people who look up dictionaries do not usually want to know how words are pronounced by, say, Geordies, Midwesterners, Australians or other regional speakers. They are more likely to want to know what they think of as the proper way of saying them.

Though it is currently fashionable to argue that one way of speaking is as good as another, this is only true within a community that understands its particular way. The essence of any code of communication is uniformity. There is no advantage in local variation, and in an era of mass communication no reason for it. Standard speech is as much a practical ideal as standard spelling and grammar, though the reality is still far short of this. The nearest we have to it is the historic mainstream of English speech, the consensus of informed speakers.

This would once have been called the educated way of speaking, but "educated" is now a devalued word, being widely equated with attendance at school. Many people today who have received their quota of British schooling pronounce words in ignorance of the traditional norm. This is particularly true of words not much in use in their home backgrounds. Their renderings tend to be guesses based on spelling or on the sound of similar-looking words. Such pronunciations used to be considered simple errors, but academics today are reluctant to concern themselves with what is correct or not correct.

The modern approach is "descriptive", as opposed to "prescriptive". By "descriptive" is meant a neutral recording of whatever is heard, a policy that gives equal weight to mispronunciations along with the correct. As this is done in the name of consensus the effect is to encourage common mistakes. Dictionaries soon record them as options, which inquiring speakers, faced with an unfamiliar word, then feel authorized to select. This is said to be evidence of a "living language", one of the few contexts where the effects of ignorance are ascribed to vitality rather than decay.

Apart from the role of dictionaries, which is less neutral than the compilers like to claim, the biggest influence in hastening unnecessary change is television and its lesser partner radio.

Announcers' mispronunciations do not seem to be subject to the same kind of editing as professional writers' misspellings.

In this Guide good spoken English is not taken to include every current aberration. Books like this exist to point out errors, not to condone them. This function is all the more necessary because a social taboo hinders one speaker from correcting another. It is an odd interpretation of good manners that a wrong name or football score is unhesitatingly contradicted, whereas a wrong pronunciation is ignored for fear of giving offence. Perhaps few are sure enough of their ground to speak up. This Guide sets out to help them.

Mispronunciations   Many words can be and are mispronounced without causing the speaker to be thought ignorant, or his social origins to be questioned. There are some mispronunciations however that dependably have these effects. They include:

Dropped aitch: In by far the majority of words spelt with an initial *h* the *h* should be sounded. Omission to do so is probably regarded more severely than spelling mistakes (to which even the educated are prone), unreasonable though this may be. In a handful of words the initial *h* is always silent (omitted), e.g. *honour/honest/ heir*. It is also systematically silent when words like *him/had* are unstressed (see VARIABLE VOWELS), and occasionally in other un-stressed syllables, e.g. *The show was (h)ilarious.* Unusually, the *h* is acceptably silent in *at (h)ome* even though the word is stressed. These exceptions apart, an omitted *h* is considered dropped (as op-posed to silent) and the following are all mispronunciations: *(h)addock / (h)aven't / (h)alf-(h)earted / (h)ope / (h)eard / (h)ide / (h)ospital / (h)urry / (h)urt* etc. So are *(wh)o / (wh)ole* etc.

The h in what etc: Is it an error to pronounce *what* as wot instead of hwot? Many people assume it is at least careless. They feel that if they were concentrating they would say hwot, and give the same treatment to similar words like *where/when/why/which.* This is a delusion. Most people have never pronounced the *h* in this way in living memory, and except among zealots and dialect speakers the *h* is silent in British usage.

North American dictionaries however uphold hw as their first-choice sound in words ranging from *whale* to *why*, though in practice this is not the principal U.S. pronunciation. The words affected include *white/wheat/while/whisk/whim.* The hw sound is still common in Scotland, Ireland and the North.

Irregular glottal stop: The glottal stop is the swallowed consonant effect common in Cockney, Scots, and other dialects (see CONSONANT SOUNDS). It is the sort of pronouncing that drops the t from *water* and the tl from *bottle*. Other consonants subject to swallowing are b/d/k/p, especially in combination with *l*. Examples: *bulb/architect/people/wouldn't/didn't*. Objection to these distortions, as to other Cockney substitutions like f for th, may be in part socially motivated, but the justification for it is surely that they produce unclear speech. At the same time it has to be recognized that even careful speakers use glottal stops more widely than they care to admit.

Intrusive r: In phrases like *law and order/china ornament/the idea is*, where vowels adjoin at word junctions, an illegitimate *r*-sound is sometimes interposed, e.g. *lawr'n'order/chinarornament/the idearis/vanillarice* etc. The intrusion occurs mainly in rapid speech and the habit is perhaps less common than it was. It is more noticeable, and so less acceptable, when the *r* intrudes inside words, as in *draw(r)ing/saw(r)ing*.

Mistaken stress: English words of two or more syllables all have fixed stresses. So putting the stress on the wrong syllable is an error on a par with misspelling. Most mispronunciations, besides the kinds listed above, are errors of stress. Words prone to mistreatment include the following, where the required stress on the first syllable is more demanding than a stress on the second (common enough to be listed as an alternative in many dictionaries):

adversary	*demonstrable*	*hospitable*	*reputable*
applicable	*despicable*	*lamentable*	
comparable	*exquisite*	*preferable*	
controversy	*formidable*	*primarily*	

In the negatives *irrefutable/irreparable/irrevocable*, which should all be stressed on the second syllable, there is a similar tendency to go for the next one.

Stress cannot be reliably deduced from that of a similar or connected word. Thus *contribution* (kontrib*U*shn) is no guide to *contributing* (kən*trib*Uting) – which varies a vowel too. A common error is to render *contribute* (and similar words) as *kon*tribUt instead of kən*trib*Ut.

In STRESS SHIFT (q.v.) words are listed in which the stress distinguishes the verb from the noun, e.g. *Your conduct* (*kon*dukt,

noun) *is how you conduct* (kənd*ukt*, verb) *yourself.* Such pronunciations are not interchangeable.

Punctuation Each of the usual punctuation devices is considered
individually in separate entries. These will be found in Part II under

APOSTROPHE	FULL STOP/PERIOD
BRACKETS	HYPHENS
COLONS	INVERTED COMMAS
COMMAS	OBLIQUES
DASHES	QUESTION MARKS
ELLIPSES	SEMI-COLONS.
EXCLAMATION MARKS	

There is also a related entry for CAPITAL INITIALS. Mentions of
punctuation points in other entries are cross-referenced.

In general writers think of punctuation in terms of what they
are trying to make the words say, typographers in terms of the look
of the printed page, and publishers in terms of the attention span of
their customers, the readers. The three viewpoints are not easily
reconcilable. Writers want punctuation to save them from recon-
structing their intractable sentences. Typographers want
ornamental rows of regular characters, unblemished by dots or
type contrasts or paragraph indents. Publishers want text with as
many signposts as it takes to keep their readers from getting lost or
tired. In an alleged dictum of Lord Beaverbrook's, "Ten lines and
they need a rest". These are all legitimate concerns.

There is a limit though to what punctuation can do for anybody. It cannot improve bad grammar or repair clumsy composition. It cannot signal the grammatical progress of a sentence except
by getting in the way of the reading. It cannot indicate the stresses
and intonation of speech. The best it can do is to give the reader an
unobtrusive nudge in the right direction whenever the meaning is at
risk. This calls for a policy of restraint.

Punctuation is as much a matter of style as of grammar, and the
number of marks used will vary according to whether the text is a
legal document (hardly any), a reading primer (umpteen), or something in between. The spread of newspaper and periodical reading
during the 20th century has led to simpler writing. Sentences and
paragraphs have become shorter, constructions less elaborate. The
style of expression has moved closer to that of ordinary speech, so
that punctuation is now sparing, even if it is still short of the

principle of as many marks as are necessary but as few as are possible. Speech, we forget, has no capital letters or semi-colons or full stops, but achieves all its signposting with nothing more than pauses and changes of emphasis and pitch.

(See also STYLE: PARAGRAPHS.)

Puns   A form of word play traditionally received with a groan, the pun is esteemed on much the same level as ALLITERATION (q.v.). It is enjoyed by ordinary people (whose groans are usually feigned) but despised by the literary. The pun plays on words that sound the same but have different meanings, as in the story of the allergic beekeeper who broke out in *hives*. Arthur Koestler quotes Groucho Marx's remark about a safari in Africa: "We shot two *bucks* but that was all the money we had". Koestler calls this "the most primitive form of human humour: two disparate strings of thought brought together by an acoustic knot". The knot is not necessarily acoustic, since puns work in print as well as in speech. Undoubtedly, though, puns tend to change the subject, a distraction that probably accounts for the traditional groans.

Before the 1960s puns were banned by most British newspapers, not for being primitive but for being too subtle to be appreciated by readers. Readers are evidently regarded as more sophisticated nowadays, as puns have become staples of newspaper headlines – one of the few places where they escape prejudice. This return to fashion yields such specimens as: *Breaking the Bond of Friendship* (on the transfer of a football manager named Bond)/ *Nelson et Lumière* (on a *son et lumière* show aboard H.M.S. *Victory*).

Questions   See INVERSION.

Question marks (**?**)   These replace full stops at the ends of sentences that ask questions:

Who is there?
Why did the chicken cross the road?
Anyone for tennis?

When the question is part of quoted speech the mark goes inside the inverted commas, where it may be equivalent to a comma in force:

"Who's there?" she called.

When the question is indirect, i.e. is alluded to but is not quoted, no question mark is needed:

Instead of asking who is there, open the door and see.

When the question is direct, but is not a direct quotation, the mark goes at the end of the sentence, not at the end of the question:

Who is there, they ask? (not *Who is there? they ask*)
Why does this happen to us, we wonder?

As question marks have the strength of a full stop they should not appear anywhere in a sentence except at the end unless they are isolated by parenthesis, such as quotes or brackets. So quotes should be supplied when a direct question is introduced by words like *the question/the issue*, as in

To revive the question "Who killed Kennedy?" takes tenacity.

Alternatively the question mark can be eliminated with an indirect construction:

. . . the question of who killed Kennedy takes tenacity.

Reported speech   This is the reporting of a speaker's or writer's words, as opposed to their direct quotation. Though often taken to concern only the past it can also occur in the present, e.g.

Waiter to diners: *"Your table is ready".*
First diner: *"What does he say?"*
Second diner: *"He says our table is ready".*

No change occurs in the second diner's tenses, which remain in the present. If the question had been put in the past (*What did he say?*) the reply would have been *He **said** our table is ready*. When something that was said in the present tense remains true when it is reported there is no need for a change of tense – hence *is ready* rather than *was ready*. This is the point most often muddled in reported speech.

A more typical example of direct speech might be:

"Most wild animals avoid man", the gamekeeper told me.

This should be reported as

The gamekeeper told him (that) most wild animals avoid man

or (depending on who reports) *The gamekeeper told me . . . .* The main verb stays in the present tense. A change to the past as in *The gamekeeper told him most wild animals avoided man* raises a doubt about whether they still do. Similarly *She **told** me there **are** bargains in the market* is normal unless the reporter knows the bargains have gone.

Generally, reported or indirect speech requires a shift of tense by its main verb a stage further into the past. Thus *asks* becomes *asked*, *asking* becomes *was asking*, *asked* becomes *had asked* etc. But no further regression is possible if the verb is already in the past perfect (*had asked*). So there is no change in *"Things had looked so promising", he said / He said that things had looked so promising.*

In conversation the tense shift often gets no further than the past simple, as in *You said you bought it in the market* (instead of *had bought*). This is hardly noticed and even occurs in print. But the present perfect (*have asked*) must shift to its past counterpart, i.e. past perfect (*had asked*), as in *I've bought a car / He said he'd bought a car.*

Other changes: The auxiliary verbs *shall / will / can / may* shift when required from present to past, but as *should / would / could / might* are their only past forms no additional shift is possible. *Must / ought* remain unchanged, having no other form. So does *used (to)*, i.e. there is no "had used to".

Of course changes to words other than verbs may be involved. Thus *"How can I finish it today?" said Veronica* becomes *Veronica **asked** how **she could** finish it **that day*** (or whatever the specific day). Adjectives / adverbs liable to need changing include (substitute shown in brackets):

ago (before)	*this (that)*
here (there)	*these (those)*
last night (the previous night)	*today (that day)*
now (then)	*tomorrow (next day).*

Semi-colons (;)   There are those who consider the use of semi-colons a minor art form, and those who consider it an unnecessary complication. The semi-colon is prized less as a stop than as a form of conjunction. If we take the two related statements *don't do it like that* and *do it like this* they can be expressed in writing in several possible ways:

Don't do it like that. Do it like this.
Don't do it like that, but do it like this

Don't do it like that; do it like this.
Don't do it like that – do it like this.

It is a matter of taste which arrangement is preferred. Probably most writers still choose the semi-colon. E. B. White says of it: "This simple method of indicating relationship between statements is one of the most useful devices of composition". He adds that the semi-colon is "still required" even if the second statement is linked by a conjunct like *accordingly/besides/then/furthermore*. It is often so used, but it is hard to see why two useful devices, the semi-colon and the CONJUNCT (q.v.) should both be required for the one purpose. The desired indication of relationship seems to be amply achieved in the form: *I'd rather go this way. Besides, it's quicker*.

H. W. Fowler, a passionate partisan of the semi-colon, and a tireless exponent of its use, contended that shorter separate sentences with full stops were too demanding of the reader, who was left to work out the relationships himself. This can only be true, surely, of bad writing. When thoughts are arranged in logical sequence their relationship becomes obvious. Within a paragraph moreover every sentence is related in some sense to the one before. Are they all to be linked by semi-colons? As a matter of fact this happens all too readily. Fowler himself thought nothing of stringing four sentences together regardless of the differing degrees of relationship, which a sequence of semi-colons cannot indicate. Once started on this relationship tack, however, it is hard to know where to stop.

What is more, the semi-colon cannot be relied on. It is often used just because a sentence has become too overloaded to be kept afloat with more commas. A specimen quoted by *Webster's New Collegiate Dictionary* as an example of the semi-colon in approved action illustrates this lifeboat technique: *Thus our search was for people who could think in very fundamental ways, who could buttress their views with careful analysis; people who were able to hang in during deliberations with their own ideas, but who could also comfortably and effectively work within the confines of a small group.* That ship was already listing dangerously by the time the second *people* was hoisted hopefully aboard.*

Because of these problems much of today's writing – probably

*Why not *Thus our search was for people who could think in very fundamental ways, buttress their views with careful analysis, hang in during deliberations with their own ideas, but also work comfortably and effectively within the confines of a small group?*

most – is done with little or no use of the semi-colon, as is this Guide. It may or may not be a useful device, but it is certainly not an essential one.

Sentence patterns Words are put together into sentences in accepted patterns. There are set sequences for statements (declarative sentences), for questions (interrogatives), for commands or instructions (imperatives) and for exclamations. The components forming these patterns are discussed under ANALYSIS. Other entries touching on sentence patterns include:

> IDIOM   LINKING VERBS
> IMPERATIVES   WORD ORDER.
> INVERSION (q.v. for questions)

This entry outlines the theoretical basis of the commoner types of sentence, by way of prompter for those inclined to try and make sense of their construction.

How far language is shaped by thought, or thought is shaped by language, is something that cannot be gone into here. But in a statement like

> *They* (subject) *rang* (verb) *the bell* (direct object)

the sequence of components seems – at least to native English speakers – the same as the order in which the thought occurs. Most English statements fit into arrangements of similar simplicity. Only seven permutations are discerned by scholars accepting the six sentence components set out under ANALYSIS:*

> (i) *Subject* + **verb** (typical of intransitive verbs)
>
> *The bell* **rang**
> *The bell* **was ringing**
>
> (ii) *Subject* + *verb* + **complement** (of subject – see LINKING
>   VERBS)
>
> *That was* **the bell**
> *You are* **right**
>
> (iii) *Subject* + *verb* + **adverbial**
>
> *The bell rang* **next door**
> *It was* **on a Wednesday**

*Others not recognizing the "adverbial" as a component arrive at a still smaller count.

(iv) *Subject + verb +* **direct object**

They rang **the bell**
Dan heard **them**

(v) *Subject + verb + direct object +* **complement** *(of object)*

Noises make me **fidgety**
You'll think me **a fusspot**

(vi) *Subject + verb + direct object +* **adverbial**

They put their bell **behind the staircase**
An electrician fixed it **last week**

(vii) *Subject + verb +* **indirect object** *+ direct object*

The loudness gave **me** *a shock*
I'll fetch **you** *the mail.*

Complications begin when more than one of these patterns occurs in the same sentence, as in

You are right (ii) **that** *noises make me fidgety* (v).
When *the bell rang next door* (iii) *Dan heard it* (iv).
I'll fetch you the mail (vii) **if** *it's on a Wednesday* (iii).

Each of these examples is a sentence in the usual understanding of the term – a complete grammatical utterance written with an initial capital and ending with a full stop or equivalent. But each is composed of two parts, a main sentence and what is termed in this Guide a *subsentence*. The subsentence is the part introduced by a connecting word (*that/when/if* etc). The effect of most subsentences (traditionally called subordinate clauses or dependent clauses) is to modify the sense of the main sentence, either limiting it or extending it.

An exception is when a subsentence functions as a noun equivalent, as in

How much I like her *does not concern you* (subject)
I've admitted **how much I like her** (object)
The question is **how much I like her** (complement).

Here the subsentence and its function in the sentence is shown in italic.

Some sentences do not fit convincingly into any of the seven basics. For example:

Patterns with it/there   The pronoun *it* or the adverb *there* often function as dummy subjects. Examples:

> *It's lovely in Greece*
> *It's silly to pay the full fare*
> *It's pouring outside*
> *It doesn't matter how wet it is.*

Here *it* is a pronoun without any noun to stand for. Similarly:

> *There's nothing doing*
> *Once there were three bears*
> *There's been a lot of talk.*

Here *there* does not refer to place. (This may be seen in the sentence *There's nobody there*, where *there* has to be repeated to bring in a sense of place.)

The purpose of these constructions is to enable the speaker to (a) impart information in the fragmentary order in which it occurs to him (*silly . . . pay* etc), or (b) build up to the point he wants to emphasize (*. . . three bears / . . . lot of talk*). *It* provides a dummy subject permitting the usual grammatical order to be honoured, and *there* similarly plugs a gap in the subject position even though as an adverb it cannot function as a noun equivalent.

Grammarians account for these anomalies by regarding them as "variations" on the nearest basic sentence pattern. So *It's silly to pay the full fare = To pay the full fare is silly*. But this dodge does not work with *It's pouring outside*, unless an invented subject is substituted, like "The rain". For practical purposes then these are additional patterns. So are sentences beginning *It seems . . . / It appears . . .* etc. Then there is a third use of dummy *it* as found in the so-called cleft sentence: *It turned out to be Alan who . . . / It was then that . . . / It'll be you who . . . .*

Apposition   Two noun equivalents are often placed together with no connecting device except proximity, as in

> *My **brother Esau** is a hairy man*
> *Why don't you invite **that girl at the office, Mr Smith's secretary**?*

Here *brother / Esau* are nouns referring to the same person and standing in the same relation to the rest of the sentence (i.e. subject). They are said to be in apposition. Similarly with *that girl at the office / Mr Smith's secretary*, both of which function as direct objects of their sentence.

Absolute construction   Proximity is also the only grammatical link in this kind of construction:

The hot water supply being mended, she took a bath.

Here the sense implies a sequence but there is no grammatical link between the two descriptions, which are said to be absolutes. (See STYLE.)

Simile See IMAGERY.

Spelling In the overwhelming majority of English words there is no choice of spelling. With few important exceptions one form is accepted for each word. Even the variants of AMERICAN ENGLISH (q.v.) are minor. So the concept of a spelling mistake remains little challenged in an era of muddled meanings and pronounce-as-you-please. Scholars who contend it hardly matters how much a word varies when spoken still seem to acknowledge the obvious advantage of uniformity in writing it. Schemes for spelling reform, though often proposed, make few converts – at present there is no agreed style for disputed words even in British government publications.

Of course there is no denying that the alphabet has nowhere near enough symbols to represent the basic sounds. It makes spelling at best a limited guide to pronunciation and vice versa. The surprising thing is that the illogicalities this leads to pass largely unnoticed, which does not suggest that they trouble the native. If misspelling is widespread, as today it is, it is more likely because modern schooling devotes so little attention to the mechanics of English, rather than because spelling is impossibly irregular. Certainly the commonest errors tend to occur with a relatively small number of words. Many will be found among the following.

Common misspellings (shown in brackets)

accidentally (accidently)
accommodation (accomodation)
authoritative (authoritive)
bachelor (batchelor)
believe (beleive)
born (borne)
borne (born)
business (buisness)

castor oil (caster)*
comparative (comparitive)
consensus (concensus)*
dessert (desert)
dependant, noun (dependent)
dependent, adjective (dependant)
divergences (divergencies)
embarrass (embarass)

exercise (excercise)
expatriate (ex-patriot)*
forty (fourty)
gauge (guage)
glamorous (glamourous)*
grateful (gratefull/greatfull)
harass (harrass)
humorous (humourous)*
idiosyncrasy (idiosyncracy)
its, possessive (it's)*
license, verb (licence)*
maintenance (maintainance)
mantelpiece (mantlepiece)
parallel (paralell)
particularly (particuly)
past, adjective/adverb/
    preposition (passed)

Philippines (Phillipines)
playwright (playwrite)
principal (principle)*
principle (principal)
privilege (priviledge)
publicly (publically)
receive (recieve)
separate (seperate)
stationary (stationery)
stationery (stationary)
supersede (supercede)
Tangier (Tangiers)*
theirs (their's)
there's (theres)
twelfth (twelth).

*See entry for this word in Part 1.

Endings Many words like *choosing (choose)/hummed (hum)/crazy (craze)/adjustable (adjust)* are formed from others by the addition of a standard ending or suffix. The spelling of the join, though not always predictable, generally follows a pattern, as summarized in these notes.

(i) *Doubled consonants*: The process of doubling the final consonant when adding a suffix applies when the join is made with the endings *ed/en/er/ing/ible/able/y*. These cover most verb inflections and the formation of many adjectives. Hence

hum but *hummed/humming/hummer/hummable*
compel but *compelled/compelling*
submit but *submitted/submitting*
fat but *fatter/fattest/fatten*
mud but *muddy* etc.

Exceptions like *veil/veiled* are accounted for by the following rules. No extra consonant is required in:

(a) words with more than one consonant at the end, like *paint/painted/painter* etc,

(b) words with more than one vowel before the final consonant, like *veil/train/beam*,

(c) words of more than one syllable with no spoken stress on the last syllable, like *sharpen/gather/covet*. An exception here is words ending in *l*, which double the letter even if the last syllable is not stressed, as in *revel/revelled/reveller* etc.*

(d) In this reckoning *y* and *w* do not count as consonants.

(ii) *Words ending in silent e*: Many words, like *refute/convalesce/persuade/scrape*, end in an *e* that is not pronounced. In forming others by adding suffixes to such words the silent *e* is left out. Hence

refute + ed gives *refuted* (not "refuteed")

refute + ing gives *refuting*

refute + able gives *refutable* (with of course no doubling of the consonant such as occurs in *rebut/rebuttable* etc).

Unfortunately there are awkward exceptions to this pattern. The spellings *mileage/likeable* are the commoner forms though the *e* is unnecessary. But then so it is in *vengeance/changeable* etc, where it is alleged to "keep the *g* soft", a function somehow not required of it in *avenging/changing* etc. We are stuck with all these but can still resist *moveable* (compare *removable*), for the spread of which Ernest Hemingway's title *A Moveable Feast* is to blame.

An area of comparable error is the spelling of adjectives formed from nouns by adding *y* (*cream/creamy, rain/rainy, show/showy*). These, besides following the doubled consonant rules, also shed any final silent *e*. Hence

gore/gory   spike/spiky   stone/stony

ice/icy   sponge/spongy wave/wavy.

But there seems to be a temptation to spell such words with *e*, as in "dicey"/"pricey". See DICE in Part I.

(iii) *Verbs ending in ize/ise*: This issue is a matter of choice. It arises in verbs formed by adding *ize/ise*: to an existing word, as in *standardize* (*standard + ize*). Pronunciation and etymology (word origins) both favour *ize*, which has the support of the *Oxford English Dictionary* and the Oxford University Press, *The Times* of London, the *Encyclopaedia Britannica* and North American usage, and this Guide. It must be acknowledged though that in British usage the *ise* spelling is much the more usual.†

---

*In U.S. usage the forms *reveled/traveling* etc are common. It does not affect pronunciation, so it hardly matters.

†The Oxford support for *ize* is a lapse from the supposed academic neutrality of the "consensus" policy (see Introduction). Evidently dictionary compilers do give rulings on other grounds when it suits them.

The difference is of long standing and shows no sign of being settled, though this would be one of the easiest English inconsistencies to put right. It is complicated by the existence of a batch of staple words properly spelt with an *s* but pronounced as though they were spelt with *z*. These include *advertise/analyse/compromise/devise/revise/supervise/surmise*. But, as can easily be seen, none of these consists of an existing word with *ise* added. They are all formed by adding *e* to words or word stems happening to end in *s*. Verbs to spell with *z* are those like *atomize / immortalize/ nationalize / personalize / polarize / regularize / standardize / terrorize / vandalize / visualize* in which the basic word is unmistakable. Then there are those in which the basic word has lost a few letters but can still be identified, e.g. *antagonize / categorize / communize / emphasize / immunize / jeopardize / sympathize*.

(iv) *Past inflections in ed/t*: The past tense or participle is normally formed with an added *ed*, as in *groan/groaned, like/ liked*. But a number of older words take *t* instead, as in *bend/bent, sleep/slept*. Still others offer a choice between the two: *burn/ burnt/burned, dream/dreamed/dreamt, spell/spelt/spelled*. See IRREGULAR VERBS for a list. It is sometimes supposed that these differences reflect differences of pronunciation. In fact the words spelt with a *t* are pronounced as such, and many of those spelt with *ed* are pronounced *t* too – specifically all those ending in any of the sounds f/k/p/s/sh/tsh or th as in "earth". Examples: *reached/ asked/helped/passed/liked/rushed*. In other verbs spelt with *ed* the pronunciation is d (*aired/dragged/failed*). If the verb's final sound is either d (as in *code*) or t (as in *post*), the *ed* is pronounced as a separate syllable, id (*coded/posted*).

(v) *Adjectives ending in able/ible*: These are formed by additions to verbs or nouns on the pattern of *detestable* (*detest+ able*) or *reducible* (*reduce + ible*). The spellings are not interchangeable, but there is no discernible (or *discoverable*) rule for the need for one ending rather than the other. Nor is there any difference of pronunciation – both are əbl, with the *l* syllabic (i.e. a trace of ə vowel before the *l*).

(vi) *Words ending in ary/ery/ory*: As with *able/ible*, endings as in *cemetery/cursory/legendary* differ in spelling but are not phonetic. If the third-from-last syllable is stressed (as in *machinery*) the pronunciation is əri. Otherwise the vowel is silent, giving ri (as in *legendary*, lejəndri).

(See also CLAMOUR in Part I for the derivations on the lines of *clamorous* etc and PLURAL FORMS for plural changes.)

Stress shifts   Verbs of two syllables like *rebel* keep the same spelling for other grammatical functions but change their stress. Hence the two different sounds for *rebel* in *What a **rebel** does is to re**bel**. As noun, or adjective (*the **rebel** leader*), the word is stressed on the first syllable, as verb on the second. This is usual, but there is no universal pattern.

In the following selection the words can all be nouns or verbs. As nouns all are stressed on the first syllable, as verbs all on the second. Those that can also be adjectives (*the present time / a subject race*) match the noun. Note that the vowel of the first syllable often varies along with the stress e.g. *kon*test / k*ən*test.

abstract	contrast	incense	refill
accent	converse	incline	refit
affix	convert	increase	refund
combine	convict	insult	refuse*
commune	desert*	misprint	reject
compound	digest	perfume	subject
compress	discard	permit	survey
concert	discount	pervert	suspect
conduct	discourse	present	torment
confines	entrance*	proceeds	transfer
conflict	escort	produce	transform
conscript	export	progress	transplant
consort	extract	project	transport
construct	ferment	prospect	upset
contest	import	protest	
contract	impress	record	

Some irregular stress shifts include those of

absent (adjective 1st syllable, verb 2nd)
compact (noun 1st, verb or adjective 2nd)
content (as *compact*, except that in the sense of contentment, as in *to her heart's content*, the noun is stressed on the 2nd)

*Only one kind of *desert* belongs here (i.e. *He would de**sert** in the Sahara **Desert***). The other kind of *desert*, the noun of *deserve*, is stressed on the second syllable. *Entrance*, the noun, is a different word in origin from in*trahns*, the verb. *Refuse* (like *use*) changes its z sound to s when it becomes a noun.

frequent (adjective 1st, verb 2nd)
minute (noun 1st, adjective 2nd)
respect (noun and verb both 2nd)
undress (noun and adjective 1st, level stress as verb).

Similar stress shifts occur in some three-syllable words:

alternate (verb 1st, adjective 2nd)
animate (verb and adjective both 1st, but verb only has
    secondary stress on 3rd – *animAt*)
consummate (verb 1st, adjective 2nd)
delegate (verb 1st, with secondary stress on 3rd, noun 1st
    without)
invalid (noun & adjective 1st, verb 3rd, but adjective in
    sense "not valid" 2nd).
overthrow (noun 1st, verb 3rd)
postulate (as *delegate*).

Compare these shifts with the change of pronunciation of the *s*
in *use/abuse/misuse* – *s* for nouns, *z* for verbs.

Style The pursuit of style as though it were some kind of literary
membership card is based on a misunderstanding. Style depends as
much on subject matter as on the author. A novelist's writing may
be recognizable in his novels but his admirers are unlikely to be able
to detect his authorship in, say, a tale for under-fives, a collection of
poetry, or an application for a bank loan. Writing changes when its
purpose changes. What the aspiring or self-improving writer needs
is not a distinctive style but a practical facility for arranging words.
He can set himself no worthier literary goal than to make words
express what he means. Plain accurate prose, as Bernard Shaw said
of common sense, is most uncommon.

The trouble is that before words can be made to say what an
author means he must first decide what he means to say. These are
two separate processes, but they tend to occur at the same time. The
forming of the thoughts blends with the composition of the sentences. The writer, not yet sure what he wants to say, may try out
various forms of words to see how they help his thoughts. If
inexperienced or undecided he will be more tempted by words that
fit together well than by words that fit the points he ought to be
making. His thoughts become sidetracked and the composing
becomes progressively harder.

The writer who knows what he wants to say has none of these

difficulties. He knows the points he wants to make and they probably suggest a natural sequence of presentation. He can concentrate on wording them clearly. Less clear-minded writers – and probably every writer's mind is a blank at one time or another – should try listing all the points their piece of writing needs to cover. To the unpractised such note-making may seem like a prolongation of the agony, doing the writing twice. In fact it eases the task. The writer can often see which points to group together, what order to present them in, and where gaps need filling. Good writing is much more a matter of clear exposition than of stylish expression.

Since style is no more than a manner of writing, nearly all the entries in Part II of this Guide touch on it. Among those especially concerned are CLICHÉS / ELLIPSIS / IMAGERY / CONTRACTIONS / PUNCTUATION / WORD ORDER. Some other aspects of clear composition are discussed below.

Sentences and paragraphs How many sentences make a paragraph? The only practical general answer to the question is: as many sentences as make an easily digestible piece of reading. This number will depend on the length of the sentences, on the complexity of the message, on the reader's attention span, on the circumstances of the reading. E. B. White, expressing a traditional view, contends that a subject breaks down into topics and that a paragraph is the natural unit for each topic: "The beginning of each paragraph is a signal to the reader that a new step in the development of the subject has been reached". But how long is a step? What constitutes a topic? Paragraphs are essentially a convenience for the reader, not the writer. It is no use going on with a step beyond the reader's inclination to digest.

Apart from dividing text into digestible pieces, paragraphs make it easier for a reader to find the place. Bookmarks may mark the page but not the place in the text. In magazines and newspapers, whose reading is likely to be subject to all sorts of interruption, frequent paragraph indentation is an essential marker device. It also makes the text look less daunting. When it falls at the foot of a column, which is considered untidy, the indentation is commonly eliminated by resetting the line to join up with the one before – a practice laymen never even notice, so little are they conscious of a "topic" requirement.

Each important stage of an exposition or narrative and each distinct change of topic does require a fresh start with a new paragraph, but the reader should not be kept waiting for these intervals. Fresh starts may be required at many intermediate points just because it has been long enough since the last one.

A similar general point can be made about sentences. There are writers who can and do write a sentence half a page long, but it is rarely a sentence in a genuine sense. It is more likely a series of sentences disguised by punctuation, i.e. several complete grammatical statements separated by semi-colons instead of full stops. It is more of a paragraph than a sentence. The natural length for a sentence is no more than can be comfortably spoken without pausing for breath. That is obviously true of speech and there is no reason for working to a greater length in writing. On the contrary it is only sensible to write to the sort of length readers are used to, since people are more receptive to the familiar. Unusually long sentences need to have a special justification for not only taking the reader's attention for granted but imposing extra demands on it.

Starts to avoid   Public speaking's classic openings (*Unaccustomed as I am . . ./I should just like to tell you how honoured I feel to be here today . . .*) have their counterparts in writing, only there are more of them. They all amount to attempts to put off getting on with whatever the author has to say, probably because he has not yet thought out what that is. An opening sentence is not a warm-up for the author but an appetizer for the reader. It should engage his interest by plunging straight into the subject.

The following examples of common delaying tactics assume the subject to be euthanasia:

> *The editor has asked me to write about euthanasia . . .*
> *When I was asked to write about euthanasia . . .*
> *Faced with the task of discussing euthanasia, my first*
> *   thought . . .*
> *The dictionary definition of euthanasia . . .*
> *To begin at the beginning, euthanasia . . .*
> *So euthanasia is back in the news . . .*
> *Euthanasia. The very word provokes . . .*
> *At 3.10 on the afternoon of Saturday 23 October, the death*
> *   by euthanasia occurred of . . .* (note: unless the exact time
> *   and date are significant in what follows this kind of
> *   opening is a false prospectus).

Ploys often attempted in the body of the text as well as in openings include:

It is an interesting fact that euthanasia . . .
An interesting aspect of euthanasia . . .
It has often been said of euthanasia . . .

Clearly anything that has often been said before is unlikely to grab the reader's attention. Similarly the reader is entitled to assume that anything written for him to read is considered interesting.

Constructions better replaced Various constructions, though grammatically correct, are weeded out by careful writers as too wordy, awkward or archaic.

(i) *the fact that*: This is innocent when the intention is to point out that something is a fact, but it is more often a rigmarole for introducing what is already acknowledged to be a fact, as in *They resent the fact that you're insisting.* Here *your insistence* could replace everything after *resent*, with a clear gain in simplicity and economy. But there may be no suitable noun available, as in *They made allowance for the fact that he's an orphan.* This could become . . . *for him/his being an orphan*, or it could be rephrased with a new verb: *They took into consideration that he's an orphan.* There is always a way out and it is always an improvement.

(ii) *with the result that/result in*: These are another unwanted complication. Consider *He fell off the swing, with the result that he broke his arm/His fall off the swing resulted in breaking his arm.* Why not just *He fell off the swing **and** broke his arm*? Or *His fall off the swing broke his arm*? Apart from such obvious simplifications there is no shortage of everyday verbs for the sense of *result in*, e.g. *cause/lead to/produce.*

(iii) *being that*: *Being that you're ready to go, I'll leave this.* This is still heard, perhaps as a spillover from dialect. It sometimes occurs as *being as* or *being as how.* The phrase is a conjunction and amounts to just a wordy and quaint way of saying *as/since/because.*

(iv) *seeing that*: *I'd better go first, seeing that I know the way.* This is common colloquially but less so in writing. Another version is *seeing as.* The phrase is interchangeable with *considering/as/since/because*, all of which are more modern.

(v) *were we etc to*: *Were we to start making exceptions, heaven knows where it would end/Were he to find out he'd complain.* This inversion is an archaic subjunctive. The modern form, regrettably wordier, is *If we were to start . . ./If he were to find out* . . . etc. Similar inversion is sometimes used instead of *If I had* . . . etc, as in **Had I** *but known*/**Had he** *but stopped to think*, another diehard archaic form.

(vi) *it being late, etc*:   As in *It being late, they stopped work*/ *You feeling frail, we'd better not go*. These constructions are known as "absolute". The participles (*being*/*feeling*) each have a subject (*it*/*you*) and complement (*late*/*frail*) and form part of a subsentence with no connection, other than juxtaposition, with the main sentence. This is an established construction (comparable with apposition), but often an awkward one, especially when *it* is the subject. Even with *it* a more natural wording is always possible, as in *The clock is worth keeping, because it's ornamental* (. . . *it being ornamental*).

But some absolute constructions, though stilted, do save words: *They parted, he forgiven and she reassured*/*We'll arrive on time, all being well*. Sentences like *She stormed out, eyes ablaze*/*He drove off, foot hard down on the accelerator* look similar but are elliptical (i.e. . . . , **with** *eyes ablaze*/**with** *foot hard down*).

Confusions to beware of   The apostrophe-*s* and the pronoun *it* are capable of various senses, which can conflict when they occur in the same sentence, especially in writing.

(i) *'s in more than one sense*:   *'s* may be short for *is* or *has*, or show possession. Confusion is common in combinations with *one*/ *it*, as in *One's disappointed but one's done one's best* (*One* **is** *disappointed but one* **has** *done one's best*)/*It's true it's been years since it's worked properly* (*It* **is** *true it* **has** *been years since it* **has** *worked properly*).

(ii) *it in more than one sense*: Besides acting as a normal pronoun standing for a noun, *it* often acts as a dummy subject standing for nothing (as in *It's raining*). Consider *The kitten perched on the vase, and it toppled over, spilling the flowers it had taken so long to arrange*. Here the *it* in *it had taken* is a dummy but could easily be taken as standing for *kitten* at first reading. If a sentence needs rereading to identify an *it*, it should be reworded.

Next time they will pay the bill, but last time it was free. Another example of *it* on the loose. The word seems to refer to *bill*, but what is meant is not *bill* but whatever the bill was for. This should be named, replacing *it*.

(iii) *Faulty coupling of subsentence*:   Apostrophe-*s* is often a cause of this confusion, as in *The puppy is Joan's, who leaves me to clear up after it. Who / which* etc cannot stand for a possessive like *Joan's*. Reword to read *The puppy belongs to Joan, who . . . .* Similarly:

>*Feeling generous, Bruce's spending was lavish.*

Feeling generous cannot refer to the possessive *Bruce's*. Reword to . . . *Bruce spent lavishly* or *Because he was feeling generous, his spending was lavish.*

Another coupling fault occurs when *and / but* intrude before *which / who*, as in *It was an honour he'd looked forward to, but which he didn't deserve.* Either *but* or *which* is an intruder. Several rewordings are possible: . . . , *but he didn't deserve it/ . . . , which he didn't deserve.*

But which is only possible if a balancing *which* is inserted: . . . *an honour* **which** *he'd looked forward to, but which . . .* This is an awkward solution though, since the defining context calls for *that*, as shown by the original omission (see THAT / WHICH in Part I).

Sentences with *and / but* before *which / who* should be looked at twice for simplified rewording. For instance: *His savings, intended for his old age, and which he kept in a shoebox, had vanished.* This can be much improved by use of parallel constructions: . . . *savings,* **intended** *for his old age and* **kept** *in a shoebox, had vanished.*

Similarly the change of construction in the following sentence after *and* unbalances it: *She cares about diet and that she gets regular exercise.* Reword to . . . *about diet and* **about** *getting regular exercise.*

Style for dates and numerals   Numbers can be written as figures or spelt out. Whichever method is chosen it should be followed consistently. As figures are just as clear and take up less space there is no good reason for insistence on spelling out. A sensible convention, widely used in publishing, is to spell out just the single-figure numbers (one to nine inclusive) and use figures for numbers from 10 up. Similarly *first* to *ninth* can be written out, but *10th / 11th / 21st / 100th* etc. With plurals this system yields *twos / threes* etc but *10s / 20s / 30s* (for decades *the 1980s* or *the '80s* etc).

It is already standard to write figures for titles like *Subsection 5 / Volume 10 / 154 Regiment / Room 504 / page 131,* and for dates, e.g. either *10 May 1982* or *10th May 1982.* Arranged in this way a date needs no comma (as it does in *May 10, 1982,* the American preference). Similarly in addresses there is no need for a comma after the building number, e.g. *8 Crowstone Road*, not *8, Crow-stone Road.*

Mainly for beginners   Writing cannot be reduced to a formula but various basics in good writing can be pointed out. For the beginner probably the best general advice is to write as though telling a friend, i.e. without slang but naturally, and not in imitation of any particular style.

[1] Construct sentences with words rather than phrases. The wording cannot be fresh if it consists of standard phrases.

[2] Prefer nouns and verbs to adjectives and adverbs. Un-adorned nouns and verbs, aptly chosen, are more vivid than the shadings achieved with adjectives and adverbs. So *The bus lumbered off* is more effective than *The big bus moved heavily off.* Similarly, why *desperate* in *Jim stumbled, cursing with desperate fury?* Fury can be imagined but how can it be differentiated from *desperate* fury?

[3] Use as few words as necessary. Choose the shorter expression – not *in view of the fact that* but *because.* Not *in actual fact/a brief glance* but *in fact/a glance* (all facts are actual and all glances are brief). Exploit ELLIPSIS (q.v.) and substitution (see PROFORMS). Prune all words contributing nothing but extra lettering – not *The inspector had visited the premises at an earlier date* but ... *the premises earlier.*

[4] Assert rather than suggest. Prefer the specific – not *The outlook could have been better* but *The outlook was bad.* Prefer the positive – not *The car was not a fast one* but *The car was slow.* Prefer the active to the passive – not *His mother's cooking was missed by them all* but *They all missed his mother's cooking.*

[5] Delay the climax of the sentence till the end. This is the expected position for new information or whatever the writer wants to build up to. The verb is not a fulcrum of a sentence – what goes after it tends to outweigh what goes before. Secondary emphasis is achieved by a position at the start of a sentence, before the subject (see INVERSION for emphatic effects).

These are basics of sentence composition, but equally important – and less amenable to rules – is the framework or arrangement of the whole message. If this is nonfiction and is so planned as to present the information it consists of in a logical sequence, the composing of the sentences will in turn be easier. A sound principle for a framework, whether for a piece of writing or a speech, is the venerable

Tell them what you're going to tell them,
Then tell them,
Then tell them what you've told them.

In other words, have a beginning, a middle and an end. Start by outlining what the message is going to be about. Then deliver the message. Then finish by summarizing its essentials.

A few don'ts may be listed.

Don't mislead the reader with false scents, Fowler's apt term for wording that seems to be heading in one direction and turns out to be heading in another. A sentence that requires rereading is a failure. Consider *He would have written but for the baby's arrival was due any day chose to wait for news.* Here the lack of commas (after *but* and *day*) causes *but for* to be read as the common phrase meaning *except for.* So *but for the baby's arrival* raises false expectations of "if it hadn't been for the baby's arrival".

Don't let careless repetition of the same word cause uncertainty whether some special significance is intended, as in *In his lecture he* **made** *clear that he is not going to* **make** *a habit of* **making** *films of this kind, though they all* **make** *money.* Here the repetition of the same verb is both tiresome and unnecessary. Similarly with *past* in *It was half* **past** *two and* **past** *time for her appointment. She had always been punctual in the* **past.**

Don't position words ambiguously, as in *The quickest way to the airport is by tube in the rush hour* (i.e. . . . *to the airport in the rush hour is* . . .), or *While they were waiting for a bus he asked her to marry him outside the church of St Clement's* (i.e. . . . *for a bus outside the church of St Clement's he asked* . . .).

Don't weary the reader with monotonous sentences of all the same length or the same construction. Vary the length by interspersing long sentences with short ones or vice versa. Avoid too many sentences constructed with two statements joined by *and/but* etc, as in *The annual outing is planned for Saturday 31 July, and all members of the staff are invited. The destination is Westsea, and one guest per person may be brought. The coaches will leave the office car park at 10.30 a.m. sharp and it is hoped to spend several hours on the beach, weather permitting. The Entertainments Committee is devising an alternative scheme for if it rains, and a fish supper will be served in Westsea at The Skipper's Cabin* etc.

This sort of thing can be improved by at least grouping similar points in the same sentence, but the monotony can only be relieved with some reconstructed sentences of a different pattern.

Manuscripts There are elementary conventions for manuscripts intended for publication, and some of them ought to be followed in all manuscripts intended for reading by other people. Margins of at least an inch should be left all round the text. This is particularly important for the left-hand edge, where the pin/clip/staple goes. If the margin there is too narrow the text may be obscured when the sheets are turned. This makes for awkward handling for an editor – some editors refuse to work on below-par MSS. An inadequate margin at the top is equally inconvenient, as it leaves no room for directions to the printer or for the printer's own markings.

In typewritten MSS not only should the proper margins be allowed but the lines of type should be double-spaced. Here again the spacing is essential to leave room for corrections, printer's directions and editing.

Only ignorance or bad manners can account for neglect of these simple precautions, which is not limited to beginners.

Subjunctives/conditionals Subjunctive verbs seem an unnecessary complication for any language, and English has helpfully shed most of the traditional forms. Still, some relics survive to puzzle the observant:

Be that as it may
Come what may
Come midsummer (etc) *the weather will change*
Far be it from me to . . . .

These may be regarded as standard phrases, not open to variation. Verbs in general only use a subjunctive form when they occur in a *that* construction after verbs like *ask/demand/suggest*, as in

The Under-Secretary proposed that firm action **be taken**
    (. . . should be taken)
The Minister asks that a suitable official **inspect** *the site*
    (. . . should inspect . . .).

As the examples suggest, this is a formal use of subjunctive, and the rewording in brackets is more modern. Other rephrasing is also possible, e.g. . . . *proposed firm action/ . . . asks for an official to inspect* . . . .

Subjunctives are essentially verb forms for expressing hypothesis, and hence wish. Exhibit A is *If I* **were** *you* (or *If he* **were** *in your shoes*). This is an unmistakable hypothesis, since *I* cannot be *you*. The alternative way of putting it is *If I* **was** *you*, which looked like becoming the norm some years ago. But *were* is still the more usual choice, especially in educated use. It occurs also in the phrase *as it were.*

Apart from these surviving uses, subjunctives are generally evaded by resort to the devices of conditional sentences, as in

> *If something **should go** wrong . . .*
> ***Should** something **go** wrong . . .*
> *If something **goes** wrong . . . .*

These refer to a future possibility and all require a future tense in the second half of the sentence, e.g. *. . . we'll come at once* (unless the verb is imperative, as in *. . . **call us** at once*, or uses an auxiliary that has no future tense, as in *. . . we **can** come at once*).

The simple past tense, used as a conditional, refers to a more distant hypothesis, as in

> *If you **went** about things differently, you'd **upset** fewer people.*

Here the second verb has to be formed with *would ('d)* or *might*. If the reference is to a past possibility the simple past is changed for the past perfect tense, as in

> *If you **had behaved** better, you **would have been invited** again.*

The second verb this time is always formed with *would ('d) have* or *might have.*

Other devices with a subjunctive effect are *let* and *may*, as in

> *Let politicians be damned* (instead of *Politicians be damned*)
> *May thy will be done* (instead of *Thy will be done*).

Tenses English verb variations seem to be widely regarded as too simple to need study. This may explain why it is so hard for the native to study them. Dictionaries do not set out the forms and permutations in such a way that they can be looked up and compared. It is rare to find an appendix on irregular verbs, rarer still to find a marshalling of the numerous auxiliary verbs like *can/do/ must/should.*

With tenses, not only are the names now in doubt after repeated revisions, but the definition of the term itself is questioned. Modern exponents of linguistics restrict *tense* to the meaning of time as indicated by inflection. On this basis there are only two English tenses: the simple present (*I go* etc) and the simple past (*I went* etc). All the others are formed by combining the verb with auxiliaries. How this distinction contributes to enlightenment is not clear, especially at a time when the same academics are extending the definition of *verb* to include escorting prepositions and adverbs. If regular combinations like *will ask / will have asked* are not to count as tenses, as they have done for centuries, a new term will be needed – because no other exists.

English tenses (apart from those of *to be*) never have more than five basic forms and usually have fewer, e.g. *ask / asks / asked / asking* is the gamut of the verb *to ask*. But irregularities complicate the scene, as does the range of AUXILIARY VERBS (q.v.) used in combination with the basics to produce traditional tenses. To these must be added the workhorses *going to*, one of several supplementary future devices (*I am going to ask*), and *used (to)*, which does comparable service for continuous time in the past (*I used to ask*).

This entry tabulates the principal tenses. For a list of other aspects of verbs treated in separate entries, see VERBS.

Verb inflections Other full verbs have four forms if regular, or anything from three to five if irregular. In the following summary irregular verbs (see separate entry for detailed list) are grouped in three categories:

Verb forms	Regular verbs	Irregular verbs		
		Class 1	Class 2	Class 3
Infinitive Present tense except 3rd person singular Imperative	*look*	*shut*	*leave*	*tear*
Present tense 3rd person singular	*looks*	*shuts*	*leaves*	*tears*
Past tense	*looked*	*shut*	*left*	*tore*
Past participle	*looked*	*shut*	*left*	*torn*
Present participle	*looking*	*shutting*	*leaving*	*tearing*

Tenses Tabulated In the following tables the regular verb *to ask* is shown in the traditional tenses, which are given a choice of labels:

Present

	Simple Indefinite	Imperfect Continuous Progressive	Perfect Perfect simple	Perfect continuous Perfect progressive
Infinitive	*to ask*	*to be asking*	*to have asked*	*to have been asking*
1st person (I)	*ask*	*am asking*	*have asked*	*have been asking*
2nd person singular (thou)	(obsolete. Plural form now used in singular sense)			
3rd person singular (he/she/it)	*asks*	*is asking*	*has asked*	*has been asking*
1st person plural (we)	*ask*	*are asking*	*have asked*	*have been asking*
2nd person plural (you)	*ask*	*are asking*	*have asked*	*have been asking*
3rd person plural (they)	*ask*	*are asking*	*have asked*	*have been asking*

Past

	Simple Indefinite	Imperfect Continuous Progressive	Perfect Perfect simple	Perfect continuous Perfect progressive
1st person singular (I)	asked	was asking	had asked	had been asking
2nd person singular (thoū)	(obsolete. *Plural form now used in singular sense*)			
3rd person singular (he/she/it)	asked	was asking	had asked	had been asking
1st person plural we)	asked	were asking	had asked	had been asking
2nd person plural (you)	asked	were asking	had asked	had been asking
3rd person plural (they)	asked	were asking	had asked	had been asking

Future

	Simple Indefinite	Imperfect Progressive Continuous	Perfect Perfect simple	Pluperfect Perfect continuous
All persons	'll ask	'll be asking	'll have asked	'll have been asking
or 1st person	shall/will ask	shall/will be asking	shall/will have asked	shall/will have been asking
Others	will ask	will be asking	will have asked	will have been asking

Future-in-the-past tenses are also known as conditionals:

All persons	'd ask	'd be asking	'd have asked	'd have been asking
or 1st person	should/would ask	should/would be asking	should/would have asked	should/would have been asking
Others	would ask	would be asking	would have asked	would have been asking

The commonest future forms in speech are those using *'ll*, which is also increasingly used in writing. The traditional use of *shall* following *I/We* is dying out. *Will* is now common with all persons, though *shall* survives in 1st-person questions (*Shall we dance?/ Where shall we go tonight?/What shall I tell them?*). Even here *will* is often preferred. Questions like *How will I know you when we meet?/When will we ever find the place?* are no less common. *Shall* is sometimes used to indicate insistence, as in *It shall be done!/The tenant shall have the right* etc, but these are formal expressions. Insistence is more often conveyed in speech by *will* spoken with emphasis (see SHALL/WILL in Part I). There are other ways of expressing the future with verbs, besides the tenses set out above – see FUTURE IDIOMS.

The following tenses are also known as Conditionals:

Future-in-the-past tenses are those that refer to future time as viewed from the past, as in

> *I knew **I'd win***
> *It was obvious the fugitives **would escape***
> *Some hoped **we'd be staying** with them.*

These tenses also occur in conditional contexts, as in

> *If I had known the trouble **I'd have asked** for your help.*

Here again the tradition of reserving a form (*should*) for use after *I/we* is no longer generally observed. In speech *'d* is usual for both singulars and plurals, unless the verb needs emphasis, in which case *should/would* becomes a matter of personal preference. But *should* tends to be avoided because it can also carry the separate sense of *ought*. *I knew I should win* could mean either *I knew I **was going to win*** or *I knew I **ought to win***. As *'d/would* do not carry the *ought* sense they tend to be preferred.

Active and passive   All the tenses so far set out are in the so-called active voice, which expresses action by the subject, as in *I ask*. Most tenses also have a counterpart in the passive voice, which shows the subject as the recipient of the verb's action rather than as the initiator (*I am asked*). Passive tenses, easily identified, all consist of the tenses of the verb *to be* plus a past participle, e.g. *I am + asked/he was + asked/we shall be + asked/you have been + asked/they were being + asked*. The tenses of *to be* are too well known to need setting out in full. By way of prompts the passive tenses of *ask* are shown in just the first person:

> Present simple *I am asked*
> Present imperfect *I am being asked*
> Present perfect *I have been asked*
> Past simple *I was asked*
> Past imperfect *I was being asked*

Past perfect *I had been asked*
Future simple *I'll / shall / will be asked*
Future perfect *I'll / shall / will have been asked*
Future-in-the-past simple *I'd / should / would be asked*
Future-in-the-past perfect *I'd / should / would have been
   asked.*

Note that passive uses are possible for a number of active verbs, e.g. the verb *to look* means "to regard" / "observe" but *She looks good* does not mean she is observing or regarding. It refers to what other people see when they look at her. Similar two-way verbs of this kind include *feel / smell / taste / read / sell.*
(See also SUBJUNCTIVES / CONDITIONALS.)

U-speech   This term refers to the distinctive vocabulary of members of the British upper class, as perceived by Professor Alan S. C. Ross and popularized in a book (*Noblesse Oblige*, 1956) in which he collaborated with Nancy Mitford. He coined the terms "U" and "non-U" to describe what he contended were expressions used by the upper class and equivalents used by the rest. U words tended to be more direct, the down-to-earth expression rather than the euphemism or the salesman's contrivance. Examples:

U	Non-U
scurf	*dandruff*
woman	*lady*
what?	*pardon?*
sweat	*perspire*
helping	*portion*
lavatory / loo	*toilet.*

The Ross research was generally found accurate and the publicity it attracted caused many a social climber to stop saying *notepaper / serviette / lounge / dentures* etc and take up the U equivalents (*writing paper / napkin / drawing room / false teeth*). Since then the cult of the common man has led to a perverse preference for the non-U among the young of the upper classes, which is perhaps more noticeable in pronunciation.

In 1978 however Ross maintained that most of the U vocabulary persisted, while the number of non-U newcomers (like "jacket potatoes" for *baked potatoes*) had tended to reinforce the division (*U & Non-U Revisited*, published by Debretts). This matter is of more interest as a social comment than as a pointer to good English. No doubt there have always been preferred expressions among people of similar background. The U vocabulary is useful for its reminders of the simple alternatives to many of the elaborations and evasions that have passed into ordinary speech.

Variable vowels   In a counterpart of consonant changes discussed in CONSONANT CONFLICTS (q.v.), vowels vary according to where they fall in spoken sentences. The natural rhythm of English speech tends to squeeze out unstressed syllables, as in *gen(e)ral / mem(o)ry / practic(a)lly*, and it also changes unstressed vowel sounds. So in *an apple for the teacher* vowels of *an / for* become ən / fə. Variable vowels are found in 30-odd common one-syllable words like these (*and / but / can / the / does / some* etc). For each of them two different pronunciations are possible, called weak and strong.

The strong way is how you would say the word separately, or perhaps in reading aloud for dictation or in broadcasting details of gale warnings to ships at sea – it occurs in singing too. The weak is an unstressed version found in a conversational word sequence, with the vowel shortened, usually to ə. Weak forms are found only among articles, conjunctions, prepositions, pronouns and auxiliary verbs – other verbs of one syllable and nouns, adjectives and adverbs are not affected.

The requirements of stress also influence the use of contractions like *we'll / we'd / won't* (for list see CONTRACTIONS). But native speakers interchange strong and weak forms without giving them a thought, and the only reason for setting them out here is to reassure those who worry about such things that the variations are perfectly normal and not elocutionary lapses:

a (*give us* ə *kiss*)	does (*where* dəz *it go?*)
am (*I'm ready*)	for (*wait* fə *me*)
an (*have* ən *apple*)	from (*she's* frəm *overseas*)
and (*up* ən *down*)	had (*the train* əd *been late*)
are (*dogs* ə *faithful*)	has (*the rice* əz *boiled*)
as (*large* əz *life*)	have (*prices* əv *gone up*)
at (*look* ət *that*)	he (*won't* i *come?*)
be (*please* bi *quick*)	her (*send* ə *these flowers*)
but (*yes,* bət *when?*)	him (*let* im *go*)
can (*you* cən *go*)	his (*take* iz *coat*)
do (*what* də *they want?*)	is (*what's happening*)

must (*we* məst *go*)   the (thə *power and* thə *glory*)
not (*don't go*)   them (*let* thəm *off*)
of (*one* əv *ours*)   to (tə *have* tə *go*)
shall (*I* sh'l *insist*)   us (*do let*'s *go/Give* əs *a kiss*)
some (*have* səm *bread*)   was (*the corn* wəz *green*)
than (*more* thən *before*)   will (*that*'ll *be enough*)
that (*be sure* thət *you do*)   would (*some* əd *say so*).

Some of the words have additional forms, depending on ad-jacent letters, e.g. *is/has* are sometimes pronounced *s* when weak, sometimes *z*, as in *what's* (*s*), *who's* (*z*).

(See also STRESS SHIFT/VOWEL SOUNDS.)

Verbs The basic form of every verb, except a handful of historic auxiliaries, is its infinitive, which is the form traditionally used for referring to the verb, e.g. *to see*. It is normally an action concept. The verb's other forms or inflections, e.g. *sees/saw/seen/seeing*, are derived from the infinitive to denote the time of the action (see TENSES). The infinitive is sometimes used in its full form (with *to*) and sometimes in its bare form (without *to*), as in

I hate to see the evening sun go down
I must see you soon.

For the rules about infinitives see INFINITIVE CONSTRUCTIONS. For other aspects of verbs see the following entries:

AUXILIARY VERBS	LINKING VERBS
CONTRACTIONS	PARTICIPLES
ELLIPSIS	PHRASAL VERBS
ENDINGS	REPORTED SPEECH
FUTURE IDIOMS	SUBJUNCTIVES
IMPERATIVES	STRESS SHIFT
INVERSION	TENSES
IRREGULAR VERBS	VARIABLE VOWELS.

Vowel sounds There are 20 or so vowel sounds in English – some phoneticians reckon 21, others 22 – but only five alphabet letters to represent them. This explains why it is not much good going by spellings. There is an International Phonetic Alphabet, which was supposed to be going to standardize the way sounds are rep-resented, but after nearly a century its application to English still seems unsettled. At any rate phonetic keys using it rarely agree (different versions, the outcome of various revisions, are shown below). Probably speech has too many subtleties of sound to be represented by any system intelligible to the ordinary person who looks up a dictionary. Hence this Guide relies mainly on rhymes and parallels.

The list that follows offers several words as examples of each sound. Some of the sounds are dipthongs (pairs of linked vowel sounds contained in the same syllable). All the examples are meant to be pronounced with the word spoken in isolation, not as it might be in sentences – which can change the sound (see VARIABLE VOWELS).

Usual alphabet symbol	IPA symbol(s)	Vowel sound as found in words like
a	ei/eɪ	*able / made / maid / stayed / steak / they / vein*
a	ae/a	*add / ant / shall / have / fan / gaffe / gather*
a	ɑ/a:/ɑː	*ah! / art / heart / vase / father / farther*
–	eə/ɛə	*air / fare / fair / there / wear / mayor*
e	i:/i	*be / bee / sea / seize / ski / key / quay / people*
e	e/ɛ	*egg / get / bet / head / berry / bury / them / said*
–	ə	*er . . . / ago / about / china / pleasure / better*
–	ɜ:/ə:/ɜ	*herd / heard / bird / sir / fur / infer / worm*
i/y	aɪ/ai/ɑi	*I / eye / tie / sigh / buy / by / bite / ice / wise*
i	ɪ/i	*in / it / fit / fiddle / silly / busy / women*
–	ɪə/iə/	*ear / real / here / beer / pier / idea*
o	əʊ/ou/	*oh! / so / sew / tone / solo / though / mauve / beau*
o	ɒ/ɔ/	*on / off / cough / ox / got / laurel / yacht*
–	ɔ:/ɔ	*all / awl / lord / awe / taught / four / floor*
–	aʊ/ɑu	*how / now / brown / out / doubt / drought*
o	ɔɪ/ɔi	*boy / boil / noise / oil / soya*
u	ʌ	*up / cut / mother / son / come / touch / blood*
–	u:/u/	*too / true / do / whom / blew / move / soup / food*
–	ʊ/u	*put / push / good / wolf / would / foot / full*
–	ʊə/uə	*poor / sure / tour / dour*

To these vowel sounds can be added those found in words where three linked vowel sounds occur, often skipping a silent *w* or *y*. Some of these sequences are always pronounced as two syllables (*knowing/chaos*), but others vary. Most of the following are usually one syllable, especially those in words ending on a vowel.

aɪə	*fire/desire/riot/choir/flier/tyre/quiet*
aʊə	*our/hour/flower/power/coward/glower*
əʊə	*goer/mower/slower/grower*
eɪə	*player/betrayal/crayon/greyer*
ɔɪə	*employer/destroyer/royal*

What may strike the reader coming fresh to these problems is the large number of sounds not consistently spelt with any particular letter combination. Closer inspection also reveals gaps in dictionary conventions, which lump differing sounds together.

The words *rule/school/fool* all have the same vowel sound. But according to the *Oxford English Dictionary, Webster's New Collegiate Dictionary,* the *Longman Dictionary of Contemporary English,* and *Collins Dictionary of the English Language* this sound is the same as in *food/woo/do/rude/roof.* These words are all represented by the same vowel symbols. The Oxford has o͞o, Webster's has ü, Longman and Collins use the IPA u:.

Yet it is plain that there are two different sounds and that the vowel of *food/rude* etc is distinct from that of *fool/rule* etc. The distinction is unmistakable in *foolproof – fool* as in "school", and *proof* as in "roof"/"rude".

The trouble is that there are three different vowel sounds in *fool, full,* and *food,* but the phonetic conventions can only cope with two. *Fool* is in effect a longer version of *full,* just as *pool* is a longer version of *pull.* The nearest longer vowel in the phonetic conventions is the *oo* of *proof/food* etc.

In some regional accents and in the sort of refined accent even educated people regard as affected, words like *fool* are in fact given the same vowel as *food.* Attentive listeners, noticing this, might well check with their dictionary, only to be misled into believing this sound is standard – and not only for *fool/school/rule* but for *ghoul/cool/drool/spool/stool/tool* etc.

Another vowel misrepresentation to be found in dictionaries is that of the words *eel/feel/seal/steal/steel/peal/peel/meal/reel* etc. These of course are all pronounced like "real", but not in the dictionaries cited. While *real* is shown with a diphthong (*Oxford English Dictionary* rĭəl, IPA rɪəl), *reel/meal* etc are shown with a vowel as in the name of the letter E (Oxford ĭ, IPA i:). If this were accurate *eel* would sound like the French "il"/"ils"/"île". Except in some local accents like Irish, no such sound occurs in modern English.

This discrepancy arises from the nature of the *l* sound. When *l* occurs after a vowel and at the end of a syllable it needs its own introductory element of vowel to make its pronunciation possible.* This introductory sound is called an ə-glide, and this kind of *l* is called a dark *l*. The vowel effect is particularly marked after the E-sound, producing a diphthong indistinguishable from that of *real*. Phonetic systems in most dictionaries do not indicate differences in *l* sounds, so the inquirer is given to understand that he ought to say *reel* differently from *real*. After a few efforts with *a reel of real cotton* he is likely to give up trying to follow phonetic keys.

Another vowel difference not indicated in dictionaries concerns *o* before *l*, as in *whole/hole/hold/gold/bold/coal/dole/* etc. The *o* sound in these (a diphthong, roughly əwO) differs from the more usual O of *holy / go / boat / dough / foam / slow* etc. The difference is only partly attributable to *l* – at least it is no harder to say *whole/ stole* with the same *o* (i.e. O) as in *holy/slow* than with the distinctive vowel, which is pronounced further back in the mouth. Still, the difference is general and there is no way of discovering this from dictionaries. The inquirer noticing the different *o* and wondering which sound is right wastes his time looking it up, as dictionaries acknowledge no difference.

(See also VARIABLE VOWELS.)

Word order   This term refers to the sequence of words in a sentence. Once the words have been selected the order in which they can be arranged in English is open to little or no choice. Sentences fit settled patterns, defiance of which changes the meaning, makes nonsense, or offends idiom. The patterns, composed of concepts such as Subject/Verb/Object, are discussed under ANALYSIS, SENTENCE PATTERNS and elsewhere. Where they can be varied it is along settled lines such as INVERSION (q.v.). Adverbials are unusually flexible as in

I haven't told her yet.

Here the adverbial *yet* can be repositioned without harm:

I haven't yet told her.

---

* Many consonant sounds cannot be uttered without an element of attached vowel, depending on where they occur in a word.

But in sentences as simple as the following no change at all is possible:

> *Your car has been laid up longer than you expected*
> *I hope they do the work properly*
> *The bald Cypriot mechanic in the outsize boilersuit was*
> *trained by the Army.*

Besides the requirements of sentence structure as revealed by analysis, word order is also shaped by the arrangements of accepted phrases and by the constructions required by individual words. Some of these rules, as they affect adjectives and adverbs, are discussed here. Others are touched on in various entries, e.g. IDIOM, INFINITIVE CONSTRUCTIONS, IMPERATIVES, INVERSION.

Adjective positioning The usual position for an adjective is in front of the noun it describes (**new** *girl* / **fast** *car* / **stale** *bread*). Or so it is said. But there are regular exceptions where the adjective follows the noun, as in *something* **old,** *something* **new,** *something* **borrowed,** *something* **blue.** All the words ending in *thing* / *one* / *body* / *where*, like *anything* / *anyone* / *everybody* / *somewhere*, normally go in front of any adjective applying to them. Also a few set phrases or senses require the adjective after the noun, as in *heir* **apparent** / *chairman* **elect.**

Where the adjective is extended by an adjectival phrase it usually follows the noun instead of preceding it. So *a car* **fast** *enough for anyone* / *preparations* **essential** *for success* / *a figure* **shapelier** *than most* / *a neighbour* **reluctant** *to complain.*

With verbs like *be* / *become* / *seem* / *grow* a placing after the verb is common, as in *The bread is* **stale** / *The car was* **fast** / *The trip seemed* **short.** Here the adjective is linked to the noun it describes by the verb. This arrangement, though extremely common, occurs with only a handful of verbs, those known technically as LINKING VERBS (q.v.). Such verbs, unlike most, do not denote action of some sort (the extreme specimen is *to be*) but the general state of the subject. They include *feel* (*I feel* **cross**) / *remain* (*She remains* **hopeful**) / *go* (*I shall go* **mad**) / *sound* (*That sounds* **unlikely**).

Not all adjectives however can follow a verb in this way. Some are confined by sense or idiom to preceding their noun, especially those which put a limit on its meaning, like *only* (*the only excuse*). Similar adjectives include *former* / *chief* / *main* / *principal* / *sole.*

Some adjectives change sense when separated from the noun by a verb (*that* **particular** *candidate* = specific / *That candidate is* **particular** = fussy).

Adjective sequences A series of adjectives may describe the same noun, but which goes where? The order of precedence is important to the clarity or sense of the sentence. This is especially so if the adjectives are placed before the noun (rather than in a complementary position after it) e.g. *a funny old man* does not mean the same as *an old funny man*. Even if the attributes denoted by the adjectives are merely arranged in an unexpected order the effect is puzzling. In *A black small overpriced second-hand Italian rusting sports car* the unfamiliar arrangement makes the sense indigestible. When the words are reshuffled the message becomes clear enough:

> *An overpriced small black rusting second-hand Italian sports car.*

But this is not the only possible arrangement. If the speaker wanted to emphasize the corrosion his description could start *A rusting . . .* , in which case *overpriced* would probably be transposed to the vacated position. The characteristic uppermost in the speaker's mind is likely to have first place after any preliminary words like *the/some/real/next* etc. In a clear arrangement the other characteristics may seem to follow in a natural succession, but in fact no immutable order can be formulated. There is room for exercise of individual preference. Though the beginnings and ends of the sequences are reasonably settled there is uncertainty about the more general adjectives, which tend to reflect the speaker's viewpoint.

Examination of the sports car example will show however that fixed characteristics are placed nearest to the noun. The thing in question is immutably a car of the sports variety, Italian and second-hand. What the other adjectives are describing is a second-hand Italian sports car. Such core characteristics tend to be clustered, though the perception of them may vary with the observer.

The order of precedence tabulated here is based on models proposed by several grammarians, but it should not be regarded as more than a guide.

It hardly needs pointing out that a sequence filling every category of adjective is unimaginable. Even the example fills too many for comfort. Most sequences would fill only a few.

Though a participle often occurs in the position so labelled, a participle may also be placed as a general adjective (e.g. *overpriced*). When *big* or *beautiful* are among the adjectives they tend to muscle into the "general" category, as do other superlative-type words like *marvellous/great/lovely*. Some of these can occur

Adjectival order of precedence

Determiner (*a* / *his* / *some* etc)	*An*	*His*	*Some*
Intensifier (*real* / *definite* / *utter* / *slight* etc)			*slight*
Post-determiner (*only* / *second* / *next* / *last* / *other* etc)		*other*	
General adjectives	*overpriced small*	*cheerful*	
Age indicator and / or *little*		*little*	
Colour indicator	*black*		
Participle	*rusting*		
Source / style indicator	*Italian*		*local*
Adjectival noun	*sports*	*night*	
Material indicator			*cultural*
Noun	*car*	*nurse*	*event*

together, as in **great big beautiful** *doll* (*great* has priority over *big*, but *beautiful* is movable – *beautiful great big bouquet*). *Little* usually goes after the general adjective and immediately before an age indicator (*little old*, not "old little"), but it could fill the general spot if desired (*a little grey wizened lady*).

Punctuation: when an adjective sequence is properly composed, by which is meant digestibly arranged and not overloaded, no need will be felt for intrusive commas, as the words will fall into familiar groups. No comma is necessary in any of the specimen sequences.

Adjectival noun sequences   Nouns are so widely used as adjectives in contemporary English that mixed sequences of nouns and adjectives or sequences of nouns only are common. In *Easy fit kitchen scales wall mounting template*, all the preceding words contribute to the description of *template*. Two hyphens remove the obscurity:

Easy-fit kitchen scales wall-mounting template. Kitchen scales are recognizable as a compound and do not need a third hyphen, though it would do no harm.

In *Factory personnel prototype documentation security* the inhumanity of the words freezes the understanding. Again hyphens can make the sequence more tolerable:

Factory-personnel prototype-documentation security.

This assumes that the prototype is of the documentation rather than the security, which is the natural sense, as each such noun modifies the next. If *prototype* applied to the security, then the punctuation should be . . . *prototype documentation-security.* More hyphens are a simple key to clarifying these forbidding groups of nouns.

Positioning of adverbs   The typical placing of CONJUNCTS/DISJUNCTS has been noted in that entry (q.v.). Among adjuncts there is a difference between those qualifying verbs, and so functioning as sentence components, and those qualifying other kinds of word such as adjectives or other adverbs. The normal position with an adjective or another adverb is in front of it, as in ***fairly*** *reliable/* ***generally*** *reliable/* ***exceptionally*** *reliable* (adj.), ***fairly*** *gently/* ***unusually*** *gently/* ***so*** *gently* (adv.). But a few adverbs, like *enough,* follow the word they qualify, e.g. *good* ***enough****/gently* ***enough****.* So do those able to qualify a noun phrase, as in *a holiday* ***abroad****/the shed* ***outdoors****/the rollcall* ***tomorrow****.*

With adverbs in their notionally main role of qualifying verbs, three positions are possible: at the beginning of a sentence, mid-sentence, or at the end. When the intention is to emphasize the adverbial qualification the beginning is preferred, as in ***Rather reluctantly****, Mr Smith enrolled.* The end position may be considered the norm: *Mr Smith enrolled* ***rather reluctantly****/She worked for my boss* ***temporarily****.*

But the mid-sentence position is usual for adverbials like *always / almost / hardly / just / often / quite / still,* i.e. those indicating frequency, relative time, or degree. When the verb consists of auxiliary and participle, like *have told/have been hoping,* these adverbials slot between them: *I've* ***always*** *told you/They've* ***just*** *been saying.* If the verb is a single word the commonest position is in front of it, as in *You* ***often*** *ask . . ./ . . .* ***quite*** *expect . . ./ . . .* ***usually*** *succeed . . . .*

Positioning of prepositions   Uprooting prepositions from the ends of sentences is something the poet Dryden is blamed for. He started a fad that still has followers nearly 300 years later – an influence he might prefer for his literary works. But prepositions were accepted at the ends of sentences long before his time, and they remain so today. The sort of phrasing in question is *What he says is nothing to go by*, instead of . . . *nothing by which to go*, or *Here's something to get on with*, instead of . . . on *with which to get*. Far from being doubtful grammar this is one the features of the language. It is the construction used by everybody in speech, if not always in writing, and it is virtually indispensable:

> *What is the alloy made of?*
> *She's such fun to be with*
> *This sounds worth looking at*
> *What a faint hope he's clinging to*
> *I was advised how much to hold out for.*

Only one of these can stand simple reshuffling: *Of what is the alloy made?* The others would need rewording to resite the preposition, because shifts as in *She's such fun with which to be/ To what a faint hope he's clinging* produce stilted English. Besides, who is confident of when the word in question is a preposition or an adverb particle? The reshuffled *I was advised for how much to hold out* leaves a suspect *out* at the end. Is this another offender? In effect *hold out* is a PHRASAL VERB (q.v.) and *out* ranks as an adverb particle, but a specialist dictionary mildly comments:* "The same particle can serve as a preposition or adverb and a student can easily confuse these functions". So this is a prohibition that takes a learned faddist to comply with it.

Some stylists apply it to specimens like the following, which they rearrange even though the preposition does not fall at the end of the sentence:

> *The inspector's visit was prepared for weeks in advance*
> *The thing I'm most concerned about is the long-term effect*
> *What they long for is peace and quiet*
> *The courses to choose from were rather restricted.*

Here the preposition still occurs in the sort of construction that is objected to, with ellipted pronoun. So we get instead *The thing about which I'm most concerned . . ./The courses from which to choose . . . .* The other examples cannot be rearranged like this without unwanted changes of emphasis.

Nearly all the rewordings etc give a more formal or artificial

---

*Dictionary of English Phrasal Verbs by Tom McArthur & Beryl Atkins (Collins).

effect than the natural originals, which is enough to show the general weakness of the Dryden tradition. There is one situation though where a preposition-at-end can be worth avoiding.

In spoken English the tone of voice can inject emphasis regardless of where words fall in a sentence, but in written sentences the words the author wants to emphasize tend to be placed at the end (e.g. *No matter how long it takes I intend to finish the job* puts the emphasis on the determination to finish the job, and the effect is less emphatic in *I intend to finish the job, no matter how long it takes*). A preposition at the end of a sentence is hardly ever stressed. So it may be held to detract from or weaken the intended emphasis, e.g. *The Royal Navy, in which we serve* has more impact than *The Royal Navy, which we serve in.*

Apart from the end-of-sentence issue there is no problem about the placing of prepositions. They go in front of the noun or pronoun they govern (*at table/on time/for you*) or after the phrasal verb they escort (*listen to/hear of*). More flexible is the placing of prepositional phrases (i.e. preposition followed by the words it governs, as in *at table/for playing golf/from where I sit*). Such phrases are counted as adverbials in sentence structure and are capable of several positions. (See the previous subsection, POSITIONING OF ADVERBS.)